GOVERNMENᴛ AND SOCIETY IN LOUIS XIV's FRANCE

Edited by

ROGER METTAM

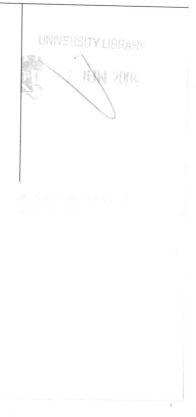

First published 1977 by
MACMILLAN PRESS LTD
Houndmills, Basingstoke, Hampshire RG21 6XS
and London
Companies and representatives
throughout the world

ISBN 0–333–06802–5 hardcover
ISBN 0–333–21430–7 paperback   1000800197

A catalogue record for this book is available
from the British Library.

11 10   9   8   7   6   5   4   3
04 03 02 01 00 99 98 97 96

Printed in Hong Kong

CONTENTS

Contents

INTRODUCTION

The conflicts which troubled the internal history of France in the seventeenth century almost all had one element in common—they were caused, or were at least prolonged and invigorated, by the unceasing struggle of the crown against the independent powers of the varied groups who formed the privileged orders in French society. At court the king and his small circle of ministerial advisers formulated endless plans to extend royal control into new fields of administration and to make the will of the king a more effective force in those areas where royal interference was familiar but unwelcome. The heart of the resistance to these ambitions often lay, ironically, with the very royal agents and officials on whose loyalty and devoted service the king ought to have been able to rely. While the favoured ministers at the centre had undoubted freedom to initiate whatever policies they chose, subject to royal approval, they lacked the effective executive arm which was necessary for imposing their wishes on the king's subjects. This book discusses the battle between central authority and provincial privilege in the years 1661–83, when one of the most celebrated French ministers, Jean-Baptiste Colbert, devised plans for expanding monarchical government which were more far-reaching than ever before, and was accordingly confronted with more persistent, if at times more subtle, opposition than many of his predecessors and successors. This span of years began in the spirit of hope that at last the king had taken control of affairs into his own hands and that no more omnipotent ministers, like Richelieu and Mazarin, would be allowed to tyrannise his people. In 1683, the year of Colbert's death, the mood was one of growing disillusionment, as reforms foundered, wars overburdened the economy and the king proved himself to be no reincarnation of his glorious ancestor, Henri IV.

In the unending war of attrition waged by crown and localities, it is not easy to apportion praise and blame. Each side might well be able to justify its actions in acceptable legal terms, even though their claims conflicted. On the one hand the power of the king was widely regarded as being in many respects unlimited and of divine provenance, while on the other there was general agreement that some of the principal privileges of various institutions and social groups were firmly founded in tradition and could not be overridden by anyone, not even the monarch. Neither side, therefore, dared to make a wholehearted attack on the rights and claims of the other, resorting instead to more underhand methods of encroachment, bargaining and compromise. It is only in recent years that historians have concentrated their attentions on this provincial resistance, and their conclusions about its extent and effectiveness have led to quite drastic revision of earlier generalisations about the rapid growth of 'absolutism' in seventeenth-century France. No longer is the reign of Louis XIV seen as one of dynamic change in government, guided by men from the newly emergent *bourgeoisie*. Advance is now recognised to have been painfully slow, with the privileged orders, especially the venal bureaucracy, retaining their hold on society and administration. Even the royal ministers, and the intendants for whom such sweeping claims have been made in the past, have been found to have their origins in the bureaucracy, not in the middle classes.

Many fields of French administration reveal this dichotomy of absolutism and privilege. The large and unwieldy royal bureaucracy was almost entirely composed of men who had not only bought their offices but also, by paying the annual dues of the *paulette*, had acquired the right to bequeath them to their heirs, which had long given rise to clashes between their personal interests and their professional duties. This was a particularly acute problem in connection with law and justice, where the king had unrestricted freedom to make laws, but had to rely for their execution on law courts composed of these venal office-holders. Nor had he at his disposal any independent forces which could police the kingdom and impose order, save for the army whose own loyalty was far from unwavering and whose presence in a province was always expensive and usually more disruptive than helpful.

The bureaucracy occupied a special place in the hierarchy of French society. Long service in its ranks or shorter service in its higher strata conferred nobility on an official, and its topmost echelons were positions of very considerable prestige. Although nobles of ancient lineage might loudly decry a nobility whose origins were professional rather than inherited, they were sometimes prepared themselves to accept suitable posts in the administration, while, more importantly, it was the ambition of every wealthy commoner to purchase an office and eventually acquire nobility. Because commerce was considered by the law to be incompatible with noble status, the wealthy who invested some of the profits of trade in an office had to abandon their earlier calling, spending their remaining resources on buying land. This gave them a new source of income and a greater degree of respectability, but it deprived commerce of funds which were essential for expansion and prevented the cherished commercial and colonial schemes of the royal ministers from prospering to the full. Faced with such an influential body of privileged men, the success of Louis XIV and Colbert in increasing effective central control over the whole administration could be at best partial.

In order to illustrate the impact of their policies on French society, and the way in which social pressures from institutions and groups of individuals inspired, changed, curtailed or defeated those policies, this book closely examines the day-to-day administration of France, for it is on that level that the inefficiency or plain obstructiveness of royal agents and ordinary subjects is revealed. On paper—in the memoirs and memoranda of the king and his chief ministers and in the instructions sent to the royal bureaucrats in the provinces—these government plans and summaries of past achievements sound impressive, not surprisingly when it is remembered that much of this material was designed to make a strong impact on the recipients rather than to expound an accurate assessment of a problem and a detailed course of action for solving it. The historians who have confined their researches to this massive body of propaganda have been able to tell of an unprecedented overhaul of administrative machinery and extension of royal control throughout the realm. But, when the fate of these edicts, decrees and dispatches is noted, the picture changes. It would be grossly unjust to deny all success to the remarkable Colbert, but it must be concluded that the way was often more tortuous than some have imagined, that the same orders had to be reiterated year after year because they were not being observed, that all kinds of favours, bribes and concessions had to be granted to win the goodwill of influential men, and that an advance in one field might well mean a compromise or even a retrogressive step elsewhere. Moreover, during the 1660s, when Colbert and his officials were primarily concerned with the accumulation of information about the kingdom and had not begun to formulate the great reforming ordinances for which he is remembered, the forces of opposition in the bureaucracy learnt that it was not difficult to outwit the royal government when it issued unpopular instructions. As a result they decided to change their method of attack from open and vocal criticism at the centre, which of necessity provoked some response from the ministers, to successful delaying tactics in the routine of administration in the localities. This shift of emphasis has led some historians to assume that such opposition had been silenced and therefore crushingly defeated, whereas recently more than one author has suggested that the struggle went on tirelessly beneath the surface.

The basic cause of this perpetual battle between the centre and the localities was the variegated nature of France itself. The kingdom was merely a rather improbable agglomeration of disparate provinces, some

more loosely joined together than others, whose local provincial boundaries frequently made more social, economic, political and legal sense
that did her national frontiers. Local customs and institutions, family
and marriage ties, privileges and the rules of professional associations
held greater sway over the minds of the king's subjects than the pronouncements of his ministers in distant Paris. Much of the routine of
local government could be seen by the inhabitants to be carried out by
men of their own area, officers of the law courts, towns, diocese and in
some provinces of the representative Estates, whose local ties the people
trusted and the king suspected. Any orders or new officials coming direct
from the capital seemed always concerned with new financial demands
for projects which seemed irrelevant or harmful to the best interests of
the province, thereby adding a new imposition to the load of an already
heavily burdened populace. Paris thus became equated with innovation
and hardship, the local officials with stability, tradition and protection.

The overall pattern of French society changed little between the death
of Mazarin in 1661 and that of Louis XIV in 1715. The privileged preserved much of their prestige and influence, keeping their immunity from
the more unpleasant financial burdens imposed by the state. It has often
been said that the independence of the nobility was broken by Louis XIV
at Versailles, but this generalisation, which stems from a failure to ident-
ify exactly which nobles suffered this fate, is a gross exaggeration. It is
true that a small and powerful group of aristocrats, containing the princes of the blood royal and certain other very high nobles, who had led
every major revolt during the seventeenth century but who had ultimately lost support on each occasion because their aims differed from
those of other nobles, had to be deprived of power. This was essential
because they constantly sought a share in political authority and policy-
making at the centre, which Louis XIV could not and did not allow.
Such men were rendered impotent. The remaining large majority of the
nobility, whether those of the sword who had inherited their rank or
those of the robe who derived it from office-holding, was too vast to be
treated similarly and there was no reason why such action should be
needed. These men wanted no share in central royal authority, but
simply wished to safeguard their positions as *seigneurs* and officials.
Although the crown felt that they could and should be made to be more
cooperative, there was no possibility of replacing them. Among other
reasons, they were the most effective, probably the only available,
means of controlling the unruly rural and urban populations, even if at
times they showed themselves to be effective inciters to revolt of those
same elements. It was on a local level that these nobles were influential

and many of them seldom came to court or remained there for very short periods. In some ways it was in their own interests to cooperate with the crown and it was Colbert's principal task to increase their devotion to national interests at the expense of personal position and family prosperity. The only method available to him was a slow and unsystematic one—the discovery, pursuit and punishment of the highly corrupt few in order to alarm the less corrupt majority, who would thus become a little more attentive to the commands of Paris.

If the venal bureaucracy were the sole feasible means of ruling France, it had advantages as well as drawbacks. Sons might be quite efficiently trained by the fathers whom they succeeded in office, and the whole system brought in some revenue—through the actual process of purchasing and retaining offices and in the form of sums which officials could be bullied into giving or lending to the crown—from a social group which was otherwise exempt from direct taxation. Although the peasantry bore unaided the burden of the principal direct tax, the *taille*, these other members of society shouldered some of the fiscal load and therefore had good reason to express grievances in times of hardship.

The plight of the peasantry was so serious because they rarely had the economic reserves to survive a major crisis, and even the attempts of the government to reduce the *taille* and increase indirect taxes helped them little, as those who paid the new levies passed much of the load on to the men beneath them in society. Yet the peasants, the chief body of taxpayers, had no voice at the national level. There were no national representative institutions, and those that had existed in the past had been abandoned because their component orders were seldom able to devise, from their varied provincial interests, any proposals which all members would be prepared to support. This was in some ways unsatisfactory from the point of view of the king, who was therefore prevented from solving his financial difficulties by the means which had been or were to be employed in other countries, where the ruler was able, at a price, to enlist the cooperation of the representatives of the people in estates, parliaments and diets. Thus, ironically, it appeared to outsiders that the French king, free from these potentially disruptive bodies, was in a stronger position than their own ruler, but these observers saw only a glittering and civilised court, an idolised monarch leading powerful armies throughout Europe in pursuit of his own glory. They neglected to realise the almost total lack of effective channels by which the French crown could make itself obeyed within France. There the increasing demands on the royal finances could be met only by cajoling, bullying or threatening the population, either to provide ready cash for immediate expenditure or to finance those schemes by which it was hoped to over-haul and revive the economy as a whole, thereby solving for ever the shortage of revenue. Unfortunately advances in this direction could be made only during prolonged periods of peace, and war was all too fre-quent and inevitable in this century.

Although most groups in French society—nobles of the sword and of the robe, clerics, municipal officials and the ordinary men of town and countryside—sometimes showed considerable hostility to each other, it was against the central government that their most vigorous protests were directed. Thus revolts were aimed at changing ministerial policies, only very occasionally containing any element of social reform or revol-ution. Even the Fronde affected the balance within French society in no significant way. The levels of the hierarchy were defined partly in terms of function but equally importantly by the privileges associated with them, and yet these often extensive rights were not a source of grievance among those who did not possess them. They were regarded as legal facts, and it did not occur to people that they should resent them or deem them unjustified. Everyone knew the specific privileges which would fall to him should he reach any particular point on the social ladder, and this acted as an incentive towards upward mobility. Even the royal ministers were aware that such rights must be openly respected, although it might be possible secretly to undermine them at the same time. It was therefore usually preferable to find convincing reasons for imposing a new tax than to attempt to abolish exemptions from an existing one.

The key figure of the following chapters is Jean-Baptiste Colbert. Firstly it is only during his ministry that the archives of Louis XIV's adminis-tration are sufficiently complete for the purposes of a volume in this series, whose main premise is that the documents should tell the story, with a minimum of editorial introduction. After his death in 1683, a greater division of ministerial responsibilities and persistent disruption of government by war and economic crises prevented the continued ac-cumulation of these large and coherent deposits, while administrative activity was brought down to the lower level of personal rivalries and short-term expedients. No one was able to further the Colbertian vision of a completely reformed bureaucratic machine, which he had been able to do so little to realise during his own life. Much of his unfinished work was not or could not be carried on. A second reason for confining this study to the years 1661–83 is that the range of Colbert's interests was so broad that it is almost impossible to do justice even to them in the space available. Occasionally a topic is discussed after 1683, in order to conclude a section more satisfactorily, but the problems of his successors are excluded.

There are further arbitrary limitations to the scope of this book. In the first place it is intended that this series should include two further collections of documents on the reign of Louis XIV, one on religious, the other on military and foreign, affairs. A more historical reason is that those aspects of government were of a very different kind from the daily workings of the internal bureaucracy which was the chief concern of Colbert. When a Frenchman thought of the monarch as 'absolute', he meant that the king was free from limitation in the fields which were traditionally the prerogative of the monarch—religion and the making of war and peace. (It is true that the persecution of the Huguenots would eventually become more widely debated than other religious matters and would dominate government attention at the expense of almost everything else, but this was the case only in the 1680s.) Foreign affairs always aroused little interest in French society. Men might complain bitterly about the burden of taxation and of serving in the army, but would not oppose the policies which prompted the wars for which the taxes were designed. The king was at liberty to declare war—their sole concern was that he should finance and staff his campaigns by means which cast no increased load on them. Although to Colbert himself war was the principal consumer of revenues, the army was a perpetually disruptive force in the provinces where it was quartered and the conscription of troops took humble taxpayers away from their lands, his detailed interest in military matters was confined to the painstaking acquisition of the necessary financial resources, and that is therefore the limit of our interest in the subject too. By contrast, the administration of taxation, finance, commerce, industry, justice and order was both Colbert's prime concern and affected the daily life of every Frenchman. On these topics, the minister was continually swamped with lists of grievances and complaints from the more eloquent members of society. It is this interchange between the minister and the people of France which forms the substance of this book.

The grievances were nothing new, and neither were the revolts in which they sometimes reached a climax. The policies which provoked them were familiar too, the direct legacy of Sully, Richelieu, Mazarin and their advisers. It is not the intention here, however, to unearth the antecedents of Colbertian policy or of social opposition to it. Rather it is to examine the whole of the internal administration of France during the twenty-two years when it was at its most efficient. The result of this investigation may point to a degree of centralised control which, if it was on the increase, was far from absolute. But it must be remembered that no seventeenth-century monarch or minister would have expected to exercise the kind of undisputed authority which a modern ruler might think appropriate to his position. The propaganda and the plans were never thought to be capable of total realisation, and Louis himself would often have regarded as successes those things which the reader of the following pages may often be tempted to call the failures of the royal ministers.

A few words must be said about the mechanics of this book. Chapter One begins with an introductory section on the problems facing the young king in 1661, taken from his own memoirs, and this is followed by a general survey of the administrative machinery with which he sought to solve them. Then follow chapters on individual aspects of governmental activity—taxation, finance, justice, commerce, industry and agriculture; and on those groups of officials and administrators who proved least amenable to obeying ministerial orders unquestioningly—the provincial Estates and the town councils. The final chapter, on revolts, offers a résumé of these various aspects when they are seen to come together at moments of crisis.

Many of the extracts are unavoidably brief. In a single letter from an intendant to Colbert a number of topics might be discussed, each meriting only a short paragraph, because the two men were continuing their debates in frequent letters. Here the extracts have been grouped according to subject matter, so that paragraphs from the same letter may be reproduced in different chapters. If the modern reader or the historian may find this evidence rather fragmentary, so too did the ministers and their agents who had to formulate or implement policy on the basis of it. Much imagination, intuition and luck were required.

The volume is ideally designed for the reader who has some knowledge of the period and should not be regarded as an introductory guide to the reign of Louis XIV. The texts have been selected, wherever possible, from printed collections which are readily available in major national and university libraries outside France. Thus, although the selection published here will be adequate for the purpose of many readers, those who wish to pursue their researches further will easily be able to do so within these French collections. The reign of Louis XIV is noteworthy for the amount of source material which his proud fellow-countrymen have assembled and printed. The full titles of the compendious works from which the extracts have been taken, preceded by the abbreviation used to designate them in the text, are as follows:

Clément—Clément, Pierre (ed.), *Lettres, instructions et mémoires de Colbert.* 7 vol., Paris, 1861–82.

Depping—Depping, G. B. (ed.), *Correspondance administrative sous le règne de Louis XIV.* 'Collection des documents inédits sur l'histoire de France'. 4 vol., Paris, 1850–5.

Hamy—Hamy, A., *Essai sur les ducs d'Aumont, gouverneurs du Boulonnais (1622–1789); Guerre dite de Lustucru (1662); Documents inédits.* Boulogne-sur-mer, 1906–7.

Isambert—Isambert, F. A. (ed.), *Recueil général des anciennes lois françaises depuis l'an 420 jusqu'à la révolution de 1789.* 29 vol., Paris, 1822–33.

Lemoine—Lemoine, Jean, *La révolte dite du papier timbré ou des bonnets rouges en Bretagne en 1675: étude et documents.* Paris/Rennes, 1848.

Sévigné—Sévigné, Madame de, *Lettres.* 'Bibliothèque de la Pléiade'. 3 vol., Paris, 1953–7.

One final word of caution for the reader—the documents, needless to say, frequently record only the failures of the royal administration to function according to plan. When it ran smoothly, it might give rise to no correspondence at all. Nevertheless the sheer extent of the opposition to ministerial policies which is described in the following pages cannot but lead the historian seriously to question the 'absolute' nature of royal government under Louis XIV.

$$\textit{Note on coinage values}$$
$$1 \; \textit{écu} = 3 \; \textit{livres}$$
$$1 \; \textit{livre} = 20 \; \textit{sous}$$
$$1 \; \textit{sou} = 12 \; \textit{deniers}$$

1 *louis d'or* = 12 *livres*	These larger units
1 *écu d'or* = 6 *livres*	varied in value, so
1 *écu d'argent* = 3 *livres*	these equations are only approximate.

(A *pistole* was worth the same as a *louis d'or* during this period.)

It is difficult to relate these units to modern values. An average winter daily wage was 12 *sous* for a man, 5 for a woman, increasing to 18 and 7 *sous* respectively at harvest time, according to one reliable contemporary source. He also quoted the tariffs of typical inns as follows: 15 *sous* for dinner, 25 for supper and 15 for horsemeat; alternatively 2 *livres* for one day's lodging, meat, drink, candle and fire. 8 *sous* was the sum to be paid by the towns to their citizens as the cost of providing a billet for one infantryman for one day.

N.B.   Place names have been modernised throughout, but surnames have been given in the most usual of their various seventeenth-century spellings.

1 GOVERNMENT AT THE CENTRE

A. The state of France at the death of Mazarin

One of the first actions of Louis XIV, when he decided to assume direct control of his kingdom on the death of Mazarin, was to make a rapid survey of the state of France, in order to diagnose her most severe problems and apply some immediate remedies. The opening pages of his *Memoirs* record these initial steps in personal kingship and they are reproduced here as an introduction to the wide range of issues which were to absorb the attention of Colbert and his agents for years to come. If the king treats each topic rather cursorily, compared with the lengthy and precise accounts of military campaigns and diplomatic negotiations which form the rest of the work, this reflects a marked preference on his part and one which is seen again and again. He fully understood the importance of effective internal administration and generously acknowledged the work of Colbert, but he found the details much less to his liking than those of foreign affairs, military strategy, dynastic marriages and other paths to prestige and glory.

1. Louis XIV: Memoirs for the instruction of the Dauphin

1661

Disorder reigned everywhere. My court was, for the most part, far removed from the state in which I hope you will find it today. Men of quality, accustomed to continual bargaining with a minister who was not averse to it and who sometimes found it indispensable, were always claiming imaginary rights over anything which was appropriate to their social standing. . . .

The finances, which provide energy and movement for the whole great body of the monarchy, were completely exhausted, and to such an extent that it was scarcely possible to see a remedy; many of the most vital and important items of my personal and household expenditure had been deferred in a most unseemly way, or had been met solely by resorting to credit, the consequences of which had still to be faced. At the same time the men of business appeared to be prosperous, on the one hand concealing their malpractices by every kind of deceit, and on the other ex-

1

posing them through their insolent and audacious luxury, as if they feared that I might not notice them. . . .

The least of the flaws in the order of nobles was that it contained innumerable usurpers, without any title or with one which had been acquired by payment and not through service. The tyranny which they exercised over their vassals and neighbours in a number of my provinces could not be allowed to continue, but it could be repressed only by the most severe and rigorous measures.

The passion for duelling had been somewhat reduced by strict enforcement of the latest laws, a point on which I have always been inflexible, and this proved to me that, as the cure for this deeply rooted disease was already working, there was never a moment at which one should despair of finding effective remedies.

Justice, whose task it was to reform everything else, was itself in my estimation the most difficult to reform. There were numerous reasons for this: posts filled haphazardly and for money, instead of by careful selection and merit; judges with little experience, let alone wisdom; almost universal evasion of my predecessors' decrees about age and conditions of service; corruption established by the usage of centuries, minds fertile in inventing ways around the best laws, and finally—and I consider this to have been the chief cause—those greedy men who make a living from court cases and who nurture them as if they were cultivating their private property, with no other purpose than to increase their length and number. My own council, instead of imposing order on other jurisdictions, far too often created greater disorder by the peculiar number of contradictory instructions it issued, every one of them published in my name and as if they came from me personally, which made the confusion all the more shameful.

The sum of these evils, their consequences and their effects, fell principally on the lower orders, who in addition were weighed down with taxes and in many areas were harassed by poverty, while in others they were troubled by being idle since the declaration of peace and needed above all to be given relief and work. . . .

After I had made this first brief review of what lay inside and outside my kingdom, I decided that, before investigating these matters in greater detail, I should begin by selecting carefully the tools which would help me in my work.

For above all I had resolved not to appoint a first minister, nor to allow anyone to exercise the powers of the king while I had only the title. On the contrary, I wished to divide the task of carrying out my instructions among a number of men, so that total authority should be vested in me alone.

It was for this reason that I wanted to choose persons of different occupations and talents, corresponding to the diversity of business which would regularly arise in the administration of a state, and I intended to share out my time and my confidence among them according to my assessment of their worth or to the importance of the matters I had entrusted to them.

For, from that moment, I imposed on myself the rule that I would attend to ordinary business twice daily, although I would never refuse at any other time to deal with something which arose unexpectedly.

On questions of conscience, the men I consulted most frequently were my confessor, the archbishop of Toulouse and the bishops of Rennes and Rodez.

When I had to give a decision on a judicial problem, I communicated it to the Chancellor.

For the examination of routine dispatches from within the kingdom and of petitions (which I received in large number because everything was in such disorder), I allocated to the secretaries of state two days of my time each week.

But for secret business and the most important matters of state, which required more time and effort than all the others put together, the men whom I believed were best able to serve me were Le Tellier, Fouquet and Lionne. . . .

And to tell you everything that was in my mind, I felt that it was not in my best interests to choose men of high social standing because, as I needed to give first priority to the establishment of my own prestige, it was important for the public to realise, by remarking on the rank of those whom I made use of, that it was not my intention to share my authority with them. . . .

I ordered the four secretaries of state to sign nothing whatsoever without consulting me, telling this also to the superintendent of the finances and instructing him to authorise no transaction without recording it in a book which was to remain in my possession, together with a brief abstract, so that I could see at a glance and at any moment the level of funds, the payments which had been made and those which were due.

The Chancellor was given a similar order, which was that he should seal nothing except when I had commanded it. . . .

Many people were convinced that before long one of the men who were close to me would gain a hold on my mind and on my administration.

The majority thought of my devotion to work as a fever which would soon subside. . . .

But time has at last shown them what they should believe, for they have seen me follow this same course without faltering: wanting to hear about everything that happens, listening to the prayers and complaints of my humblest subjects, always knowing the strength of my army and the state of my defences, dealing promptly with envoys from abroad, receiving dispatches, preparing some of the replies myself and giving my secretaries the substance of others; supervising the revenues and expenses of my kingdom; ensuring that those who hold important positions shall report to me personally; keeping my own counsel, distributing favours to people as I alone choose, reserving to myself all authority, and maintaining those who serve me best in a position of humility far removed from the exalted rank and prestige of first ministers. . . .

Of all the things which I noticed in making this personal review of my realm, there was nothing which touched my heart and soul more deeply than my realisation of the complete exhaustion of my peoples, due to the immense burden of taxation which they had to shoulder.

Thus, although the principal schemes which I had formulated for striking at the root of this evil could not be carried out so soon, because everything was in short supply and there were heavy debts which I had to meet, I nevertheless resolved to make an immediate reduction of three million *livres* in the *tailles* for the following year; telling myself that there was no better way for me to begin to implement my plans for growing rich than by preventing my subjects from falling into the ruin which seriously threatened them.

But in order that even the nobles and the inhabitants of the larger towns, who would derive no benefit from the reduction in the *taille*, should also receive some advantage from my early labours, I wished to curtail by various edicts the ruinous extravagance caused by their luxurious purchasing of foreign lace and gold and silver embroidery.

After meeting this, the principal need of my subjects, I could see nothing more ripe for reform than the abuses of justice. For this precious repository, which God has given into the hands of kings and which participates in His wisdom and His power, was so distorted by human corruption that it had degenerated into mere dishonourable trafficking.

But because it would have required time to draw up with the necessary caution all the many orders which ought to be given on this topic, I contented myself for the moment with reforming where it was most

4

urgently needed, and primarily with curbing the extensions of jurisdiction which the courts of justice had until then often granted to themselves.

As the *cour des aides*[1] had in some instances exceeded its powers, I removed a number of its more audacious members for a while, being convinced that it was wise to begin my administration by showing my readiness to take swift and severe action, in order to confine the other courts of the kingdom to their proper courses of duty.

And, as I had expected, the *parlements*,[2] who until then had raised difficulties about submitting to the orders of my council, received, with all the deference I could have wished for, the decree in which I forbade them to continue this abusive practice, allowing them to complain to me only when they believed that my council had issued a command which was contrary to justice or to legal procedure.

So too the assembly of the clergy, which was then still in session in Paris, and which claimed the right to defer the execution of my order that it be dissolved until I had issued certain edicts which they had earnestly requested of me, no longer dared to maintain its position once I had made known that it displeased me.

Meanwhile the office of colonel general of the infantry had fallen vacant on the death of the duc d'Épernon, and I resolved to suppress it because its powers seemed too extensive, and I did not believe that a sovereign should give to a single individual the right to carry out his orders and to have creatures in all the regiments which form the principal strength of his state.

It was also from this time that I began to moderate the excessive authority which had belonged for many years to the governors of frontier towns, who had so far forgotten the respect which they ought to feel for the king's authority that they had extorted the same dues from my subjects as they had from my enemies, and had dared to claim as a right and to negotiate for all the privileges which they thought fitting for someone in their position.

And as the reasons why their control was so absolute in their towns were that they had been given the right to distribute the revenues

[1] The *cour des aides* was the principal court which dealt with cases about the allocation of all kinds of taxation. It also received appeals from lesser taxation courts, but against its own decisions there was no appeal. The king is referring here to the Paris court, which was the worst offender, but other troublesome *cours des aides* existed in twelve other provincial centres.

[2] Louis particularly detested these, his most prestigious and influential law courts, because of the leading role they had played in the revolts of his minority.

from taxation, and that they were free to make up their garrisons from troops who depended on them, I determined slowly to take both these powers away from them and to send into all the important towns, from time to time, troops who took their orders exclusively from me. . . .

Meanwhile I ordered the continuation of the fortifications at the castle of Bordeaux and the citadel of Marseille, not only to remind these towns of their duty, but also to set an example to others. I vigorously repressed all movements which appeared to be veering towards disobedience, as at Montauban, at Dieppe, in Provence and at La Rochelle, where I insisted that my instructions be carried out with whatever severity was necessary, and I even commanded that there be sufficient troops to quell any degree of resistance which might be shown towards them. . . .

Of all the various crimes which I have enumerated, the people are always the sole victim; it is only at the expense of the weak and the poor that so many men have been able to build up their massive fortunes. Instead of the single king whom the people should have, they have a thousand tyrants at once, and with this difference: that the commands of the rightful prince are always mild and temperate because they are based on reason, whereas the orders of these false sovereigns are inspired only by their unbridled passions and are therefore always unjust and harsh. . . .

Although Louis XIV had decided to dispense with a first minister, he soon realised that one of his senior officials, the superintendent of the finances, Nicolas Fouquet, was still a man of immense power and independence. Fouquet deliberately thrust his massive wealth, his elaborate *châteaux*, his luxurious way of life and his ambition in front of the king's eyes. Louis XIV decided that he must be swiftly removed. How, therefore, were the legitimate functions of the superintendent to be divided up now?

In addition to the councils of finance which had been meeting for a long time, I wished, in order that the duties of the superintendent might be carried out more scrupulously, to establish a new council and to call it the 'royal council'. I appointed to it the maréchal de Villeroy, two councillors of state (d'Aligre and Sève) and an intendant of the finances (namely Colbert); and it is in this council that I have laboured incessantly ever since, unravelling the terrible confusion into which my affairs had fallen. . . .

The thing which I was most impatient to reform among this widespread corruption was the use of *ordonnances de comptant*,[1] because they

[1] *Ordonnances de comptant* were orders sent to the Treasury, authorising payments in cash, but not giving the name of the recipient nor the reason for the transaction. They could, therefore, become a costly and dangerous weapon in the hands of an unscrupulous minister.

had without doubt contributed more than anything else to the dispersion of my funds. For in this form one could give money unceasingly and without limitation to whomsoever one wished, and create, without fear or shame, a drain on my resources which should never have been permitted. To avoid this confusion in the future, I decided that I would personally fill in and keep a record of the details of every *ordonnance* I signed, so that from this time there would not and could not be any payment made for which I did not know the reason.

I also wanted to reallocate the tax-farms, which until then had not been distributed at a fair price; and in order to avoid the frauds which were often perpetrated on these occasions, either because of the corruption of the judges who allotted them, or because of secret conspiracies among those who ought to have been making higher bids, I went in person to the auction, and this first attempt of mine at intervention increased my revenue by three million *livres*, in addition to which I announced that the payments for these leases should be due monthly instead of annually in arrears, which straight away gave me the means of meeting very urgent expenditure, and enabled me to spare the state the loss of fifteen millions a year which had until then been consumed in interest on sums which it had borrowed.

As for the contracts for the direct taxes made by the receivers general, I decided that, instead of allowing the commission of five *sous* which was formerly granted, it should be reduced to only fifteen *deniers* in the *livre*, a reduction which, taken over the whole of the kingdom, added up to a sum so large that it gave me room, notwithstanding the exhausted state of my reserves, to decrease the *tailles* by four millions. . . .

Louis then describes his plans for sharing the resources of the richer provinces with their poorer neighbours in time of famine, and tells of the great warmth which his people feel for him as a result of this generosity. He also considers the *rentes*, which were government bonds, and summarises the improvements already effected in the fiscal system during his first year of personal government. Thus he could claim that, by 1662, there had been a corresponding improvement in cooperation between the central administration and the provinces.

1662

It was easy for me to see that my peoples responded to my affection in the most distant provinces just as in the nearest. . . .

The *pays d'états*[1] who, in the matter of taxation, formerly considered

[1] The *pays d'états* were basically those provinces where the old representative provincial Estates still met; although it was accepted that some sizable taxes would be paid to the state, they had the right to negotiate the exact amount, and this sum was still known, as in the days when it was truly optional, as the 'free gift'.

themselves to be independent, began to use this freedom for nothing more than to offer me their most willing obedience. . . .

It was also during this year that, continuing my plan for reducing the authority of fortified towns and provinces, I resolved never again to appoint any new governor for more than three years, reserving to myself alone the power to prolong this term by further letters of reappointment whenever I thought it desirable. . . . I have observed this rule ever since, and I have found that it produces two good results: the first is that those who serve under the governors no longer become so attached to them nor go to such lengths as they were used to do; secondly the governors themselves, knowing that they will remain in their posts only by keeping my goodwill, behave in a much more submissive way.

Louis then returns to a topic which had concerned him greatly in 1661, the need to increase the crown's income and thereby to reduce the burden of taxation on the people.

I realised that there were two important ways in which I might bring some very necessary relief to my overburdened subjects; one was to diminish the number of men in the provinces who were exempt from paying the *tailles*, and whose own load was therefore added to that which the poorer people had to bear. I attacked this abuse by each day suppressing and reimbursing the holders of many small, new and utterly useless offices, to which this right of exemption had been attached during the war in order to encourage men to buy them. The second was to examine more closely the exemptions claimed by certain parts of my kingdom, and which they possessed not so much by right or because of the great services they had rendered, as by the irresolution of the kings our predecessors or the weakness of their ministers. The Boulonnais was among this number. The inhabitants of that area have been hardened to warfare since the Hundred Years War, and even had a kind of militia which was divided up among the various towns of the province, was quite well trained and could easily be called together when needed. For a long time they had used this as a pretext for contributing nothing to the *taille*. I wished to impose a very small sum on them, simply to show them that I had both the right and the power to do so. Initially this had a very bad effect; but I have turned it to such good use that, although it has caused me considerable pain and sorrow, it will be of great advantage in the future. The ordinary people, either frightened of something which seemed new to them or secretly stirred up by the nobles, raised a commotion against my orders. My remonstrations and the gentleness of those whom I had chosen to convey them, being mistaken for timidity and feebleness, increased the tumult instead of appeasing it. Up to six thousand rebels gathered together in a number of places; their anger could no longer be ignored. I sent in troops to punish them; the greater part of them then melted away. I readily pardoned those whose retreat signified their repentance. A few, more obstinate in their wrongdoing, were taken with their arms at the ready and were delivered into the hands of the law. Their crime deserved the death penalty; I made sure that most of them were condemned only to the galleys, and I would have even excused them this punishment had I not believed that in this confrontation I should follow my reason rather than my inclinations.[1]

Most of the rest of the memoirs are devoted to the details of military campaigns, foreign policy and diplomacy; yet there are a few passages which do refer to the internal state of the kingdom.

1666

I was also preoccupied with another matter which chiefly affected men of fashion, but whose results were spread widely throughout the kingdom. I was aware that enormous sums were being laid out by private individuals and were perpetually leaving my realm, through the purchase of lace and other foreign manufactures. I observed that the French lacked neither the labour nor the materials to produce these goods themselves, and I did not doubt that, if they were made on the spot, they could be sold at a much more favourable price than those which came from so far away. Because of these considerations I decided to establish factories here, whose effect would be that the nobles would experience a reduction in their expenditure, the lower classes would gain from the money which the rich were spending, and the large amounts of currency which had been leaving the country would be retained and would steadily lead to great wealth and plenty. Beyond that, it would provide employment for many of my subjects, who had until this time been forced either to decay here through idleness or to go and seek work among our neighbours. . . .

In a short while many manufactures, such as cloth, glass, mirrors, silk stockings and the like, were established in my kingdom according to this plan.

I was carefully searching above all for means to expand and safeguard maritime trade on behalf of my subjects, making existing ports safe and locating sites for new ones. But I also conceived another plan at the same

[1] This revolt in the Boulonnais, the province centred round Boulogne, is one of the three insurrections considered in some depth in Chapter 8—see pp. 255–60.

time, which was no less useful: this was to build a canal which would join the Ocean to the Mediterranean, so that it would no longer be necessary to travel right round Spain in order to pass from one sea to the other. This would be a large and difficult enterprise. But it would have immense advantages for my kingdom which would thus become the centre and arbiter of trade throughout Europe. And it would be all the more glorious for me who, by carrying out this project, would be raised above all the greatest men of past centuries who had unsuccessfully attempted it. . . .

(*Mémoires de Louis XIV*, ed. C. Dreyss, 2 vol., Paris, 1860)

B. Decision-making: The king or the ministers?

The new central conciliar system which Louis XIV rapidly instituted at the core of his administration had a practical and a symbolic function. Firstly it was to be a small body of trained professional ministers, who would gather immense amounts of detail about the resources and state of the kingdom and from whose meetings with the sovereign would come major decisions of policy. Secondly it was to be a perpetual reminder to the people that the old criteria of birth and hereditary position counted for nothing in the selection of the highest counsellors. Even loyalty and devoted attachment to the service of the king were not enough by themselves—royal favour, an easily revocable gift, was the *sine qua non* of success. The arrest of Fouquet underlined this point dramatically, and the members of the bureaucracy realised from these first days of the personal rule that the king would show no mercy towards others who used their official position to gain excessive advantage and power for themselves and their families. That was also the crime which led him to deprive the princes of the blood royal of their great influence. A number of distinguished aristocrats, who were trusted friends of the monarch, did remain or become advisers whom the king consulted frequently, doing so informally in the course of daily life at court, but it was the council of more humble ministers, with its regular meetings and its concern with routine as well as counsel, which was the most obvious manifestation of the new order.

These ministers were usually drawn from the small group of secretaries of state who had been an increasingly important feature of French central government and of some other European administrations since the sixteenth century. Under the Valois kings they caused little resentment among the people, but when in the seventeenth century the crown began to extend their range of competence and when their responsibilities became more clearly delineated, they started to arouse the hostility of the privileged orders. In particular they offended because they rose rapidly to positions of considerable influence solely through the elevating force of royal favour, without following the traditional routes of promotion which governed advancement in the rest of the bureaucratic hierarchy. Nevertheless the secretaries of state who served Louis XIV were men from administrative families and were not, as many historians have assumed, 'bourgeois'.

That was simply a slander put about by jealous and vituperative courtiers like the duc de Saint-Simon. It was their service in the lower levels of the bureaucracy which had brought men like Colbert and Le Tellier to the notice of the king and his ministers in the first place.

If these counsellors and makers of policy, both aristocrats and new ministers, kept their place solely through their talents and the continuing favour of the king, they contrast sharply with the officials who had bought their offices and who were the executive agents by whom policy had to be implemented. Before considering the extent to which the royal ministers were able to dominate this unwieldy bureaucracy, an attempt must be made to discover how far these ministerial policies were evolved in close consultation with the king and whether these powerful royal servants had much freedom to initiate courses of action within their own departments. Secondly it is important to appreciate the minute detail in which topics were discussed by the ministers, and the lengthy, accurate reports which were demanded from their agents in the provinces. Such precision was a novel factor in French government. Louis XIV and Colbert were prepared to devote most of their time to the business of ruling, and expected their officials and clerks, especially the intendants, to do likewise. They knew that a government is as good only as its sources of information, and were far ahead of many contemporary rulers in acting upon this knowledge.

An estimate of how much initiative lay with the king, how much with the ministers, is not easy to reach. Although Louis XIV did not intend to appoint a 'first minister', and although he kept a watchful eye on all his close advisers, he obviously allowed them considerable latitude. He was influenced by their ideas, and might quote them as his own—the views of Colbert are clearly evident in the king's *Memoirs* for the year 1666[1]—and there were often times when it was almost impossible for him to reach an independent assessment of a situation without his information having first been filtered through ministerial minds. To the average Frenchman, it was certainly the ministers who were responsible for unpopular royal policies, not the much-loved king.

The following group of documents illustrates some aspects of the relationship between Louis and Colbert, but it is not possible to paint a clear picture. Many of their discussions took place unrecorded, behind closed doors, and throughout his correspondence Colbert regularly attributed to the king statements and orders which are really his own, thus adding the weight of his master's authority in a way which the king would of course have approved. Those reproduced here consist of an early public statement of Louis XIV's trust in his minister (2), a typical report from Colbert to the king with the latter's comments in the left-hand margin (3), a warm letter to the minister by Louis, and the celebrated rebuke which the faithful servant received from his royal master and which reveals that the king was no mere cipher to be used by the ministers at will (4); finally (5) there is a letter in which he tells a group of erring subjects that he has deliberately withheld news of their offence from the king and that they would be well advised to change their attitude before he informs his royal master.

[1]See pp.9–10 above.

11

2. Colbert to all intendants and *trésoriers de France*

20 November 1662

As the king has been pleased to inform you of his wishes regarding the finances of your generality,[1] in the letter of credence for me which you will find enclosed, written in his own hand, I have therefore thought it my duty to add these few lines to assure you that I shall not fail to make an exact report to His Majesty of all that you do me the honour of sending me as a result of his orders, and to represent to him your zeal, your determination and your diligence in everything you do which concerns his service.

(Enclosure):

Louis XIV to all intendants and *trésoriers de France*

16 November 1662

Having made known to all the 'commissioners sent out into the provinces'[2] last year, when I myself took control of the conduct and administration of my finances, that my intention was for them to learn my wishes on this subject through the letters that Monsieur Colbert should write to them on my behalf, which I instructed them to accept completely and without question, I am very glad to repeat to you the same point once again, and to say that I wish you to show the same acceptance towards all that he writes to you. . . .

(Clément, vol. II(i), p. 235)

3. Colbert to Louis XIV

SCEAUX, *24 May 1673*

It must be done as soon as possible.

All the merchants have been asking me if it please Your Majesty to allow the circulation of Spanish royals, at 3 *livres* 58 *sous*, as

---

[1] The *généralité* was the area administered by an intendant and by the local financial officials—the *trésoriers de France*. It was divided up into a number of *élections*, each under the supervision of an *élu* (see p.106, note 1).

[2] This is a literal translation of the phrase 'commissaires départis dans les provinces', by which the intendants were frequently designated.

Good.

was fixed in the last decree published in Your Majesty's presence, and I believe this to be a necessary step.

The edict about the alienation of the tax on timber in the province of Normandy has been registered by the courts.

Whichever you think is better.

I estimate that this will yield between four and five million *livres*. It is necessary for me to know if Your Majesty wishes it to be farmed out at a discount of one-sixth, or if it should be collected direct. Farming is the surer method, and the tax-farmers would show greater determination than the royal agents we would have to send out; but perhaps, by direct collection, we could economise somewhat on the amount of discount.

It is for you to judge which is better.

My advice would be to farm it out; I await Your Majesty's instructions.

The ordinances are signed.

I also ask you to sign the enclosed ordinances.

I am very keen to have news of Versailles.

I am now going to Versailles; I will report to Your Majesty tomorrow about the progress of the building works there.

(Clément, vol. II(i), p. ccxxxii)

4. Louis XIV to Colbert

VERSAILLES, *15 April 1671*

I have been told that you are not in very good health, and that your keenness to return here will only be harmful to you.

I am writing you this note to order you to do nothing which will prevent you from serving me when you arrive, in all the important tasks which I shall entrust to you. In a word, your health is so vital to me that I wish you to conserve it, and to believe that it is my trust in you and my friendship which makes me speak in this way.

(Louis XIV, *Oeuvres*,[1] vol. V, pp. 477–8)

[1] 6 vol., Paris, 1806, edition.

CHANTILLY, *24 April 1671*

I was sufficiently master of myself, the day before yesterday, to hide from you the pain I felt on hearing a man like you, on whom I have heaped kindnesses, speak to me in the way you did. I have felt a great friendship for you, which is borne out by what I have done; I still feel like this, and I am showing you a striking example of my affection when I tell you that I restrained myself for a moment for your sake, and that I did not wish to say to your face what I am now writing to you lest you displease me even further. It is the memory of the service you have given, together with my friendship, which lead me to give you this advice; profit from it and do not take the risk of angering me again, because, when I have listened to the opinions of you and your colleagues, and made my decision on what course should be followed, I do not wish the subject to be mentioned again. If the navy is not agreeable to you, if it is not to your taste, if you would prefer another post, speak out freely; but after I have given my judgment, I do not wish to hear a single complaint. I am telling you what is in my mind in order that you may work on a secure basis and that you will not take any wrong decisions.

(Champollion Figeac,[1] vol. II, p. 519)

5. Colbert to Pellot, first president of the *parlement* of Rouen

SAINT-GERMAIN-EN-LAYE, *8 January 1672*

I have reported to the King on the information contained in your letter of 4 January, about the registration of the two declarations concerning the roll of summonses and fines; but I must warn you that all the difficulties which your court is making will assuredly incur His Majesty's irritation, and I can inform you with certainty that, over the carrying out to the letter of the ordinances which His Majesty has published, there is no task to which the principal officials of these courts should apply themselves more vigorously, because His Majesty is so sensitive that it is almost impossible to ensure that, no matter what colour one paints these modifications, they will not provoke a show of indignation on the part of His Majesty. I must therefore tell you that the King has not yet been informed of the amendment clauses contained in the judgment of the *parlement* of Paris and that, if His Majesty had been, he certainly would not

[1] *Documents historiques inédits*. Publiés par M. Champollion Figeac, Paris, 4 vol., 1841–8.

have permitted them. But as the remonstrances drawn up by the *parlement* of Rouen have prompted His Majesty to wish to be informed in greater detail of all that happens in this matter, if he were to find out that they included some modification or that the ordinance had not been carried out to the letter, I can assure you that this step would be so hazardous that I would advise you to persuade your court to obey with the deference and respect which they owe to him, or, if you cannot bring this about, to take steps to make it clear to the King that you yourself have had no part in their refusal.

(Clément, vol. II(i), p. 79)

2 THE INTENDANTS

The historians who have exaggerated the effectiveness of centralised government under Louis XIV have tended particularly to inflate the importance of the intendants, whom they have seen as the very basis of the absolutist régime they have described. These chroniclers of change, always looking for the rise and fall of social groups in history, have added the intendants to the ranks of their 'new men' which also include the secretaries of state—in fact the holders of both offices came from established bureaucratic families. An intendancy was becoming an important rung on the ladder of promotion within the sovereign courts of justice, although it was not a position which could be bought and was therefore one from which the holder could easily be dismissed. The tasks which he would have to carry out made it imperative that he be of some status within the hierarchy of the judiciary.

The crucial point about the post of intendant was that, unlike all other bureaucratic offices, it was always given to a man who was not a native of that generality, and who therefore had no personal vested interest in the life of the area. Yet, if the intendant knew that this enforced period of residence in a strange province would benefit his career, he nevertheless hoped that his exile from his family, his local influence, his estates and his investments would be as brief as possible. He would accordingly use every legitimate means, and sometimes others, to demonstrate the efficiency of his administration and his suitability for higher office in his home district. As a result, Colbert wisely placed no more confidence in the intendants than he did in the rest of the bureaucracy and, if their duties were novel in their very nature, they were allowed no more licence than other officials in exercising their authority. There was soon evidence that some of these officials were not above corruption, and that others showed genuine sympathy for the grievances voiced by their provincial charges both against local officials and also against the royal government to which they were required to communicate all such petitions and complaints. In order to reduce this personal involvement in the life of their generality, intendants were often moved to a different intendancy after a few years in any one post.

Earlier French kings and ministers had often tried to introduce new grades of functionaries, who would be more efficient and loyal than those then in office, but on each occasion these recent creations had acquired the attitudes of the administrative class as a whole, preferring personal and local interests to state service. The intendant was somewhat different. He was designed to be primarily an observer of existing officials rather than a replacement for any of them. Colbert knew that there was no alternative system to substitute for the vast ranks of venal office-holders and that efforts must be concentrated on improving the efficiency and devotion to duty of those who already held office. There was insufficient

16

money to buy these men out of their posts, and there would have been no more reliable men of adequate training to replace them.

During the ministry of Colbert the intendants were used more extensively than ever before, not just to spy on the bureaucracy but to send in highly detailed reports about every aspect of provincial France. Throughout the kingdom they acted as the eyes and ears of the Paris ministers, and were therefore in some ways the blinkers round which the ministers could not see. If the king's independence of action was limited by his reliance on the secretaries of state as sources of his information, so too these senior counsellors relied on evidence which had been filtered through the minds, biases and prejudices of the intendants. Sometimes the intendants were sent on general tours of inspection in their area, on other occasions they were asked to investigate specific problems. The implementation of the policy decisions which resulted from their reports was usually entrusted to the ordinary members of the bureaucracy, but the action consequent upon an unusually important decision might be assigned to the intendant himself, in which case he was allocated special powers to deal with this particular matter only. Had he been given general and permanent powers of execution, instead of simply having general rights of examination and interrogation, he would have been one of a corps of potential tyrants which no royal minister could have tolerated. The ministers had to rely so extensively on their reports than it would have been madness to concentrate the tasks of sending information and enforcing royal decisions in the same hands. By keeping the two distinct, the ministers provided themselves with the best possible, although far from perfect, standard by which to judge others. A further drawback to this central system of conciliar decision-making was the sheer size of France, and lengthy delays were caused by the considerable time taken for information to travel to Paris and for the ministerial response to be conveyed to the localities.

The intendants were no novelty. They had been used spasmodically but increasingly during the sixteenth and seventeenth centuries, until they became a major grievance of the Frondeurs. Yet this outcry seems to have been caused less by the realities of their power at that time than by its implications and possible development in the future. The Frondeurs were opposed to the whole idea of an official who came from a distant area to a province where he was not part of the closely knit network of administrative families, and who might therefore be subject to very different, and from their point of view undesirable, pressures from outside. Once again the realities of the system, when the intendants were extended and their powers more clearly formulated by Colbert, were less frightening than the officials feared and the government hoped.

The intendants will appear throughout the subsequent chapters, from which it will be seen that they did indeed improve the efficiency of the administration, but slowly and only to a partial degree. In the *pays d'états* and the larger municipalities, where the elected Estates or town councils played an important and semi-independent part in local government, they were able to do less than in the *pays d'élections*, which were administered by venal officials directly responsible to the crown, but throughout France they did root out the worst examples of corrupt officialdom, although much sharp practice remained. It would never be possible to ensure that all royal and municipal officials perpetually put the interests of their sovereign before their own, especially so because the borderline between the legal and the illegal exploitation of office was hard to draw exactly. In addition, as the intendants were given more and more tasks by the royal ministers, they were able to do everything less thoroughly.

This chapter discusses the role of the intendant in general terms, leaving the details of their activities until later chapters. It considers their function as conveyors of information, the agents they employed, their relations with other royal officials, and finally it discusses the one official who was a viable alternative to the intendant in certain areas.

A. The duties and qualities of an intendant

The annual instructions from the central government to the intendants, whose wording varied but little from year to year, give the best idea of the scope of the activities required of them (*6*), although further exhortations, urging unceasing labour, increased speed, more detail, greater impartiality and the avoidance of inconvenience to the people were often needed (*7–9*). When their opinion was asked and information sought on more specific matters, it was often because the government hoped to introduce some innovation. Secrecy might be vital here, if the ultimate purpose were to be the undermining of local privilege or authority (*10*), although the motive behind the ministerial enquiry might also be kept secret from the intendant himself.

6. Colbert to all intendants

FONTAINEBLEAU, *1 June 1680*

The King has instructed me to repeat most strongly to you the orders which His Majesty has given you, in every preceding year, about the inspection of the generality in which you serve. He wants you to apply yourself to this task even more vigorously than you have in the past, because he wishes there to be equality in the allocation of taxes and a reduction in all kinds of abuses and expenses, thus bringing further relief to his peoples in addition to that which they have received from the lowering of taxation.

The King intends that, as soon as you have read this letter, you should begin your visit to each of the elections in your generality:

That, during this tour, you should examine with the utmost care the extent of landed wealth, the quality of livestock, the state of industries and in fact everything in each election which helps to attract money there; that you should seek out, with the same diligence, anything which might help to increase animal foodstuffs, to expand industrial production or even to establish new manufactures. At the same time, His Majesty wants you to journey to three or four of the main towns in each election, excluding those which you have chosen in earlier years, and in these places to call before you a large number of the tax-collectors and leading inhabitants from the surrounding parishes; to take pains to find out all that has taken place concerning the receipt of the King's orders, the nomination of collectors, and the allocation and payment of the *taille*; to ferret out all the malpractices in these procedures; to try to remedy them yourself; and, in case you find some which can be treated only by a royal judgment or decree, to send me a report in order that I may inform His Majesty. . . .

Listen to all the complaints which are brought to you about inequalities in allocation on the rolls of the *tailles*, and do everything which you consider appropriate to stamp out these iniquities and to make the allocation as fair as possible. Examine with the same thoroughness the expenses which are incurred, both by the receivers in relation to the collectors and by the collectors in relation to the taxpayers. As this is something which has always been open to endless trickery, you cannot show too much determination in trying to expose it. One of the most effective methods which His Majesty wishes you to use in repressing these abuses is to suspend the receiver of the *tailles* who seems the most culpable in your generality, and to entrust his duties to someone else for the next year. This punishment will assuredly cause the disappearance of many of these evil practices. His Majesty will also offer a reward to the receiver who has run his election the most effectively, and who has incurred the least expenses.

His Majesty likewise requires that you should report every three months, without fail, on the number of prisoners who have been arrested concerning the *taille* or the various indirect taxes.

He further wishes you to prevent, in so far as this is possible, the receivers general of the finances, and the receivers and collectors of the *tailles* from impounding livestock; because on the multiplying of their numbers depends a large part of the kingdom's prosperity, not to mention the ability of the people to make a living and to pay their taxes. . . .

You must also inspect in each election the amount of the taxes collected to date, both for last year and for this, giving all the necessary orders for hurrying up the whole process, and must join the receivers of the *tailles* in searching for means of regulating collection so that the taxes are paid during the current year or within the first three months of the following one at the very latest.

With regard to the nomination of collectors, see that the rotas of collectors have been properly drawn up, and that they are implemented promptly. Check that there is no corruption involved in this method of naming collectors, and if there is you must decide how to remedy it.[1]

(With regard to the nomination of collectors, it is evident that this procedure, which involves the bringing of many legal actions before the *élus* and by appeal to the *cour des aides*, causes widespread abuses, and you should therefore in the first place examine the ways of preventing this; and among these methods, you might well consider whether the rota system as it is practised in Normandy would be a good alternative and would bring some benefit to the people.

I am sure that you know how these rotas are compiled in each taxable parish. The first contains the names of the richest inhabitants, the second those of the less wealthy. Those who are included on these lists take it in turns to be tax-collectors, without the need for nominations; and there are already rules laid down for the drawing up of the lists.)

Having explained to you His Majesty's intentions concerning the *taille*, I am further instructed to tell you that he wishes you to investigate, at the same time, all the disorders which have arisen in collecting the indirect taxes; to which end he requires that, as soon as you become acquainted with some abuse, you should report it to the agents who have been appointed in each generality or election to collect these dues; that you should listen to their explanations, and should send me an exact account of all you have discovered together with your views on the most suitable remedies which should be applied.

He further tells me to inform you that he will be able to see, from the places and dates at the head of your letters, whether or not you have carried out his orders promptly.

His Majesty has already made known to you at such length his intentions for the liquidation and repayment of the debts of the communities,[2] that is enough for me to say simply that he wishes you to devote adequate attention to this task, which you must undertake for each election as you have been told to do. He also requires you to keep watch over everything involving the coinage throughout your generality, which is to say that only coins authorised by royal edict and decree may be in circulation. On this same subject, His Majesty wants you continually to ascertain that

---

[1] The contradiction between this paragraph and the two which follow is explained by the fact that this is a circular letter, in which some passages refer only to certain generalities.

[2] See pp. 68–73.

there are no mints producing false coins; and, if you should find one, to send word immediately, so that His Majesty may issue the necessary orders for bringing the culprits to trial without delay, because there is no crime which is more prejudicial to the interests of the people than this one.

(Clément, vol. II(i), pp. 131–5)

7. Colbert to Foucault, intendant at Montauban

VERSAILLES, *14 July 1682*

I have submitted a report to the King about the memoir you have sent me, describing your inspection of your generality; but as you have not given an account of your tour election by election, and have produced a general survey instead, His Majesty is not satisfied with it, because it was his intention that you should visit each election in your generality, allowing yourself plenty of time to do so, and should inform him in detail of your findings concerning the points which are contained in my dispatches; this is an order which every intendant must obey, and it is the only way to please the King. His Majesty is not content with your general statement that livestock has greatly increased throughout your generality, as it is important that His Majesty should be able to see, from the reports which are sent to him, the exact number of animals in each election. . . .

I will write to you in more detail about each election after you have sent your report to the King.

(Clément, vol. II(i), p. 199)

8. Colbert to Ménars, intendant at Paris

VERSAILLES, *17 July 1682*

I have received your letters and memoirs of 20, 23, 27 and 30 June, and 3 and 5 July, describing your visit to the elections of Nemours, Sens, Joigny, Saint-Florentin and Tonnerre. I am sure you would wish me to tell you that to visit five elections in fifteen days is no way to satisfy the King, for it is impossible to carry out in so short a time all that His Majesty requires of you, as contained in the orders and letters I have sent to you. You should not have led yourself to believe that His Majesty would put any faith in your memoirs, when it is obvious that they have been prepared so hastily. You were asked to examine so many problems that you would quite clearly have been unable to carry out unaided all the investigations which you have put in your reports, and it is almost impossible to believe that you have done any more than consult some local officials about these matters, and have based your conclusions on what they told you.

(Clément, vol. II(i), pp. 200–1)

9. Colbert to Marle, intendant at Riom

VERSAILLES, *23 September 1672*

. . . It seems that I must say to you once more what I have said so many times before, that you are much too eager to order general investigations during the course of your work, and that these large-scale enquiries serve only to vex the people, forcing them to come from the farthest corners of the generality in order to bring their papers to your office, thus loading you with endless amounts of documents and discussions which promote neither the service of the King nor the welfare of the people. You must eliminate this desire once and for all, so that I shall be spared the trouble of mentioning it to you yet again. . . .

(Clément, vol. IV, p. 75)

10. Colbert to d'Aguesseau, intendant at Toulouse

SAINT-GERMAIN-EN-LAYE, *3 March 1679*

. . . In the meantime the King wishes that you should apply yourself with the utmost diligence and secrecy to compiling a thorough and detailed list of all the communities in the province, arranged in order of dioceses, to include all the taxes which are levied in each diocese on the instructions of the Estates, for the free gift, for military provisions, for the expenses of holding the Estates, for local administration, salaries, fees, bounties and in general all levies which are imposed by the diocesan assemblies[1] or by the town councils to finance the tasks with which they are

---

[1] The dioceses and diocesan assemblies of Languedoc were administrative divisions and committees, with no religious function. The secular and religious dioceses were usually identical in area, but not always.

concerned; this must be done lest there be some dues in certain communities which have not been authorised by the proper body.

It is also essential that, in this same list, you report on the acreage of each community, including the number of properties which have been valued for taxation, and those which have been classed as noble and which enjoy exemption from all taxes. I know that this list will cause you considerable trouble, if it is to be drawn up with the necessary precision and secrecy; but you will also be aware that these labours will not be fruitless. . . .

(Clément, vol. IV, pp. 127–8)

B. Limits of his powers and relations with other officials; use of sub-délégués

The powers of the intendant were carefully defined by the central government, and he would be sharply reprimanded if he exceeded them. He was to work in harmony with other royal officials where possible, making sure that they did not exceed their duties (*11*), but avoiding unnecessary criticism of them as a body (*12*), and he was never to encroach upon the rightful power of other administrative officers and provincial institutions (*13*). If the intendant were to discover flagrant abuses of royal authority, he should not take action himself but should inform the king at once; then he would be sent a commission to deal with that specific instance. On the other hand he should not report matters within his competence to Paris, to avoid making decisions himself, nor should he show fear in time of trouble (*14*). Above all he must never appear to favour his generality, because the unique quality of the intendant was that he did not have personal ties with the area he administered, and ought to be outside the network of local influence and patronage.

Yet, even the most honest, loyal and conscientious intendant needed assistance in carrying out the ever-increasing number of tasks which were being thrust upon him, and he thus began to appoint deputies called *sub-délégués*. These men were, of necessity, natives of the generality, and their local links and preoccupations often conflicted with the policies they were required to implement. Therefore, although some delegation of powers was inevitable, the royal ministers strongly opposed the widespread use of these *sub-délégués* (*15–6*).

11. Colbert to Chamillart, intendant at Caen

SAINT-GERMAIN-EN-LAYE, *15 April 1672*

I was very surprised to learn, from your letter of 11 April, that the collector of tolls at Valognes has ordered the arrest of a Dutch vessel in the port of Cherbourg, on the grounds that war has been declared against the

States of the United Provinces. It is not the place of these toll-collectors to meddle in such matters; but, seeing that the ship has been seized, the master must be permitted to ask that it be returned to his charge. However, it is now your task to inform the collector in private that I have pondered over this event and have decided that, for an action of this kind, I should put the culprit in a dungeon, with his feet in irons, for a period of six months, to teach him that it is not his privilege to use force in this way and on his own initiative, and that he should show greater wisdom in the future.

I ask you to tell him this in private because it is not appropriate for the people to believe that there is dissatisfaction with some of the men who collect taxes for His Majesty.

(Clément, vol. II(i), p. 250)

12. Colbert to Feydeau de Brou, intendant at Montauban

SAINT-GERMAIN-EN-LAYE, *10 February 1673*

... I cannot refrain from telling you on this occasion that I have noticed, in all your letters, an excessive eagerness to think ill of all those who are employed in the collection of the King's taxes, or, to put it rather better, that you believe too readily whatever you hear said against them. You know well enough that, in every situation, no matter how trivial, there is nothing more dangerous than to allow oneself to be biased. As the business of collecting public taxes is always burdensome for the people, and is therefore detested, it is important not just that you should take care to believe and think ill of these men only when you have reliable evidence, but that, even when you have such proof, the people should not hear a public official like you openly condemning and blaming the agents who are instructed to carry out this task. . . .

(Clément, vol. II(i), p. 272)

13. Colbert to Creil, intendant at Rouen

PARIS, *23 December 1672*

... With Monsieur Pellot,[1] who is the head of all justice in the generality in which you serve, you must maintain an intimate and frank relationship, for that is very necessary if the King's interests are to be fur-

[1] Pellot was first president of the *parlement* of Rouen.

thered; and apart from this general reason it will please me if you treat him amicably, because of the lengthy friendship which he and I have shared, and because your unity will be fruitful when you are dealing with the policing of Rouen, to which matter you must both apply yourselves in order that the province may benefit. . . .

(Clément, vol. IV, pp. 85–6)

SAINT-GERMAIN-EN-LAYE, *3 February 1673*
I have seen and examined the memoir which you have sent me about the matters you have investigated and which have caused the *cour des aides* of Normandy to lodge complaints. . . .

I believe that I have already told you to be careful that you take cognisance only of those matters which are within your competence. . . . But on this last occasion, it is your own memoir which has done you the disservice which you usually blame on others, because the account it contains shows clearly that you have concerned yourself with affairs about the *tailles* which are under the jurisdiction of the *élus* and the *cour des aides*. To bring this business to a close, you must take care to contain yourself within the limits of your powers as granted you by the council in its decrees, and, with regard to the *tailles*, by the regulations which have been registered in the *cour des aides*. Over and above that, if the *élus* and the *cour* give bad decisions, tell me, and await the appropriate powers to remedy them. . . .

(Clément, vol. II(i), p. 270)

14. Colbert to Bidé de La Grandville, intendant at Limoges

PARIS, *15 November 1674*
I have received your letter of 10 November, concerning the sedition which certain men have been fomenting in the countryside around Angoulême, and I have read it to the King. But I must tell you that His Majesty was astonished to hear that you had shown such great alarm that you had doubled back in your tracks, more especially because His Majesty thinks it likely that this undesirable action on your part will have given the rebels a boldness which they hitherto lacked.

I must point out to you that not only should you have remained at Limoges until you were better informed of what was happening, so that you need not have exposed yourself to danger at the wrong moment, but that having advanced you should not have retreated, for nothing is more serious, at a time like this, than to show signs of fear to the people. . . .

It is the duty of those who have authority in the provinces to reveal not the slightest alarm, and even to take chances on such important occasions in order to tell the people where their duty lies, and also to make known to them the severity of the punishment which will fall upon them if, through disobedience and rebellion, they interrupt for a few moments the flow of victories and noble actions of our master. . . .

(Clément, vol. II(i), p. 360)

15. Colbert to Sève, intendant at Bordeaux

PARIS, *18 May 1674*

I feel bound to tell you that, of all the matters concerning the behaviour of the intendants in the provinces, the one which causes the King the greatest distress is the large number of subdelegates whom they have created in all the towns of their generalities; these men, on their own initiative, have arrogated to themselves the authority to take cognisance of every sort of business, and very often abuse this power which they do not understand, and which they extend in whatever way their fantasies, passions and interests suggest to them. . . .

It is true that your commission gives you the right to appoint subdelegates; but it was the King's intention that this faculty should be used, as it has been until now, in connection with ephemeral matters to which you were unable to attend, because of the need for you to devote yourself diligently to other affairs of greater importance which had arisen at the same time. Thus I would advise you that you could do nothing more pleasing to His Majesty than to suppress this large group of subdelegates, and to use them in future only in the way which I have just described to you.

(Clément, vol. IV, p. 108)

16. Colbert to Dugué, intendant at Lyon

PARIS, *21 November 1681*

. . . I have recently examined a report on the liquidation of debts in the town and election of Montbrison. . . .

On which matter, I am eager to point out two things to you:

Firstly, that this liquidation has been carried out by one of your subdelegates, and it is not the intention of His Majesty that the subdelegates of the intendants should deal with liquidations, because His Majesty has decided that it is too dangerous to entrust such a task to men from the same province, who would always have interests and desires which would run counter to the course of true justice. . . .

(Clément, vol. IV, p. 150)

C. An aristocratic alternative to the intendant: The provincial governor

The intendant found it no easy task to watch over the bureaucracy and daily life of any province, but in the *pays d'états*, where the elected Estates were still responsible for the overall supervision of everyday administration in their area and for a decision on the exact amount of taxation to be paid to the crown, his job was even more difficult. In the *pays d'états*, most of which were the more remote provinces, far from the court, the king therefore often appointed one of his close and trusted aristocratic friends as provincial governor. This post existed in all provinces, but in many of them it had been reduced to an honorary and ceremonial function, simply because in the past it had offered its holder the opportunity of creating a dangerous and independent authority over his region, based on the troops he commanded, which was virtually beyond the control of the central government. Yet the Bourbon kings and their ministers recognised that this almost unlimited power over a piece of the kingdom could be used not only for evil as it had been, notably during the civil wars of the sixteenth century, but also for good, and aristocratic governors accordingly played a significant role in extending the authority of the crown into the more distant provinces throughout much of the seventeenth and eighteenth centuries.

In order to master his dissident provincial subjects, the governor needed more than his extensive powers. To gain their respect he had to be an aristocrat of considerable prestige, who already had property and influence in his province. In contrast to the intendant therefore, he was meant to be personally involved in the economic and political life of his *gouvernement*. When Louis XIV decided that governors should henceforward be appointed for a limited period of three years,[1] thereby giving himself the ready means of removing an ill-chosen one and at the same time issuing a warning to all that excessive independence of action would not be tolerated, he did not intend to reduce every governor to impotence nor to change the holders of governorships every time their tenure of appointment expired. Some of them were renewed again and again, for one spell of three years after another, and their sons were allowed to succeed them in office, because these were men whom the king trusted and who were ruling their province effectively. This is another of the many instances during the personal rule of Louis XIV where the power and privileges of a social group were destroyed or limited

[1] See p. 8.

but where certain individuals within the group retained their position, although it no longer rested on any hereditary or social right but on royal favour alone.

Whereas Louis and Colbert put no more trust in the intendant than in any other bureaucrat, their faith in their carefully selected aristocratic governors was sufficient for them to permit these officers to act on their own initiative and to make important decisions without reference to Paris. This avoided the lengthy delays caused by sending messengers to and from the capital, which was an impossible method of administration in these distant and separatist *pays d'états* where the stormy sessions of the Estates gave rise to problems which required instant action or intervention. Moreover the high social position of the governor put at his disposal the powerful weapons of clientage and influence by which he could mould the opinions of the leading inhabitants. In some ways he was almost a living embodiment of royal authority in the province (*17*). Being more closely involved in provincial life than the intendant, who was usually concerned to do what he thought Paris would like best, he sometimes supported the genuine grievances of the people and might well produce a change of heart on the part of the royal ministers, while on other occasions he was able to persuade his province to be more amenable to the demands or actions of the crown (*18*). The intendant tended to have much weaker powers of persuasion both in Paris and in his generality. The governor often took a leading part in economic development,[1] and his reports could be just as detailed as those demanded from the intendant. He also initiated discussions on points which he thought would interest Colbert, whereas an intendant seldom did more than to reply to the precise questions and carry out the specific tasks required of him by the ministers. Even a distinguished prince and soldier like Condé took his administrative responsibilities seriously (*19*). At times of revolt a respected aristocratic governor could often control or restrain his *gouvernement* when the presence of an intendant would have served only to inflame passions further,[2] while in some provinces there were both an intendant and an effective governor, working well together, the former having frequently been chosen by the royal ministers after consulting the latter. However, there were many conflicts between the two officials in other areas, as when the governor might refuse to mobilise the troops and thus deprive the intendant of his only real way of making his authority a reality (*20*).

Like the intendants, the governors will be seen at work in greater detail in the chapters which follow.

[1] See for example p. 184, including note 1, and pp. 212–13, 221 and 227–8.
[2] The restraining influence of the governor in the 1675 Breton revolt is discussed below, pp. 237–55.

17. Jean-Baptiste Colbert: Memoirs on the financial affairs of France in the form of a history (1663)

Chapter V

. . . His Majesty has sent out special commissions to liquidate the debts of the communities in Languedoc and afterwards in Burgundy, in which task he wishes that Monsieur le Prince [de Condé] and Monsieur le prince de Conti,[1] governors of these provinces, shall play a personal part, in order to make the people understand more clearly how deep are His Majesty's feelings on this matter, which is now being investigated for the greater advantage and happiness of the inhabitants of these provinces. . . .

(Clément, vol. II(i), p. 49)

18. Colbert to the duc de Chaulnes, governor of Brittany

SAINT-GERMAIN-EN-LAYE, *10 December 1673*

I hope that the bad humour in which you have found all the members of the Estates will be turned to your greater glory and will make even better known to the King the respect in which you are held in the province, and your hard work to bring to a successful conclusion those things which are pleasing to him and are in his best interests. . . . I feel I should tell you that the edicts which have given rise to these complaints in Brittany have been put into operation and are still in force in Languedoc and Provence, two provinces where other circumstances make them seem even more burdensome than they do in Brittany, among which is the fact that in those areas it is the intendants, whom the provinces regard as outsiders, who judge all matters arising from the execution of these edicts. . . .[2]

---

[1] It is interesting to note that, although Louis was careful to ensure that they did not regain too much independent influence, he actually encouraged some of the former princely rebels to exercise power as governors. Both of these provinces were *pays d'états* and the role of the governor was crucial.

[2] Brittany was the last province to receive a permanent intendant, at the relatively late date of 1689.

I have no doubt at all that Brittany will do the same, or even better; but I confess to you that, as I hope that this province will yet show, and more strongly than others, clear signs of its unlimited devotion to the wishes of His Majesty, I am a little concerned that I shall be obliged to tell him of such ill will in the minds of his subjects. As I am convinced that you can inspire other feelings in them, I am hoping that I shall soon have the satisfaction of bearing more agreeable news to His Majesty. . . .

(Clément, vol. II(i), pp. 309–10)

SAINT-GERMAIN-EN-LAYE, *23 December 1673*

His Majesty was not surprised, because of both your adroitness and the high regard which you enjoy in the province, to learn of the change which you have brought about in the six or eight days since you arrived there. . . .

His Majesty . . . has been pleased to learn, from your letter of the 16th, that the Estates have voted the free gift of 2,600,000 *livres* after their first deliberation. . . .[1]

(Clément, vol. II(i), pp. 315–17)

19. Colbert to the duc de Bourbon, governor of Burgundy[2]

DUNKERQUE, *24 May 1671*

I have read to the King the whole of the letter which it has pleased Your Highness to write to me about what has taken place from the opening of the Estates of Burgundy until the 16th of this month, and I must begin the reply which I have the honour to make to you by telling of the satisfaction which His Majesty feels with all that you have done in this assembly and during the time you have been in the province. . . .

His Majesty has been surprised to see the detail into which Your Highness has entered, both with reference to the industries of Auxerre, and over the repayment of the province's debts, and he fully realises the amount of skill, ingenuity and leadership needed to have prompted the

---

[1] See pp. 54–9 for the details of these negotiations by which the governor, not without difficulty, induced this change of heart among the deputies of the Estates.

[2] The prince de Condé was now known as the duc de Bourbon. He had acquired the duchy of that name in 1661.

deputies to authorise the collection of an additional tax for nine years, to be used for repaying these debts. . . .

(Clément, vol. IV, pp. 57–8)

20. Colbert to the comte de Pardaillan, governor in Upper[1] Poitou

8 September 1662

I feel I must inform you that Monsieur Pellot[2] has written to tell me that you are refusing to order the troops to go and coerce the parishes who are in arrears with the payments which are due from them, that you have forbidden them to leave their barracks for any reason whatsoever unless you have ordered it, and that you have even withdrawn from some villages those whom the said Monsieur Pellot had sent there, all of which is completely ruining the collection of the taxes and prevents the collectors from making their payments to the treasury. You will, I trust, permit me to say to you that it is vital to the success of our plans that you should issue no instructions about the billeting of troops without his agreement, and that you should give all the orders he asks of you when he feels that it is appropriate to use the soldiery to compel recalcitrants to pay what they owe; otherwise I shall have no alternative but to inform the King who, it may be presumed, will not be pleased. . . .

(Clément, vol. II(i), p. 231)

[1] The large governorship of Poitou was divided into two. Therefore, although Pardaillan was technically called *lieutenant général*, he was *de facto* governor.
[2] Pellot was intendant at Poitiers and Limoges.

3 THE PROVINCIAL ESTATES

The *pays d'états*, the provinces in which the time-honoured representative Estates continued to meet regularly, were among the more efficiently administered areas of France, although ministerial control over them was more tenuous than elsewhere. As Colbert was unable to devise any more effective alternative local government for such distant and separatist regions, he was compelled to maintain and work with these assemblies, while dreaming that one day, in a more ideal world, he could abolish them. Among their principal disadvantages, the royal ministers could cite their extensive control and supervision of much routine administration in their province, their right to dispute the amount of tax they should pay to the king, and their extensive privileges which they guarded jealously. In their favour it had to be admitted that their orders were obeyed by the people with greater speed and goodwill than the direct royal agents had come to expect in the *pays d'élections*. In the *pays d'états* the highest authority was at least one which had been elected by the populace, whereas the officials who carried out the same tasks elsewhere were regarded as the creatures of the hated ministers in Paris. Thus resistance to royal commands came at a different, and higher, level in the *pays d'états*. Once the Estates were persuaded to implement a policy, then there was a good chance of its execution. The *pays d'élections* possessed no comparable forum in which the views of the province as a whole, and of its component social groups, could be clearly voiced and brought to the notice of the central government. The only method of opposition there was the obstruction or corruption of royal officials as they carried out their orders, which was not very difficult given the scant regard paid by these agents to some of the commands they received from the ministers.

The Estates were by no means unreasonably stubborn. It is true that they had acquired a tradition of initially opposing anything that was required of them, but their aggressive and lucid statements of intent, which suggested an irreconcilable division between the views of the province and those of the crown, did not prevent the negotiation of a final compromise solution. It was accepted that each side overstated its position, bargained and ultimately resolved the matter fairly amicably. It was not possible for one party in such a dispute to override all the wishes of the other. The deputies of the Estates were particularly passionate in their defence of the vast corpus of fiscal, military and judicial privileges which the province had accumulated over the centuries and which the king was always keen to undermine. The crown had not the strength openly to annul these rights but it never ceased its attempts to erode them. In the *pays d'élections* the twin ministerial goals of increased revenue and reduced local privileges could be pursued stealthily by the intendant without causing an outcry, even if results were slow, but in the *pays d'états* such plans had to be channelled through the Estates,

32

giving rise to angry exchanges and prolonged bargaining between their delegates and the royal representatives. Although some Estates met annually, a number of the more important ones met only every few years and it might therefore be some time before king or Estates could reopen an issue on which one of them had suffered a defeat.

The Estates did not always sacrifice the interests of the state to those of their province. In time of war they were prepared to make an extra effort in providing for the increased expenditure of the king, and it is equally true that the deputies were sometimes accurate in asserting that the economic state of the province did not permit it to pay the sum required by the treasury. But, in the average prosperous peace time year, the usual course was for the crown to exaggerate its needs and the province to magnify its poverty and distress, each trying to wrest concessions from the other by fair or foul means.

Many examples of detailed administration in the *pays d'états* will be found below, in the chapters on taxation, finance, justice, commerce and industry. This chapter is concerned with the sessions of the Estates themselves, because it is in and around their debates that the nature of the relationship between the various social groups in the province and the central government can best be seen. The principal bargaining counter of the Estates was their right to negotiate the exact amount of taxation to be paid by the province. Certain taxes had to be paid in full, of course, but one important direct tax—the free gift—had to be agreed with the royal commissioners. It was accepted that a substantial sum would be paid, because it was no longer the purely voluntary grant from which it had derived its name in the past. Yet there was considerable room for manoeuvre, and these negotiations make an interesting central core in the documents which follow.

Although Colbert was determined to reduce the *taille* throughout the nation as a whole, he felt with some justification that the *pays d'états* were undertaxed and that their contribution should rise while that of others fell.[1] Thus the crown was always attempting to increase the free gift, at the same time as it was raising the other taxes paid by the province and was demanding that the Estates spend more and more on civil and military administration, on communications, commerce, industry, education and on other public works. It must be remembered, however, that the discrepancy between the fiscal burdens of *pays d'états* and *pays d'élections* is partly explained by the fact that the former had to finance such major items of local administrative expenditure directly from provincial funds, whereas the latter received considerable grants from the central government.[2] A further drain on the resources of the *pays d'états* was the sheer cost of running the Estates themselves, which was a prime cause of ministerial keenness to terminate the sessions at the earliest moment.

[1] See pp. 120–1.
[2] See pp. 201–2, 205, 207–9 and 227.

A. Composition, procedure and attitudes

The documentary evidence on the *pays d'états* is frequently more complete than that on the *pays d'élections*, but unfortunate lacunae remain nevertheless. Languedoc is particularly well served by its archives and is also the province whose administration was most widely admired in the seventeenth and eighteenth centuries as being a model of its type. Before examining the progress of the free gift in Languedoc, there is a short group of general documents to introduce various aspects of the Estates: their composition (*21*), the problem of choosing the town where the assembly should meet (*22*), and an example of the regular method of proceeding from confrontation to compromise in one of the Estates which is not discussed in detail below (*23*).

21. General memoir on the province of Languedoc[1]

The Estates of Languedoc are composed of men from all three orders, that is to say: from the church, the nobility and the third estate. The order of the church consists of three archbishops and twenty bishops, whose rank in the assembly is determined by the date of their consecration and who, if they are unable to attend, have the right to send their vicar general instead.

The order of the nobility consists of a *comte*, a *vicomte* and twenty-one barons. The *comte* is Monsieur le comte d'Alais, who occupies the first tied seat and is the first speaker for the nobles. . . . The *vicomte* is Monsieur le vicomte de Polignac, who has the second tied seat. The first of the barons is the representative of the Vivarais in rotation, that is to say one of the twelve barons of the Vivarais who have the right to attend the Estates in turn, each one therefore sitting one year in twelve. . . .

The baron in rotation from the Gévaudan has his tied seat after that of the Vivarais. . . . The other barons . . . take their seats in turn, day by day.

When the titulars of the *comté*, *vicomté* and *baronnies* cannot come in person to the Estates, they have the right to send in their place a gentleman with full powers of attorney. . . .

The third estate consists of the mayor-consuls appointed by the chief towns in each diocese[2] and by certain other places, the former having the

---

[1] Although this memoir was compiled in 1698, most of its contents apply equally well to the period 1661–83.

[2] See p. 22, note 1, for the meaning of 'diocese' in Languedoc.

right to send someone every year, the others taking it in turns according to the rota and order of rank which varies from one diocese to another, and depends on specific rules and ancient custom; and to explain this rather more precisely, the principal town in each diocese sends one or two deputies, and apart from them there are some other towns who take it in turns to represent the diocese at the Estates, with the exception of Le Puy which does not send diocesans, and seven dioceses where the towns are fixed and take their seat every year. . . .

The order of voting in the Estates is as follows: after the president has put forward the proposition, a prelate begins by giving his opinion, then a baron states his views, and after that come two deputies who are called out by the name of their towns, one immediately after the other, because the voice of the third estate alone is considered to be as great as that of the clergy and the nobility together. . . .

The bishops enter the assembly wearing their rochets and camails, the barons with their swords.

The former are seated in the raised seats on the president's right, the barons on his left. . . .

The king instructs the secretary of state who is responsible for the province of Languedoc to send letters under his private seal to the titulars of the first two orders, to the towns who are to send deputies and to the officials of the province. . . . When all the deputies have arrived, on the day appointed in the letters, the royal commissioners take their seats in the assembly, which they then declare open by reading out the king's commissions.

Throughout the duration of the Estates, the tasks of the commissioners are to receive remonstrances from the deputies on any matter they suggest, and to carry out two commissions, the first of which is called the verification of the debts of the communities and consists in effect of auditing everything which the communities have borrowed. In this province they have a great liking for running up bad debts, and it is necessary to restrict this practice by means of the annual audit, which declares a loan to be null and void if it does not conform to the rules which the council has laid down on the subject. The royal commissioners are the sole members of this commission.

The other is known as the report on the taxes, and it involves the scrutiny of the rolls of the *tailles*, in order to ensure that there have been no impositions beyond what is due; to do this, they make use of the registers which contain all the decisions made by the communities about the sums they ought to provide, and act as controls against which to check the taxes.[1]

The royal commissioners come into the Estates only on the opening day, in order to convey the permission for the assembly to meet, and to inform them of the reason for its convocation with regard to the taxes which must be levied on the people of the province; this is the day[2] on which they make the request for the free gift and, having done so, retire so that the Estates may feel free to discuss it. They appear again when it is time to decide the details of the equivalent,[3] and on other occasions when there is some matter of importance to impart or explain to the deputies. . . .

The commissioners who preside at the Estates on behalf of the king are: the governor of the province, one lieutenant general and three of the king's lieutenants, the intendant and two *trésoriers de France*, one representing the finance office at Toulouse, the other that at Montpellier.

The business which is discussed by the Estates includes the regulations for and the allocation of the sums which are to be levied on the province; the scrutiny of the closing statement by the treasurer of the general tax account,[4] and those for the army and the equivalent; and other things of a similar nature which are reported to the Estates; and in general all topics which affect the province as a whole, and especially disorders; also any happening which might diminish their rights and privileges of which the most important, and the one which the Estates consider to be their most fundamental principle, is that no tax can be levied without their consent, just as no tax can be levied without the consent of the King.

The deputation which was sent to represent the province at court then reports on everything which took place, and on the replies received from the royal council to the demands included in the list of grievances they presented to His Majesty.

[1] Apart from these two commissions, the Estates appointed a number of others from its own members, to consider extraordinary taxation, industry, agriculture, public works and other tasks whose local organisation was in the hands of the province and therefore had to be overseen and directed by the assembly.

[2] It was not until the 1671–2 assembly that it became the invariable practice to announce the sum required on the first day.

[3] The *équivalent* was a lump sum paid by the province of Languedoc, as an alternative to paying the *aides* on certain commodities. The *aides* were still imposed, but it was the province which kept the profits from them.

[4] The treasurer was appointed by the Estates to collect almost all the taxes in the province and arrange for payments to the crown.

The taxes which the Estates have agreed on are distributed among the twenty-three dioceses which make up the province, according to an ancient tariff which is recognised by all. . . .

The local assembly of each diocese has to be convened, as is prescribed by custom, one month after the meeting of the Estates in order to allocate, among all the communities in the diocese, the tax which has been demanded from the diocese by the Estates, and it is for this reason that these assemblies are called *assiettes*;[1] they consist of a bishop, a baron and the representatives of the towns of the diocese, together with the chief commissioner who has a commission from the governor to authorise this meeting on behalf of His Majesty. . . .

(Depping, vol. I, pp. 3–8)

22. The duc de Chaulnes, governor of Brittany, to Colbert

RENNES, *30 June 1675*

. . . I feel I must explain to you why I have selected Dinan as the meeting place of the Estates. My first idea was to choose Nantes, because the sight of a castle with a garrison would make the delegates more respectful. But so many other considerations cancelled out this advantage that I felt I ought to name Dinan without further hesitation. These other factors were that the Estates have never proved more difficult nor been so full of incident than in the town of Nantes, because of the fiery and uncouth natures of the inhabitants, keen arguers who are quick to flare up at the least thing.

Although the people there have accepted the presence of troops in the town without complaint, they have been none the less upset by it in their hearts and would gleefully take advantage of a disturbance in the Estates to create further discord and confusion. . . .

As one of the chief trading commodities of the Nantes region is wine, and as it is only within the Estates that there can be a discussion about the duty which is levied on it, and there is talk even of making some specific proposals about this obligation, Nantes would not be a suitable place to discuss or examine it; for there have been many occasions in the past when, in the presence of the maréchal de La Meilleraye,[2] the nobles have

[1] *Assiette* means 'allocation' or 'assignment' of a tax.
[2] The maréchal de La Meilleraye was the predecessor of the duc de Chaulnes as governor of Brittany.

drawn their swords in the assembly here at Nantes, because of differing opinions about the duties on wine, and it would be more difficult to reach agreement in this town than in any other. Moreover, Monsieur, it is upon the president of the clergy that the smooth running of the Estates depends; I believe my Lord of Nantes to be a good bishop; but I do not think you would consider him capable of presiding at the assembly unless this was a time of peace and complete calm; and the man who presides over the third estate[1] is the president of the *présidial*,[2] who unfortunately has no talent and no prestige within his social class, and it is that group which, because of the coming debate about the tax on noble land acquired by commoners, will be very hard to control; and when it pleases you to enter into a discussion about the bishops of this province, you will readily agree that my Lord the bishop of Saint-Malo is the only one qualified and able to occupy this position. . . . That, Monsieur, is why I maintain that Dinan, the only place in the diocese of Saint-Malo in which they could be held, is the most suitable in the present circumstances, because at least at Dinan we will have to surmount only the difficulties which are natural to any Estates, whereas at Nantes we would be exposed to all those which the entire population of that town were able to think up. . . .

(Depping, vol. I, pp. 546–9)

23. The duc de Bourbon, governor of Burgundy, to Colbert

DIJON, *18 June 1662*

. . . To come to the Estates themselves, the opening took place on Tuesday the 13th. . . .

Since then the Estates have had discussions every day, and the extreme misery from which the province is suffering, whether it be because of the heavy burdens they have shouldered in the past, or the recent years of dearth, or the disorders which have been creeping steadily forward for some time, has convinced them that His Majesty will give them some relief on this occasion. This is why they came to me the first time with an offer of only 500,000 *livres* for the free gift. Then, after I had told

---

[1] In Brittany the three estates deliberated separately for much of the time, in Languedoc they debated together.

[2] The *présidiaux* were local courts which dealt with the smaller offences which would otherwise have been the prerogative of the *parlements*.

them what I thought of that, which would be too lengthy to recount to you in detail, they raised it to 600, then 800, and finally to 900,000. Until then I had been resolutely insisting on 1,500,000;[1] but I realised at that moment they had almost certainly decided not to give any more, though not through lack of affection, for I can truly say that from the beginning to the end I saw them show towards the King nothing but respect, obedience and goodwill; and it was simply their fear of finding themselves unable to honour their promise which prevented them from making a higher offer. I therefore reduced it to 1,200,000, which my orders permitted me to do, and invited them to discuss among themselves yet again, telling them that I was not prepared to ask the King for a lower figure and that I believed they could do nothing better to further their own interests than to obey the King without question, showing him in this encounter the highest expression of their submission and good intentions. They have done this willingly. They came to me this morning with an offer of 1,000,000 *livres*; but they begged me to let it rest there, and to demand nothing more from them for the free gift; and when I said to them that they must provide a little more in order to give the King reason to be entirely satisfied with them, they made a great show of their poverty and begged me to explain it to His Majesty; yet, rather than displease him, they preferred to make one more effort, leaving it to me to decide how much it was necessary for them to provide. I told them that I imagined His Majesty would have the goodness to content himself with 1,050,000 for the free gift, and they gave their hands on it, all the while pressing me to convey to the King the extreme hardship of the position in which they found themselves. . . .

I must inform you that the chamber of the clergy and that of the nobility have acted splendidly in the discussion of the free gift, having raised almost no problems about any of the proposals which have been made to them. It is true that the third estate has given us a little more trouble, but that is excusable, seeing that it is they who carry the burden of almost all the taxes[2]. . . .

(Depping, vol. I, pp. 426–31)

[1] The Estates of Burgundy met every three years, and this sum for the free gift would be collected throughout that period.

[2] It was frequently the case that the third estate was more troublesome than the other two, partly because the nobles and clergy hoped for royal patronage or favour and therefore wished to keep on good terms with Colbert, even though they were prepared to stand by their province. Also they were rather more experienced in matters of state, and understood the central government's difficulties better. Colbert was careful to exploit this rift in the Estates whenever possible.

B. Languedoc: The will to cooperate—a dominant clergy and a testy third estate

This group of documents traces the daily progress of the Estates of Languedoc in some detail, especially during its debates on the free gift. In this province the deputies were more cooperative than in certain others, although the third estate was frequently tiresome. The dominant order here was the clergy, whose ranks contained both influential supporters of the crown and outspoken champions of provincial privilege, including a significant number whose vote might be cast for either side according to the merits of a particular issue. The assembly was summoned annually, usually in December. In 1661–2 it was peaceful (*24–7*); in 1662–3, a time of some economic distress, the third estate was more difficult (*28*), but in 1663–4 harmony had returned (*29*); the following winter saw heated debates at all levels in the assembly. During the war years of the 1670s the fiscal burden became too heavy and, although the Estates tried to support the increased needs of the central government, they had to borrow the money from elsewhere. Even so, the sums to which they had consented might be in considerable arrears when it came to the actual process of payment, despite the apparent harmony between the king and the deputies (*30–1*). Agreement in the assembly did not mean that commitments would or could be honoured in full.[1]

24. Bazin de Bezons, intendant at Toulouse, to Colbert

PÉZENAS, *January 1662*

The Estates are to begin tomorrow.... I have spared no effort to bring them together, and my Lord the bishop of Viviers[2] assured me today that he will make every attempt to bring the affairs of His Majesty to a successful conclusion. He is on the best of terms with all the bishops, and especially with my Lord of Albi, who is the first to give his opinion and who will help him with anything which may arise. If you wish us to spend a little money in order to expedite the King's business, please tell me so that the necessary steps can be taken in good time. . . .

(In Colbert's hand): Spend some money!

(Depping, vol. I, pp. 49–51)

---

[1] For a similar attitude among judicial bodies, see p. 139, including note 4, and pp. 147–9.

[2] The bishop of Viviers was president of the Estates in the winter of 1661–2, a session which started unusually late, not beginning until the new year.

25. The bishop of Saint-Papoul to Colbert

BÉZIERS, *13 January 1662*

Monsieur le prince de Conti, accompanied by the other royal commissioners, today made his entry into the meeting of the Estates.

He spoke very effectively and strongly in support of His Majesty's interests.

He finished his speech with these words: 'Remember that I am speaking on behalf of a King, and a King who means to govern'.

Monsieur Bazin de Bezons, whom His Highness called upon to explain the details of the royal proposals, dwelt at great length on the evil conduct of those who had administered the finances in the past,[1] and upon the good order which His Majesty was taking pains to re-establish. . . .

After a long discourse, the said Monsieur Bazin de Bezons concluded with the following proposals: a free gift of 2,500,000 *livres*, payable monthly;[2] a double payment of the equivalent,[3] in order to replace the funds which were lacking in the general treasury of the province; an increase of one-quarter on all the tax-farms, save those of the salt-tax; and the multiplication of the number of office-holders.[4]

These requests astonished the assembly, especially the third estate. . . .

The first discussion by the Estates, at which the royal commisioners hope that they will offer 1,200,000 *livres*, will not take place until the 17th or 18th of this month. That will give us time to approach each of our friends and persuade them to agree to grant this sum. Monsieur Bazin de Bezons and I decided today that, if this plan is to succeed, it is vital that it be accepted by my Lord the bishop of Albi, who speaks first in the assembly; and that it be discussed beforehand with every prelate and baron individually and in secret, without calling a general meeting, for fear that the third estate should also wish to assemble.

[1] It was only four months since the arrest of the superintendent of the finances, Nicolas Fouquet.

[2] Monthly payment was a burden, because it involved extra expenses of collection and of guarding this precious cargo on more frequent journeys to the treasury along dangerous roads; and it meant that the money had to be raised more quickly. See also p. 7.

[3] See p. 36, note 3.

[4] Those offices which were held jointly by three men, each working every third year, were now to be divided among four holders, working every fourth year, thus bringing revenue from the sale of a new post into the treasury, but reducing the profits of the existing officials.

I have no doubt that the bishops and barons will all be of right mind, from what they have said to me, with the exception of my Lord of Montpellier of whom I can speak only through the reports of others. . . . Monsieur Bidou, vicar general of Toulouse, who gives his opinion first among the vicars general, will assuredly do what is required of him, having received orders from my Lord the archbishop, whom he represents, that he should conform to our wishes. . . .

Monsieur de Saint-Martin, the envoy of the comte d'Alais, who is the first speaker after the barons, comes to see me often, and told me yesterday that he would go up to 1,200,000 *livres*. If he persists in this, as I believe he will, it will have a good effect on the other representatives; for he is very highly regarded.

As for the third estate, His Highness must talk to them, and also beg the bishops and barons to influence those that are dependent on them. . . .

(Depping, vol. I, pp. 58–61)

26. The bishop of Mende to Colbert

BÉZIERS, *16 January 1662*

Obeying the order which you gave me to inform you from time to time of the progress of our assembly, I am writing to report, Monsieur, that in a day or two we shall discuss the free gift, and there is reason to hope that on the first debate we shall reach agreement on 1,200,000 *livres*. I have four votes in my diocese; they will wait upon my decision, and will always be of my opinion. I have also received offers of support from some other deputies, and I am sure that they will do what is best for the service of the King. I think that we shall reach a solution in two or three meetings; but in case the debate becomes more prolonged, you will oblige me greatly, Monsieur, if, when you reply to this letter, you include some sign of favour towards the consuls of my diocese and towards those who are prepared to accept my judgment, asking me to send you their names, in order that you may reward them on future occasions which may present themselves, or show them some similar mark of friendship. That will give them the courage to do even better. . . .

(Depping, vol. I, pp. 66–7)

27. The bishop of Béziers to Colbert

BÉZIERS, *20 January 1662*

Yesterday we discussed the King's business, and it was decided with almost one voice to give 1,200,000 *livres* to His Majesty. My Lord of Albi and I were deputed to carry the news to Monsieur le prince de Conti, who told us that these first steps proved to him that the Estates were taking pains to give satisfaction to the King. . . .

The third estate, being less well informed than the clergy and barons about world affairs and about the needs of the kingdom, normally think only of how they can bring relief to the ordinary people, and the consuls of Toulouse, who head the parterre,[1] are accustomed to show the greatest zeal for this cause. This year, because of the care taken by His Highness . . ., the consuls were of the same mind as my Lord of Albi, and certainly produced this uniformity of opinion by their example. . . .

I imagine that Monsieur le prince de Conti will attend the Estates again next Monday, and then we shall debate during the rest of the week. He will have to try to persuade them to offer 1,500,000 *livres*, and he will need to exert considerable pressure; for my Lords the bishops of Montpellier and Montauban, who are bursting with fury because they were obliged to accede to our views in the first discussion, will do everything in their power to make the third estate adhere to the sum already agreed on; harm is always easier to do than good, but we shall be vigilant and prevent them. After we are decided on 1,500,000, I think that all we shall be able to do is to arrange for it to be paid monthly, and that it will be impossible to go further. The King must be content with their goodwill. . . .

(Depping, vol. I, pp. 63–5)

28. The archbishop of Toulouse, president of the Estates of Languedoc, to Colbert

PÉZENAS, *8 December 1662*

Since my last letter, nothing has been done in our assembly except to continue with the ordinary business of the province, which I have been hurrying along as diligently as I can, in order to find the means of closing the Estates in two months at the outside. With that end in view, Mon-

---

[1] The parterre of the assembly hall was the place where the third estate sat, and is therefore often used to describe the estate as a whole.

seigneur le prince de Conti and Monsieur the intendant are in full agreement that I should state clearly to the gentlemen of the parterre that they will receive four monthly expense payments,[1] whether they take six weeks or whether they make the business last for six months; and that, if they exceed the time permitted, they will be paid nothing for their stay. I hope that we shall not run into any difficulty and shall be finished soon. . . .

Monseigneur le Prince came to the assembly yesterday with Monsieur Bazin de Bezons, and announced the proposal for 2,500,000 *livres* in terms so gentle and civil that they really deserved to be given the sum they asked for. . . .

(Depping, vol. I, pp. 95–7)

PÉZENAS, *11 December 1662*

. . . I hope that on Thursday at the latest we shall debate the King's business, and I reckon, judging by the mood of the parterre as I see it, that in this first discussion we shall propose the same amount as last year, that is to say 1,200,000 *livres*. The real effort must be made at the second debate, in order to surpass what was offered last session; we shall do our utmost. . . . Monsieur the intendant has overlooked nothing which might encourage our parterre to do its duty, and His Highness this morning began to send for the members of the Estates one by one. Just this minute Monsieur de Chassan, consul of Toulouse and a well known advocate, has left here, he being among those who claim to be our friends. . . . I expressed to Monsieur de Chassan my astonishment that the city of Toulouse, which is a compounded town[2] and pays not a penny of the free gift, should allow its consuls to appear here regularly in the assembly as if they were tribunes of the people in opposition to the service of the King, and that one day a reason would be found for annulling their composition fee; then it would seem more acceptable that they should make so much noise to defend their own interests, whereas at the moment they can claim no motive apart from a wish to show their disinclination to please the King. . . .

(Depping, vol. I, pp. 97–8)

[1] The deputies received a payment for every month or part of a month during which the Estates met. They therefore made sure that, for example, a six week session extended into three calendar months. The fourth payment was a bonus which the president could award if the assembly had been cooperative.

[2] These towns paid a lump sum instead of certain taxes, and their contribution did not vary from year to year no matter how taxes might fluctuate.

29. The prince de Conti and Bazin de Bezons to Colbert

PÉZENAS, *29 December 1663*

This morning Monseigneur le prince de Conti came to the Estates . . . and told them that the King was pleased with the respectful way in which they had expressed their opinions at the first debate, when they had offered 1,200,000 *livres*; but that, as this sum was not proportionate to the needs of the state, he had come to ask them to conclude by a second discussion what they had begun in the first, and he was able to assure them that good behaviour was the only way to earn His Majesty's favour. . . . It was customary, after the propositions had been put by my Lords the royal commissioners, to allow five or six days for reaching some kind of agreement..., but scarcely had Monseigneur le prince de Conti left the assembly than the deputies came to him, bearing the reply that they had unanimously decided to give 1,400,000 *livres*. Monseigneur le prince de Conti replied that the King had had the kindness to grant him the power to accept this sum, in order to afford some relief to the province, and in consideration of the efforts they had made in preceding years, but that this was on condition that the payments be made monthly; when this was reported back to the assembly, the news was received with the utmost joy and warm acknowledgments of His Majesty's goodness, their surprise being all the greater because they had not for an instant believed that their offer would be accepted. . . . The whole affair ended with a unanimity of opinion throughout the entire company, and without a single dissenting voice, which has never before been seen in these Estates. . . .

(Depping, vol. I, pp. 133–4)

30. The cardinal de Bonzi, archbishop of Narbonne,[1] to Colbert

NANCY, *13 September 1673*

I have just allowed myself the honour of writing you a letter . . . about the expedition of our affairs . . . in order that the sums of money which His Majesty has done me the honour of telling me that he requires our assembly to grant this year, shall not only be agreed willingly, as our

[1] The cardinal, who had been trusted by Mazarin and Louis XIV for many years and was also highly respected in Languedoc, was the president of the Estates in the winter of 1673–4.

45

zeal and loyalty demands that we should, but shall also be able to be paid as well. For in good faith, Monsieur, and without wishing to play the part of the president who is too much preoccupied with aiding the King's subjects, I can assure you that on the day we agreed to give 2,000,000 *livres*, there remained more than 1,000,000 still to be raised of the 1,700,000 from the previous year. Our obligation to pay in the month of January forces us to borrow, in order to provide in advance money which can certainly not be collected until after the harvest at the earliest. To pay it at Paris is also a great expense for the province . . .; if the state of the royal finances permit, Monsieur, will you not let us wherever possible spend this money in Languedoc, so that all or part of the free gift may be used up here, for example in those sums which are needed for the payment of troops in Roussillon, or for the maintenance of the galleys in Provence. This would bring great relief to the province. . . .

(Depping, vol. I, pp. 295–6)

MONTPELLIER, 8 December 1676

Since Monsieur le duc de Verneuil[1] told the Estates of the request for 3,000,000, it appears that many hearts have been filled with dismay at the impossibility of paying this amount by a levy, as the payment of the 2,000,000 *livres* from last year is so far behind schedule that the prisons are full of tax-collectors, especially so because there has been no crop this year of olive oil, which is the staple product and surest source of revenue in lower Languedoc. Seeing that some wished to send a memorandum, beseeching the King to consider the misery of this province, and that even those who try their utmost to serve the King were inclined to offer 2,000,000 and to ask whether His Majesty still persisted in wanting the third million, assuring him that the Estates would use all their credit to borrow it, it seemed to me better that we should spend a few days working to unite all the opinions in the assembly in accord with the instructions of His Majesty which my Lords the royal commissioners had made known to me, rather than to allow differing views to be expressed in the debates, although fundamentally no one would wish to voice anything which would, in any way whatsoever, be distasteful to the King. By taking this precaution, Monsieur, we caused the Estates to grant His Majesty the 3,000,000 in a spirit of blind submission to his orders, without any conditions or remonstrances, and they have discussed possible ways of paying it which will at the same time place the

---

[1] Governor of Languedoc since 1666.

least burden on the ordinary people, and it seems that will be to borrow 1,000,000. . . .

The urgency of the King's needs and the hope of some relief in better times gives strength to the hearts of the men of Languedoc. . . .

(Depping, vol. I, pp. 308–9)

31. Louis XIV to the duc de Verneuil

SAINT-GERMAIN-EN-LAYE, *18 December 1676*

I have seen from your letter the sum which the Estates of Languedoc have granted to me, together with all the other circumstances which make this new expression of their loyalty the more agreeable to me. I am so satisfied with them that the almost limitless expenses which press upon me have not prevented my allowing them a remission of 300,000 *livres* on the 3,000,000 which they have accorded me. . . .

(Depping, vol. I, p.310, note 1)

C. Provence: Constant opposition—a disruptive third estate

The situation in Provence was somewhat different. During the ministry of Richelieu the Provençal Estates had been abolished, and their fiscal functions had been largely taken over by an *assemblée générale des communautés*. However, this body was no mere pliable tool of the central government. By 1666 Colbert was prompted by the attitudes of certain deputies to intervene successfully in the elections (*32–3*), but in 1671 the assembly was still far from obedient and was conspicuously unwilling to join other provinces in making some concessions because of the war effort. The minister, tired of its obstinacy and delaying tactics, warned it that an improvement in its behaviour was long overdue (*34*). Further procrastination followed, and Colbert took decisive action (*35–41*). From that moment, although the request for the free gift increased in size as the years went by, the deputies made little difficulty about granting the sum required. Of course we may wonder whether, in this province as in Languedoc, the whole sum was ever paid to the treasury, despite this mood of cooperation.

As with the more usual kind of Estates, the governor did not attend the day-to-day deliberations of the assembly. It was summoned each year and consisted of the archbishop of Aix as president, two delegates from the clergy, two more from the nobility, the two consuls of Aix who, as procurators of the people, were the influential leaders of the third estate, and the mayors and first consuls of the principal towns. The voice of the third estate was therefore a loud and important one—and these documents underline the point which has already been made, that these municipal representatives were frequently far more troublesome than the other two estates.

32. The duc de Vendôme, governor of Provence, and Oppède, intendant at Aix, to Colbert

LAMBESC, *5 October 1666*

. . . We have already told you what has been happening under the newly elected régime in the city of Aix. The procurators of the people have shown all their venom there, and have revealed themselves as men who do not wish their successors to serve the King any better than they have done, having cheated and used every kind of intrigue in order to pass on their office into hands which are unwilling to serve His Majesty; but, nevertheless, they have brought about this result with such a want of discretion that there would be valid reasons for annulling the election, and the King could therefore intervene once and for all, to safeguard his interests in the province for years to come. . . .

(Depping, vol. I, pp. 358–62)

33. Oppède to Colbert

AIX, *30 October 1666*

The decree annulling the election of the last procurators of the people, and the nomination of others in their places, was executed in the assembly this morning, and with a show of complete submission and obedience on all sides. The King will be very well served by those he has chosen. . . .

(Depping, vol. I, p. 365–6)

34. Colbert to Oppède

VERSAILLES, *25 September 1671*

. . . The King has commanded me to tell you that His Majesty strongly desires you to compel the assembly of the communities to conclude all its business within a month, the long time which it took last year being completely contrary to the good of the province and to all the orders of His said Majesty. The Estates of Brittany lasted three weeks, those of Burgundy less than that. Thus as all the other provinces conform to the wishes and the instructions of His Majesty on this point, it is very necessary and important that you should cause Provence to do the same. . . .

(Depping, vol. I, p. 387)

35. The bishop of Marseille to Colbert

LAMBESC, *11 October 1671*

The first decision of our assembly has been to offer 200,000 *livres*; we shall continue in our attempts to persuade the deputies to give His Majesty the sum he desires. . . . We would simply wish to point out to you that previous assemblies have never raised the free gift above 400,000 *livres*, save last year when they gave 450,000, on condition that the treaty of Godelot be revoked. Therefore we shall have all the trouble in the world to push them up to 500,000 this year, and we are accordingly obliged to beseech you, out of kindness to us, to suggest to His Majesty that he might well content himself this year, as last, with the sum of 450,000. . . .

(Depping, vol. I, p. 387–8)

36. Colbert to the comte de Grignan,[1] lieutenant general in Provence

SAINT-GERMAIN-EN-LAYE, *16 October 1671*

. . . I must assure you . . . that His Majesty wished to receive 500,000 *livres* from the province last year as this year, and it was only at the very last moment, because of your letters and those of Monsieur d'Oppède, that His Majesty reduced it to 450,000, for special reasons which I cannot call to mind at present; but this year His Majesty intends to have 500,000 *livres*. You can readily understand, because of the immense amount he has spent on raising troops, why it is necessary for his subjects to assist him in carrying out all his plans, seeing that this will both enhance the glory of his reign and promote the peace and welfare of his peoples. . . .

(Depping, vol. I, p. 389)

[1] The comte de Grignan was *de facto* governor, because the new duc de Vendôme was too young to exercise the functions of the governorship which he had received in succession to his father.

37. Colbert to Oppède

SAINT-GERMAIN-EN-LAYE, *6 November 1671*

The King was a little surprised to learn that the deputies of the communities have returned to their homes on the pretext of celebrating the feast days, and that, after negotiating for three weeks, you have obtained no more than 300,000 *livres*. I must warn you that I fear the King may decide to disband the assembly without taking any of this money from them.[1] His Majesty, having regard to the behaviour of other Estates, is strongly disinclined to permit these long periods of bargaining over a sum as moderate as that which is being asked of Provence, considering that there are so many powerful and pressing reasons why he could request a great deal more assistance.

(Depping, vol. I, pp. 389–90)

38. The bishop of Marseille to Colbert

LAMBESC, *18 November 1671*

. . . The deputies are continuing to progress in the way they have been permitted to do, which is to go along slowly, one step at a time, and they have decided to offer 350,000 *livres*; in a few days they will reach 400,000; meanwhile we await the return of the courier we sent, bringing your latest orders. If His Majesty has the goodness to reduce the free gift this year to 450,000 *livres*, we shall manage to carry the assembly with us, by thinking up some pretext as we did last year; but if His Majesty absolutely insists on 500,000, we shall have a great deal of difficulty, because the gift has never been as high as that. Nevertheless we shall set to work in an effort to give His Majesty complete satisfaction.

(Depping, vol. I, p. 393)

---

[1] This would be a serious blow because it would prevent the assembly from taking its customary petition to Paris at the end of the session. This document contained the grievances, usually of a specifically local nature, which the Estates had formulated, and the deputation which carried it thus had an opportunity to discuss matters directly with the royal ministers concerned. There was keen competition for places in this delegation because there was an accompanying payment of 8000 *livres* for each cleric and noble, and 4000 *livres* for each member of the third estate.

39. The comte de Grignan to Colbert

LAMBESC, *13 December 1671*

. . . You have made known to me that the King is greatly dissatisfied with the delays and the lack of affection shown by the deputies of the communities. I have sent for them all, in order to let them see this letter, and to explain to them by the most forceful arguments the harm that will befall them and the province if they do not resolve to effect with all haste what His Majesty wishes; but there are some troublemakers who are putting into the heads of the best-intentioned among them the idea that the King will be content with 400,000 *livres*; and as these weak and stupid men are only too quick at convincing themselves that what they want to believe is in fact true, I find that they change from one day to the next, and may break the promises they have made to me; therefore, Monsieur, I believe it is vital to the interests of His Majesty that you send me an order dissolving the assembly, with some letters issued under the private seal by which to punish the principal fomenters of sedition. . . . I shall use these methods only as a last resort, and when you instruct me to do so. Meanwhile, we shall work unceasingly, my Lord the bishop of Marseille and I, to calm these troubled spirits and to inspire in them by gentleness or by fear sentiments appropriate to their duty. There is no longer any problem about pushing them as high as 450,000 *livres*; but I believe that it is only this particular threat which can fill them with terror, and that they will not go up to 500,000 unless they see an order for the dissolution of the assembly.

(Depping, vol. I, pp. 396–7)

40. Colbert to the comte de Grignan

PARIS, *25 December 1671*

I have informed the King of the bad behaviour which the assembly of the communities in Provence continues to exhibit and, as His Majesty is not disposed to suffer it any longer, he has given the necessary orders for dissolving it, and at the same time for dispatching ten letters under his private seal so that ten of the worst-intentioned deputies may be sent to Normandy and Brittany. You will receive these letters and orders by the first post, and I consider it superfluous to remind you that you should carry them out quickly and thoroughly, knowing as I do how much warmth and zeal you feel towards anything which is in the King's best interests.

(Depping, vol. I, p. 398)

PARIS, 31 December 1671

I have told the King of everything which has happened in the assembly of the communities since the 20th of this month. You will see from the orders which His Majesty has sent that he has derived little satisfaction from the behaviour of the deputies this year, and that, although His Majesty has accepted the offer of 450,000 *livres*, he intends that you should still send to Normandy and Brittany, in accordance with the instructions you have received, the ten deputies who have shown the greatest ill-will towards the King's service. The whole of Provence will clearly understand to what angry extremes the obstinacy of these deputies has forced him. I do not know whether His Majesty has resolved not to summon them again for a long time to come, but, if that is the case, they will have plenty of leisure in which to repent of their evil conduct. In addition, His Majesty is well pleased with all that you have done.

(Depping, vol. I, p. 398)

41. The comte de Grignan to Colbert

LAMBESC, 9 January 1672

I have received this morning the letter which you have done me the honour of writing me, in which His Majesty orders me to dissolve the assembly and send away ten of the most evilly disposed among the consuls; but, as I have now persuaded the deputies of the communities to satisfy the King's requests in entirety, by offering 500,000 *livres*, I dare to hope, Monsieur, that you will have the goodness to obtain a pardon for them, and that the obedience they have shown on this final occasion will prompt His Majesty to forget their past conduct. . . .[1]

(Depping, vol. I, pp. 400–1)

LAMBESC, 24 December 1672

The assembly of this province agreed last Thursday, at the first discussion and without attaching any conditions whatsoever, to offer the King the 500,000 *livres* which His Majesty had asked of them. . . .

(Depping, vol. I, p. 404)

[1] It appears that the King did not carry out his threat of sending the ten deputies into provincial exile, although the assembly had been truly frightened.

D. Brittany: The royal attack on provincial privilege—the nobility leading the opposition

The Breton Estates were perhaps the most unruly of all these local representative bodies, and it is their particularly discordant session of 1673–4 which is considered in the next group of documents. Brittany was a relatively late addition to the realm of the French king, and struggled hard to preserve its independent identity and its peculiar liberties. Seigneurial justice was still a powerful force in the province, and Colbert was keen to reduce these extensive judicial rights which were legitimately held, and at times usurped or illegally extended, by the Breton aristocracy. However, his attempts at doing so had soured relations with these nobles, and it was they, not the third estate as in Languedoc and Provence, who accordingly led the opposition to the crown in the Estates. Moreover they attended the assembly in much larger numbers that was usual elsewhere. By 1673, when the Dutch War had disrupted the maritime economy of the province as well, the atmosphere was really tense, and the publication of royal edicts which further undermined the privileges of the Estates léd its members to feel that they were fighting for their very survival. Whereas the preceding meeting of the assembly, in the winter of 1671–2, had ended amicably, this one was to culminate in an inconclusive compromise—Colbert giving way on the issue of privilege and the province paying extremely heavily for its victory. Before the next session in 1675–6 the two sides would be even more passionately at loggerheads, and a full-scale revolt would have swept through Brittany.[1]

In these confrontations a crucial role was played by the aristocratic governor, the duc de Chaulnes. Brittany was the last French province to receive a permanent intendant, in 1689, but even after that date the governors were vital. In 1673 the governor was a man who both enjoyed the trust and respect of his provincial subjects, although they might not agree with all his actions and policies, and also had the confidence of the king and of Colbert, to whom he was related by a royally arranged marriage. Chaulnes was efficient and thorough in his regular inspections of his province, and often took the initiative in suggesting and in carrying out improvements. In a turbulent area he was allowed much greater freedom of action that would ever have been given to an intendant.

Against this background of conflict (*42–3*), the negotiations with the Estates dragged on (*44–9*) until the final compromise was reached (*50*), on which that staunchly loyal Breton, Madame de Sévigné, had a few harsh words to say (*51*).[2]

---

[1] This revolt is one of the three discussed in Chapter 8—see pp. 237–55.
[2] See also pp. 29–30.

42. The marquis de Lavardin, lieutenant general in Brittany, to Colbert

PARIS, *9 November 1673*

In accordance with your orders, Monsieur, I have conferred with Monsieur Boucherat,[1] who thinks as I do that it would be advisable for the proposal about the free gift, which he will make at the beginning of the Estates, to exceed 2,600,000 *livres*, and that he ought to ask for 3,000,000 in order that we may reduce it to that sum as a concession. . . .

(Depping, vol. I, p. 521)

VITRÉ, *26 November 1673*

. . . I arrived here with Messieurs de Boucherat and de Harlay on the 22nd, and we opened the Estates on the 24th although there were not yet many deputies in attendance.

During the short time we have been here, we have already come to the conclusion that the assembly will be difficult to manage, not only because of the interruption of commerce, but also as a result of the enquiries which are being rigorously made into the illegal extension of seigneurial jurisdictions. . . .

(Depping, vol. I, pp. 523–4)

43. The duc de Chaulnes to Colbert

VITRÉ, *3 December 1673*

. . . I arrived here yesterday evening, since when I have spent my time unearthing the truth about the situation here, and I can say, Monsieur, that I have found even more consternation and unfriendliness in every heart than I had been warned about or than I could ever have imagined. Two principal points seem to me to have caused this change of outlook which I have noticed here; one is the relentless pursuit of illegal jurisdictions . . ., and the other is the statement which was inserted in the council's declaration of 17 September 1672, which said, as a general regulation, that the Estates were to be denied the opportunity of criticising royal edicts which the *parlement* was to register, even when the edict was aimed at the destruction of their own privileges. . . .

[1] Also one of the royal commissioners at the Breton Estates.

54

With reference to this clause in the declaration of 17 September 1672, they imagine that it will mean the annihilation of their liberties because, although a restrictive condition was included in the agreement drawn up at the 1665 estates, when Monsieur Colbert, your brother, was present as a royal commissioner, in which a promise was given that, by confining themselves solely to matters which concerned their privileges, they would have the right to discuss all edicts which affected those same privileges, they are now to be denied all cognisance of these matters; and it will be very difficult to reassure them on this point. . . .

(Depping, vol. I, pp. 526–8)

44. The marquis de Lavardin to Colbert

VITRÉ, *9 December 1673*

. . . Monsieur le duc de Chaulnes, having noted the extent of opposition among the three orders, who have done nothing for the last four days, entered into the assembly today and, with all his personal authority and forcefulness of character, ordered that, as the discussion of other matters seemed to have ceased completely, they were now to deliberate about the free gift for the King which, he announced, would be reduced to 2,600,000 *livres*, without reference to any other considerations; and as it was by then already rather late, they will debate it tomorrow. . . .

(Depping, vol. I, pp. 529–31)

45. The duc de Chaulnes to Colbert

VITRÉ, *10 December 1673*

This morning we received the deputation from the Estates, and my Lord the bishop of Saint-Malo, who acted as their spokesman, conveyed to us, in a most eloquent speech which was both deeply respectful towards the King and loyal to the province, that the feeling and the sentiments of the Estates were most humbly to beg the King to accept, or to put it better to give whatever orders were pleasing to him about the free gift and the suppression of the edicts, and that the oppression which they (and especially the nobility) might suffer as a result would in no way limit their strong desire to contribute towards the great expenses of state; and that as an immediate proof of this they would offer 3,000,000 which, they maintained, should be divided between the free gift and the edicts. We then explained to them that the free gift to the King could not be mixed up with other such items, and that we were not able to accept on these terms either the 2,600,000 we had asked for, or the remaining 400,000 as the first part of a separate offer for buying off the edicts. Not having the authority to negotiate about this suggestion, he returned this afternoon to report to the Estates who, being convinced that they could show their respect in no better way than by offering the King whatever he wanted in return for deliverance from the edicts, were greatly enraged to learn that these offers which they thought would please His Majesty had been refused. I also decided on a plan to remove from the assembly tomorrow two gentlemen who today spoke with excessive heat, as I do not believe, Monsieur, from what I have seen here, that there is any method of governing such obstinate and headstrong spirits other than by using one's authority to make an example of an individual. . . .

(Depping, vol. I, p. 532)

VITRÉ, *13 December 1673*

. . . We had resolved to drive out two gentlemen who had distinguished themselves from the body of the noble order by their excessively pathetic accounts of the state of the province. I carried out this decision yesterday morning and, having summoned them to my lodging, I ordered them to withdraw from the assembly and forced them to leave the town in my carriage, accompanied by an officer and six of my guards. This action was reinforced by all the authority which the King has entrusted to me, and the whole of yesterday was spent in receiving three deputations asking for the return of these gentlemen. We made use of these deputations in order to fill the Estates with fear that, if they did not decide on the free gift for the King with great speed and without imposing any conditions, we would withdraw the proposal, because the glory of the King would suffer too much from begging, which is how it would seem to others, for a gift which was more glorious to give than useful to receive; and after we had enlarged upon the blind obedience which must be shown to all His Majesty's wishes, the Estates sent us word this morning, imploring us to accept the 2,600,000 *livres* which we had been instructed to ask for. The decision was made with one voice and without conditions, and it is only tomorrow that we shall receive the memoirs from the assembly against the edicts, and you will be able to judge, Monsieur, the extent of their suffering from the size of the sum which they will offer in order to be relieved of them. . . .

(Depping, vol. I, p. 537)

46. The marquis de Lavardin to Colbert

VITRÉ, *15 December 1673*

... My Lord the bishop of Rennes made sure that the decision on the free gift was approved by his order and sent it on to the third estate, where the *sénéchal* of Rennes arranged for its acceptance as well. We had helped him in a thousand little ways, even going to the lengths of preventing some communities from being there, by summoning them before us on the pretext of discussing means of liquidating their debts. . . .

(Depping, vol. I, p. 540)

47. The duc de Chaulnes to Colbert

VITRÉ, *16 December 1673*

... I had found that so much repugnance was being shown towards my advice, together with such stubborn refusals to follow it, that I had therefore despaired of persuading the nobility to grant the free gift to the King in the form of a separate sum, as opposed to the offers they were determined to make in which so much was allocated to the free gift and so much to buy off the edicts; we accordingly resolved to win over the third estate, being already assured of the support of the clergy, and by that means to carry the nobility along with them. . . . We begged Monsieur le prince de Tarente to prevent the nobles from voicing their opinions until they had heard the views of the clergy and the third estate. We instructed the president of the third estate to delay discussions within his order until he had heard the decisions of the clergy, and we asked my Lord the bishop of Rennes, as a consequence of this plan, to hurry his order into expressing its ideas. Their conclusions were then conveyed to the third estate, who adopted them as their own, and the nobility thus received the agreed decision of the other two orders before they were able to consider the matter, and therefore went along with it. . . .

(Depping, vol. I, pp. 542–3)

48. The marquis de Lavardin to Colbert

VITRÉ, *19 December 1673*

... We have spent nearly twelve hours in three discussions with the deputies of the Estates, who have made the strongest representations to

57

us on more than twenty points of which they are complaining. We answered them with all the vigour and resolution that you could have wished for, and I am sure you will not doubt this, knowing as you do Monsieur le duc de Chaulnes and my Lord the bishop of Saint-Malo. They insisted on nothing so passionately as the suppression of the chamber which is investigating seigneurial jurisdictions, as they consider it to be a new court in direct opposition to the privileges which His Majesty has graciously allowed them to enjoy. They would give more than 2,200,000 *livres*, and might even offer 2,500,000, if they believed that it would be suppressed at the same time as the revocation of the edicts which are its prime concern. . . .

(Depping, vol. I, p. 540)

49. The duc de Chaulnes to Colbert

VITRÉ, *20 December 1673*

. . . By this method we should take more money from the province than we should receive through the application of the edicts. . . . I also believe that I would be lacking in my duty if I did not inform you that the fear alone of the implementation of the edicts by the chamber has thrown the province into the utmost confusion, and the effect of actually applying them will inevitably be to provoke widespread disorder. . . .

(Depping, vol. I, pp. 543–4)

50. The marquis de Lavardin to Colbert

VITRÉ, *27 December 1673*

Praised a thousand thousand times be the name of the Lord who has shown such goodness towards his people, and who has at this moment snatched our province from the depths of dismay in order to hurl it into excesses of joy! In a word, there is no Frenchman, who loves his master, who could have witnessed what took place here today without tears in his eyes; the assembly seemed cowed but restive, and on all sides one saw no emotion save melancholy and listlessness, when Monsieur de Chaulnes, having taken his place with the other commissioners, an hour after the return of the courier, revealed to them the favour with which His Majesty wished to honour Brittany, by consenting to the suppression of the chamber and the revocation of the edicts. At once, the whole assembly interrupted Monsieur de Chaulnes with so many shouts of delight and cries of 'long live the King' that, as men forgot their dignity, it sounded as if the whole population were joining in; there has never been seen such a demonstration of fervour and gratitude; and this shouting was interrupted just for long enough to announce, with redoubled offerings of thanks, that they would give 2,600,000 *livres*—the same amount again as that already agreed for the free gift. On leaving the assembly, men ran in all directions, crying even more loudly those same words: 'long live the King! Brittany has been saved! an end to the chamber!' . . .

(Depping, vol. I, p. 541)

51. Madame de Sévigné to Madame de Grignan

PARIS, *1 January 1674*

. . . By the way, all the edicts which were strangling us in our province have been revoked. The day that Monsieur de Chaulnes announced the news, a great cry of 'long live the King' went up which made the Estates weep with emotion; men embraced each other and were beside themselves with joy; in celebration, they arranged a *Te Deum*, bonfires and a public expression of thanks to Monsieur de Chaulnes. But do you know how much we are giving to the King as a token of our gratitude? 2,600,000 *livres* and as much again for the free gift; that is precisely 5,200,000 *livres*. What do you think of that little sum? You can therefore gain some idea of the kindness which has been shown to us in suppressing the edicts. . . .

(Sévigné, vol. I, p. 665–7)

4 MUNICIPAL ADMINISTRATION

In the *pays d'états* the central government had little direct control over many aspects of local administration, which were under the supervision of the Estates. Even in the *pays d'élections* the mayors and consuls of the towns had power to organise municipal government in a manner which Colbert found intolerable. Although these urban councils could not mount the sustained opposition to royal policy of the kind seen at the Estates, they were frequently more selfish, corrupt and inefficient, and their members showed less inclination to protect the interests of the people they represented. The problem of imposing order and discipline on the town councils was one of the most difficult and time-consuming tasks attempted by Colbert, and success was far from universal. Often he could do no more than consider the needs of the state and the royal treasury, leaving the local population at the mercy of their exploiters.

It has already been stated that the municipal representatives at the Estates were more stubborn and short-sighted than their clerical and aristocratic colleagues (*23, 28*) and had little conception of the burdens which the central government had to shoulder (*27*). They revealed no greater intelligence in their handling of affairs in their town councils, and Colbert had regular recourse to bishops and prestigious nobles in the hope that they might temper urban selfishness with loyalty. The more important the city, the more outspoken were its consuls in defence of privileges which might not even affect their own municipality. The consuls of Toulouse championed every assertion of provincial independence in the Estates of Languedoc, while those of Marseille manifested a zeal for protecting local privileges which was exceeded only by their corruption, their debts and their hostility to the commercial expansion which their great port ought to have welcomed.

The daily routine of town government was thus disrupted by endless wrangling between the agents of the crown and the elected local officials, and among the officials themselves, which delayed the implementation of new policies and wasted precious resources. Many towns had extensive control over the maintenance of order and justice, and the building and repair of roads and bridges, financing them out of local taxes which they levied with the agreement of the royal council. An adequate police force and well maintained communications were two things on which the fiscal and economic policies of Colbert depended, and it was with considerable alarm that he saw self-seeking officials misusing their municipal revenues and running up enormous and often unnecessary debts which mortgaged the prosperity of their town for years to come. Sometimes these consular families had formed themselves into a closely-knit élite, whose power and dominance were virtually unshakeable.

In the *pays d'états*, the Estates regularly scrutinised the debts of the communities, the public works they had been assigned and the amount of taxes they had and should have paid.[1] In the *pays d'élections* such supervision had to be carried out by a royal official, usually the intendant. He was heavily burdened with other duties, and could keep only an intermittent eye on the activities of the consuls. He reported cases of obvious corruption to the minister, when he might be sent powers to deal with the offender, and he could use the threats of increased taxation, reduced privileges or, as a last resort, the summoning of troops to reinforce his demands for better administration. Yet the only effective way of instituting wiser government was to change the character of the consuls themselves, and put the power in safer hands. In flagrant cases of misrule it was possible to annul a local election, but that was only really feasible when the consul was himself unpopular in the town. Otherwise serious demonstrations in his favour might be provoked among the citizens. The better course was to influence the elections and prevent an unsuitable candidate from gaining office.

This slow process of increasing central control in the municipalities by interfering in the selection of officials was to reach its climax in 1692, when it was at last possible to promulgate a royal decree announcing that henceforward all mayoral appointments would be made by the king. A mere two months later the city of Dijon was allowed to pay 100,000 *livres* for the right to nominate its own mayor. Yet another ministerial victory over local privilege was thus sacrificed to the pressing needs of the royal treasury.

A. The election of mayors and consuls[2]

The first (*52–6*) of the two groups of documents on urban elections is concerned with varying degrees of royal and ministerial interference in the process of selecting municipal administrators, all in towns where the crown had established some traditional right to designate the mayor, and perhaps the consuls as well. The intention of the government was usually simply to choose worthy and loyal men, but sometimes (*56*) to find a candidate from a particular social level. The electoral pressures exerted by local factions in towns where royal influence had to be more discreetly used are described in the second group (*57–60*).

---

[1] See p. 35–6.

[2] The words 'mayor' and 'consul' have been used throughout to convey the sense of the French terms *maire* and *échevin*, and of the various alternative titles which appear in some towns.

52. Louis XIV to the duc d'Estrées, governor of the Soissonnais

SAINT-GERMAIN-EN-LAYE, *29 July 1670*

I have examined the list of those men who have been proposed by the assembly of citizens of my town of Soissons for the posts of mayor and consuls in my aforenamed town, and I am writing you this letter to inform you that I have chosen Monsieur Rousseau as mayor, and that, with regard to the consuls, I approve the four who have been elected. . . .

(Depping, vol. I, p. 811)

53. Courtin, intendant at Amiens, to Colbert

ARRAS, *1 January 1665*

I have just come back from Béthune, where I renewed the consuls. There are ten of them, of whom I allowed four to continue in their posts, because it is customary that they should stay in office for two years and these four had been appointed only last year. I chose for the other places six of the most substantial men of property in the town. The people seem to have been very satisfied with my choice and with the way the affair has been managed; for it is the first time in nineteen years that it has not cost anything to join the magistrature. . . . .

(Depping, vol. I, p. 717)

54. Louis XIV to the consuls of Beauvais

VERSAILLES, *12 August 1677*

As we wish that Monsieur Le Gay, former mayor of our town of Beauvais, should fulfil the duties of mayor in our aforenamed town during the present year, we are writing to you in order to inform you that, notwithstanding the election which has already taken place of Monsieur de La Motte, you are to assemble again in order to elect the said Le Gay as mayor of our aforenamed town, according to the customary procedure. Do not fail in this, for such is our pleasure.

(Depping, vol. I, p. 873)

1 August 1678

The services which Monsieur Le Gay, mayor of our town of Beauvais, has rendered to us since his election have been so pleasing to us that we have resolved to prolong his tenure of the said office. We are therefore informing you that we intend him to exercise the powers of the mayor for a further year, and that with this in mind you will give him your votes. . . .

(Depping, vol. I, p. 873)

55. Colbert to the bishop of Auxerre[1]

SAINT-GERMAIN-EN-LAYE, *10 February 1672*

Monseigneur le duc de Bourbon[2] keeps pressing me to tell him the men whom I consider to be the most suitable for the posts of mayor and consuls of Auxerre; and as I know no one who is more concerned than you that worthy men be selected, I ask you to send me your thoughts on the subject. But it is vital that this be kept secret, and you must above all ensure that those whom you select will be able to cooperate in the great work of setting up the hospice for the poor. . . .

(Depping, vol. I, p. 851)

SAINT-GERMAIN-EN-LAYE, *18 March 1672*

. . . I have examined what you sent to me about the men who would be suitable for the office of mayor; but the choice must be left to Monseigneur le duc de Bourbon. . . .

(Depping, vol. I, pp. 852–3)

SAINT-GERMAIN-EN-LAYE, *8 April 1672*

. . . With reference to the appointment of the mayor, I will see if I can find some appropriate moment to speak to Monseigneur le Duc; but, to tell you the truth, I shall not make a great effort to do so, because I am not very keen to meddle in this kind of matter. . . .

(Depping, vol. I, p. 853)

[1] The bishop was one of Colbert's sons.
[2] Auxerre was in Burgundy of which Bourbon was the governor.

56. The bishop of Béziers to Colbert

(November 1673)

... Monsieur d'Aguesseau, our intendant, told me that you wished one of the merchants to be given the third consulship, in order to persuade his fellow merchants to apply themselves keenly to promoting commerce. I have done my utmost to carry out your wishes and, despite the large number of procurators in Béziers, men who are accustomed to fill such a post, one of the best merchants in the town was today elected third consul. . . .

(Depping, vol. I, p. 866)

B. Quarrels and law suits among the municipal élites

If the consuls of Béziers would have preferred to exclude merchants from their ranks (*56*), in some towns there was considerable hostility between the two groups (*57*), although the former had often gained its initial wealth through the world of commerce as well; in others a single powerful resident might seek to impose his will on the elections (*58*). Confusion and even riot often accompanied the voting, and the selection as consuls of totally unsuitable men was not infrequent (*59*). As a consequence of disputed elections towns could incur enormous legal expenses, because of lengthy law suits about the validity of the procedure and of the result (*60*), thereby adding to their already extensive debts.

Having been elected and admitted to office, the mayor and consuls had no easy task. Although the central government often complained of their behaviour, which might be scandalously illegal (*61*), the citizens who had chosen them were also quick to condemn them, even when they were being conscientious. This was especially true when taxation was involved (*62*). It was thus not always their fault when royal officials and agents were obstructed or even killed by unruly townsmen.

57. The archbishop of Sens to Colbert

SENS, *29 December 1671*

The kindness which you have always shown us has prompted us to bring you all the problems affecting our town; our present difficulty is indeed an urgent one. We have elected the three men from whom His Majesty is accustomed to choose a mayor, unless he decides that other methods will suit his interests better. These three men include two judges from the presidial court, worthy and honourable candidates who do not, however, wish to accept this office, and the provost[1] of the town, who has less influence but who wants the post much more than the others. It is widely feared that, were he to obtain it, he would maltreat the merchants and anyone else who engages in trade, because he has brought legal proceedings against them and is believed in this area to be very vindictive. The only way to prevent the evils which a majority of our citizens await with dread, will be, Monsieur, for you to see fit to prolong the term of office of Monsieur Luison as mayor, who was appointed by you, and who has carried out his duties admirably both for the good of the town and in furthering those things which he knew would please you because they are advantageous to the state[2]. . . .

(Depping, vol. I, p. 844)

58. Pellot, intendant at Montauban, to Colbert

BORDEAUX, *21 April 1664*

. . . At Pamiers the new consuls are most worthy men, and support the interests of the presidial court, which is essential if that body is to establish itself firmly in the town. But my Lord the bishop of Pamiers, who thwarts the presidial whenever he can, is opposed to these nominations and would wish to have, as has been the case in the past, consuls who are dependent on him, and to that end he would wish to put forward men of humbler status in order that he may obstruct the presidial more easily. . . .

(Depping, vol. I, p. 705–6)

---

[1] The provosts or *prévôts* were the humblest of the three levels of local royal judges, and dealt with only the simplest cases. Their prestige was much less, therefore, than the judges of the presidials, who were second in the hierarchy (the *baillis* and *sénéchaux* occupying the topmost position).

[2] In at least one town it was the merchants who were in sole control of the council, using their dominance to manipulate prices and establish a monopoly in cloth—see pp. 218–19.

59. Du Saulx, public prosecutor at the *parlement* of Bordeaux, to Colbert

BORDEAUX, *11 February 1664*

I have already begun to report to you about the abuses which are being committed in the consular elections in the towns of this province, where the disorder and confusion has now reached such a pitch that two men who are condemned to death and whose effigies have been executed outside the palace of justice have been elected consuls at Nérac and Condom, so that the royal prosecutor whose task it is to pursue them has now become their colleague through this election.

(Depping, vol. I, p. 692)

60. The bishop of Mirepoix to Colbert

MIREPOIX, *26 September 1672*

The town of Fanjeaux in my diocese, which is one of His Majesty's towns and sends a deputy to the provincial Estates every year, is a place which is ruined and in debt to the amount of more than 80,000 *livres*, debts which come for the most part from law suits among the inhabitants who wish to become first consuls and to gain entry to the said Estates; and if I had not, for some years, taken care of this poor town and stopped its legal proceedings and other disorders, it would now be utterly bankrupt. But as His Majesty had been told, during the year 1668, about the extent of intrigue and clientage at the time of a consular election, he did me the honour of sending me the orders for which I had asked, so that we were able to nominate as consuls men of integrity, who were keen to serve the King and to further the interests of the town. Since then I have attempted to prevent any more law suits, and the town has been peaceful until the present moment, when it was once again time for a new consular election, on 15 August last, as is the custom there. It so happened that a gentleman from this part of the country had managed to acquire a post as a royal judge, in order to make himself master of the consulate; this judge … has appointed consuls from among a small group of citizens, who are dependent on him because he has lent them money. The lieutenant of the Lauragais, who usually nominates the consuls, determined to oppose this action, at which point I, seeing that this could cause trouble and expense to the town, wrote to Monsieur le marquis de Castries,[1] who

[1] Royal lieutenant general in Bas-Languedoc.

issued an order forbidding the judge to appoint consuls until the arrival of Monsieur the intendant. Notwithstanding all these things, the judge continued with his plans, installed his consuls and broke down the doors of the town hall. . . . The next day all the citizens, together with the lieutenant of the Lauraguais who is the lawful commissioner, obtained permission from Monsieur de Castries to nominate consuls, which was duly carried out in accordance with the traditions of the town. They chose Messieurs Marion-Lemazet, Reverdj, Mazières and Audouj, who are all worthy men, devoted to the service of their King and the well-being of their town. This double election has resulted in a law suit at the *parlement* of Toulouse where, after both sides had put their case, judgment was given in favour of the said Lemazet, Reverdj, Mazières and Audouj, the others being expressly commanded to cause them no trouble. . . .

(Depping, vol. I, pp. 859–61)

61. Herbigny, intendant at Moulins, to Colbert

MOULINS, *23 July 1667*

I am greatly displeased that the anger of Messieurs the mayors and consuls of Bourges has led them to show a want of the respect and obedience which is due towards the King's orders. A man named Gegry, who is keeper of the town hall and receiver of the local taxes, had been taxed at 1500 *livres* on the rolls of the chamber of justice and, as he had not paid this sum, was arrested last Wednesday, after which he was taken to the royal prison at Bourges. The mayor and consuls, indignant that their keeper had been taken away, seized the gaoler of the prison and held him captive for five hours in the town hall, after which they pretended to return him to his gaol; but, when they reached the gate, they took the keys by force from the hands of the warders and released their keeper. . . . I am leaving here tonight and am going straight to Bourges; in the meantime, Monsieur, I have taken prisoner the son of the town hall keeper of Bourges, who came to me here with a petition from his father, together with a report from a doctor and a surgeon, claiming that he had received excessive treatment at the hands of the bailiffs who had served the writ on him. . . . I have ordered the arrest of his father and his mother. . . . Despite all these things, the mayor is the King's advocate at the presidial court, and because of the duties of his office should therefore be specially devoted to the execution of the King's orders. . . .

(Depping, vol. I, pp. 763–4)

62. The maréchal de Clérambault, governor of the Berry, to Colbert

PARIS, *25 May 1664*

You will learn from the consul of the town of Bourges who bears this note, and from the official report which has been entrusted to him, of the unrest which has broken out between the common people of the town and the magistrates and other leading citizens about the establishment of certain duties on liquor; and, Monsieur, although I have never held anything in higher esteem than the service of the King and the execution of his wishes, I am giving myself the honour of writing to you on this occasion to ask that you not only consider the innocence of the magistrates and other leaders in this matter, but that you also reflect a little on the willingness with which these men risked their lives, in order to snatch from the hands of the mob the men who had been appointed to establish this tax. . . .

(Depping, vol. I, p. 725)

C. The attempt to liquidate the debts of the towns

Although intervention by royal agents could stamp out some malpractices in municipal administration, and might even prevent the consuls from incurring further debts, the problem of reducing the amounts which had been borrowed over the years was much more difficult. Many towns had become heavily indebted and, if some welcomed the opportunity to halt this process, they could not see a means of repaying those sums which were already outstanding. Frequently it was as much as they could afford to pay the interest.

The liquidation of these debts was a perpetual topic in correspondence between Colbert and the provinces, but it was never possible to reach a satisfactory solution. The minister felt particularly strongly about this kind of problem, because it stored up trouble for the future, committing years of revenue which could be spent more usefully elsewhere. Yet, in local as in national government, especially in time of war, such anticipation of funds was all too common. Colbert ceaselessly urged the intendants to work towards the complete repayment of these loans, and to give this task priority over almost everything else (*63*). This document shows that the issue was still causing concern after he had been steadily seeking a remedy for nearly twenty years.

Some municipal debts had, of course, been incurred to meet the urgent demands of the royal treasury, or to finance public works of the kind which would have earned ministerial approval. A large proportion were nevertheless the result of maladministration by the consuls and officials, or selfishness on the part of rich

citizens who sought to avoid paying the taxes which were designed to repay existing loans; the conflicting policies of the central government might aid them in
their attempts at deception (*64*). There were endless attempts by the crown to
restore the communities to solvency, taking care to prevent the consuls from
devising the means of repayment and from collecting the funds destined for that
purpose (*65*). Some revenues did fall into their hands, despite these precautions,
and the misuse of them was to be severely punished. Once again there is evidence
that the important towns were more resentful than others of royal interference
in their internal affairs, and that some of them were not receiving the
best possible returns from the collectors to whom they had sold the right to
collect taxes. A further source of worry for Colbert was the adverse effect of municipal debts on commercial expansion (*66*).[1] The towns were always prepared to
support their position by wasting precious resources on sending costly deputations to court, and it was accordingly decreed that this could be done only with
the permission of the intendant, thereby putting him in a position of considerable
influence which might also be a little dangerous (*67*); the large cities treated this
requirement with their usual contempt.

63. Colbert to all intendants

VILLERS-COTTERETS, *29 February 1680*

The King has already made known to you many times through my letters
that the principal and most important task which His Majesty wishes
you to undertake consists in the liquidation and repayment of the debts
of communities in all the generalities of his kingdom, to which end he
does not doubt that you will strive with all the care and devotion necessary to so great a matter, and one so dear to him and so beneficial to his
people; he now commands me to add that he wishes you thoroughly to
investigate the ways of preventing the communities from acquiring debts
in the future, and to examine the freedom they have had in the past,
which has produced the innumerable abuses that are well known to you
in the work you have already begun. His Majesty's intention is to formulate a declaration, based on the advice of all the intendants, in order to establish strict and unambiguous rules which will prevent the towns and
communities from falling into the difficult position which they are in at
the moment, even though the King has been working for twenty years to
release them from it.

His Majesty has also instructed me to tell you these further thoughts of
his on this subject, in order that you may consider them, changing,
reducing or adding to them, according to your estimate of their suitability for the task in hand. He believes therefore that all communities

[1] See p. 174.

69

should be strongly forbidden to take on any debts, except as a result of plague, or for the provision of equipment and supplies for the army, or for the repair of the naves of churches, and then only if they have been damaged by fire; and, in cases such as these, that the people should be required to assemble as a body, either in the town hall, or at the end of the parish mass, so that the deed can be drawn up with the consent of the whole community and kept at the record office in the town hall. . . .

(Clément, vol. IV, p. 138)

64. Bouchu, intendant in Burgundy, to Colbert

DIJON, *14 February 1663*

. . . We are continuing without a moment's pause in our examination of the debts of the communities, and are working at present on those of Beaune. . . . We have found that in three places which have given us a list of their borrowings there are more than 1,500,000 *livres* outstanding in debts; that is to say 500,000 at Dijon, 400,000 and more at Semur, and more than 600,000 at Beaune, in addition to what is still due for payment of the *tailles*. . . . The ill effects of wars are responsible for part of this; but thirty years of maladministration, and the confusion which has resulted, together with the deaths of many people who could have brought us their complaints or given information, or who could have been punished because they were partly responsible, and the willingness of most creditors to participate in a vicious, if universal, practice which is sanctioned and even instigated by those who ought to oppose it, all of which help these disorders to perpetuate themselves, prevent us from doing the good which we would have wished, and limit us to taking action only against the trickery and negligence of the creditors and magistrates. . . .

(Depping, vol. I, pp. 666–7)

DIJON, *21 March 1666*

. . . The chapter of the cathedral church at Autun has sent a canon to me, to deliver two decrees from the council dated the 18th of last month, in one of which His Majesty dispenses the clergy and the religious houses from paying the town dues, while the other, issued at the request of the syndic of this diocese, summons the mayor and consuls of the town before the council, but also exempts them from contributing to those same taxes. If these decrees are carried out in Burgundy, all our work . . .

in delivering the towns from the overwhelming misery which beset them, and in bringing their citizens up to a level where they had the means of subsistence and could afford to pay the *taille*, will be undone, and these communities will fall into a confusion which is greater than they have ever known, for this is the only way by which these towns can pay off their debts which amount now to nearly 600,000 *livres*. These town dues were auctioned to the tax farmers on the understanding that they would be levied on and collected from all the clergy, gentlemen, officers of the sovereign courts and other men in privileged positions; if these men are now to be exempt, the taxes will not bring in half of their original value. . . . If these decrees are allowed to stand, there is no doubt that other churchmen, gentlemen and officers of the courts will obtain similar ones for themselves. . . .

(Depping, vol. I, pp. 679–80)

65. Colbert to Ris, intendant at Bordeaux

PARIS, *26 March 1683*

. . . I must admit that the contents of your letter of 16 March, about the taxes for the repayment of the debts of the communities, caused me great distress, because it seems to me that there is a genuine cause for alarm when we learn that the people have been subjected to these taxes but that their debts have not been paid off; that is why it is vital for you to discover . . . what has become of these revenues, which result from taxes whose specific purpose is the liquidation of these debts. . . . In future, the consuls must never be allowed to lay hands on the funds collected for this purpose, no matter what pretext they suggest; on the contrary they should be collected by the receivers of the *tailles*, or by someone who has been selected and named by the creditors to collect and apportion these sums on their behalf; thus we can be certain that, after an appropriate and agreed number of years, the communities will have discharged their obligations, and the creditors will have no cause to complain or to accuse them of defaulting in their payments. You will understand the immense importance of this matter when I tell you that the King has been trying for twenty-two years to reduce these municipal debts, and yet one finds on the contrary that the towns are heavily burdened with taxes but are not repaying their creditors.

I should tell you that, in a large number of the provinces of the kingdom, preference has been given to repaying those creditors who have allowed the greatest remissions on the original capital or on the back-interest, and that you might like to adopt this procedure too if you think it appropriate. . . .

(Clément, vol. IV, p. 175)

66. Colbert to Le Blanc, intendant at Rouen

SAINT-GERMAIN-EN-LAYE, *2 April 1681*

In answer to your letter of 30 March, I confess that I am a little surprised to learn the extent of the debts incurred by the town of Dieppe, which amount to 226,004 *livres*. . . .

It is most important that you should hold the auction for the allocation of the right to collect the various town dues, in order to secure the highest possible price and use it for the repayment of these debts. Let your work be guided by the knowledge that Dieppe has always been a great trading port, and that it is impossible for commerce to recover and to increase on the scale which the needs of the state demand, when vital foodstuffs are being subjected to these duties. Therefore you must use every kind of means to deliver the town from this burden as quickly as you can.

(Clément, vol. IV, p. 144)

67. Colbert to Morant, intendant at Aix

FONTAINEBLEAU, *6 November 1682*

In reply to your letters of 24 and 28 October, I would say that you should be very cautious, or, to phrase it more accurately, that you should give no ground to the deputations which the towns wish to send here, to represent their personal interests, because you know that there is nothing which has contributed more to the ruin of many towns than this kind of deputation; and you are well enough able to judge that the attention which the King gives to such matters is easily sufficient for the solution of problems which are reported in the memoirs of the intendants, without the need for any further representations. And to show you more positive evidence of the ruinous expenses which the towns incur by sending these deputations to speak for their particular interests, let me tell you that, although I give audiences every day, it is more than three weeks or a month since the deputy from Marseille arrived in Paris and I have still not been able to see him. . . .

As you know only too well how important it is for the trade of Marseille, and therefore of great consequence for the kingdom, that its debts be repaid, in order to deliver it from the burden of the dues which have been levied for that purpose . . ., I do not doubt that you will make every effort to attain this goal. . . .

(Clément, vol. IV, pp. 164–5)

D. Misappropriation of revenues: Supplies for the army

Further examples of the way in which officials, and especially the mayors and consuls, misused their powers and misappropriated funds can be culled from the collection of the *étapes*, the furnishing of supplies for troops on the march. Colbert vigorously condemned the diversion of these funds by the municipal officers, and the two letters which follow (*68*), although separated by ten years, bear the same message and show that the problem remained unsolved. Funds to reimburse those who had supplied provisions were also being diverted, and Colbert's suggestions for supervising this process (*69*) and for punishing some offenders in order to frighten others (*70*) closely resembled his methods of trying to ensure repayment of municipal debts (*65*). Worse still, some of the troops were only imaginary, but the supplies and dues were collected nevertheless (*71*).[1]

68. Colbert to all intendants

SCEAUX, 29 August 1673

I have noticed that, in those generalities where a special officer has been appointed to collect military supplies, there is a great deal less corruption in the reimbursement of goods than where such an appointment has not been made. As it is crucial to the King's service and to the welfare of the people that the present disadvantages in the system be avoided, where funds designed for the reimbursement of these goods have fallen into the hands of mayors, consuls and leading citizens of towns and villages, His Majesty has instructed me to tell you that you should set about finding a man who will take charge of provisioning all troops who pass through any part of your generality, and at an agreed price, so much for the cavalry, so much for the infantry, which should be as low a figure as possible when the cost of the necessary commodities has been taken into account. . . .

(Clément, vol. IV, p. 95)

[1] For a further example of misappropriation of revenues, see p. 209–10.

PARIS, *15 April 1683*

His Majesty has instructed me to write to you as he wishes to know the manner in which provisioning of the troops has been carried out in your generality, since the year 1679 until December of last year; that is to say, whether there is a special officer responsible for doing this, with whom an agreement has been made; if this official has arranged for storehouses in the supply towns, and if the goods are conveyed from there to the troops by men whom he has appointed, or not; or if the official is content for the citizens of the place to convey the supplies, in return for receipts which they have to take to the receiver of the taxes; in such cases His Majesty wishes to know on what basis the price of these supplies has been agreed with the official, and on what basis will the citizens of the supply towns and other places be reimbursed.

And, in instances where there is no special officer, His Majesty likewise wishes to know on what scale the prices of goods have been calculated in the accounts which have been checked, and how the inhabitants of the towns which have supplied these provisions have been reimbursed; and in case there is a discrepancy, who has profited by this discrepancy.

As His Majesty seeks to be enlightened on these points, about which there have been many complaints from a number of generalities, you must devote all your attention to explaining these matters and must send me a memoir about them.

And as the bulk of these troubles result from the fact that in some generalities there has been no special officer appointed, His Majesty wishes you to take every possible step to find one.

His Majesty desires in addition that, in every town where the funds to pay these supplies have been given into the hands of the mayors and the consuls, and they are to distribute them to the citizens who have provided the goods, you should examine carefully whether or not the mayors and consuls have distributed them, as His Majesty has been informed that, in the majority of towns, the municipal officials have kept these funds for their own profit, which merits a severe punishment as an example to all.

(Clément, vol. IV, pp. 176–7)

69. Colbert to Creil, intendant at Rouen

VERSAILLES, *25 November 1672*

... The procedure which is observed in all the generalities of the kingdom consists, when there is a special official, in checking carefully that the agreements which have been made about the advancing of supplies are carried out, and it is then for the intendants in the provinces to scrutinise the accounts against which reimbursement is authorised to the men who have provided them, in proportion to their contribution. And when the communities and towns furnish these provisions themselves, without a special official, I never cease to tell the intendants that they should inspect the accounts of these supplies every three months, seeing that it is on the basis of these lists that money is allocated and ready cash made available out of the funds of the same generalities. Afterwards they should take care to ensure that reimbursement is made to all those individuals who provided these supplies. . . .

(Clément, vol. IV, p. 79)

70. Colbert to Bercy, intendant at Riom

VERSAILLES, *3 March 1683*

. . . The method which you suggest for the reimbursement of individual citizens in the supply towns, for the provisions they have given, is a good one; but it is not strong enough to prevent trickery on the part of the consuls, or to maintain good order. To do that, you must work hard and search out three or four of those who have been most corrupt, you must collect evidence against them and must discover certain proof of their thieving. As soon as you have this information, the King will send you the power to try them, without the right of appeal, in any presidial or bailiff's court that you choose; and be assured that you can best demonstrate the justice of this action by imposing severe punishments.

It has been remarked upon that, in five or six provinces in the kingdom where the King has authorised this type of enquiry, at the moment when the intendants have begun legal proceedings against a consul, the other municipal officials have made extensive restorations of funds in the supply towns, and since that time when someone was severely punished there have been no further complaints about this matter. . . .

(Clément, vol. IV, pp. 171–2)

71. Colbert to all intendants

SCEAUX, *23 September 1673*

His Majesty has instructed me to tell you that he has been informed of a common abuse in the provisioning of troops, which concerns the companies of cavalry and infantry and the number of men they contain; the supply officers receive orders for provisions which are based on your information from the royal reports on how many troops are passing through, but often these same troops receive other orders and do not come that way. However, the supply officer in drawing up his accounts behaves as if they had passed through and had received their supplies, a kind of thieving which merits an exemplary punishment and is something which you must be most careful to guard against. . . .

(Clément, vol. IV, pp. 95–6)

E. Law and order, private jurisdictions, urban improvement, poverty, plague and fire

The next group of documents is concerned with the more constructive side of municipal administration—the preservation of order and of the citizens' well-being. Some towns maintained a militia for this purpose,[1] although it too was a privileged body (72). The policing of cities, especially Paris, was made more difficult by the existence of private palaces in which criminals might hide; some owners cooperated with the authorities, (73–4), but a general attack on this anomaly was needed and was attempted in 1674; many years later the problem still remained (75). Hygiene, water-supplies and street cleaning were important tasks for the municipalities, but if some towns were willing to ensure that their streets were kept free from dirt and refuse (76), the consuls of Marseille, with the jealousy characteristic of officials in the larger cities, were fully prepared to destroy the work of an enterprising *bourgeois* in this field for the most selfish of reasons (77). The principle to which Colbert adhered for the financing of improvements to town amenities was that they should be paid for by those who would benefit in proportion to their gain, and that charitable institutions should also be financed on a local level (78–9)[2] The minister insisted that people who had suffered losses because of these schemes should receive just reimbursement.[3]

The remaining documents continue the theme of urban poverty in various forms. It was a subject which distressed Colbert and the king, not least because the urban poor, together with the impoverished peasants who came to the towns and swelled their ranks, constituted a potentially dangerous and rebellious element. Yet only in peace time could money be spared by the treasury to give relief to these luckless subjects. Appeals for some small respite came not infrequently from town councils, and sometimes directly from the paupers themselves. Two

[1] For the role of an urban militia at a time of revolt, see pp. 239–40.

[2] See also p. 162.

[3] Other examples of municipal administration will be found in the chapters on taxation, finance, justice, commerce and industry below. Although Colbert wished to reduce the role of the towns in local government, he actually had to increase their participation in the regulation of industry—see pp. 211–14 and 216–17.

further causes of poverty were disease and fire, both ever present dangers in the overcrowded and unhealthy streets, although in the case of the fire at Toulouse (*80*) the central government showed a total disinclination to help a great city which was reluctant to help its own citizens, possessed great wealth and was perpetually uncooperative.

72. Pellot, first president of the *parlement* at Rouen, to Colbert

ROUEN, *20 June 1675*

I am sending you a memoir on behalf of the companies of the 'fifty' and of the arquebusiers of this town, in order that they may receive their *franc salé*[1], and I have nothing to add to it save only that we need these companies on so many occasions, and they are ready for action in an instant, that we should avoid giving them any cause for complaint at the present. . . .

Memoir

The company of the fifty, which consists of 52 horsemen or officers, is very ancient, and was established to promote the service of the King and the safety of the town, and to carry out the orders of Messieurs the governor and the first president of the *parlement*, and of those who command in their absence. . . . It can trace back through 400 years, to 1222, its claim to certain privileges which it ought to enjoy and always has enjoyed.

These privileges are the right of its members to be exempt from the billeting of soldiers both in town and country; to use their patrimony to the full without paying the *taille*; to sell 10 *queues*[2] of wine over and above that from their own vines without paying any wine-duty, and, among the others which they claim, to take the following amounts of salt from the salt depot at Rouen, as follows: for each captain and lieutenant one *mine*[3] of salt and for each horseman one *mine* on payment only of the market tax.

---

[1] *Franc salé*, the privilege of being exempt from some part of the salt-tax, was a right which men were most keen to obtain. It was granted to certain officials, religious and charitable institutions, etc.

[2] 10 *queues* were equal to 15 hogsheads.

[3] A *mine* was about 78 litres.

Every one of these privileges has been confirmed by all our past kings
of happy memory, and by His Majesty, and the said company has always
exercised these rights until the present. . . .

The fifty and the arquebusiers labour night and day to preserve the
security of the town, and to carry out the orders which are given to them;
for every night a brigade of these men marches during the greater part of
the night through the streets, acting as officers of the watch, and every
day they execute the instructions they have received concerning both the
King's service and the peace of the town, as well as implementing the
requests of the judicial authorities. In fact they do everything. If there is
some disturbance, they are ready at once, they can be called upon immediately, and they can be used not only in the town, but also in the
countryside when there is need. . . . They follow all the instructions which
they are sent with precision, loyalty and intelligence, because there is no
part of the town which they do not know well and where they do not
know what is happening. Also, because of them, the thieves, vagabonds
and other men of evil purpose find no profit in staying here, and Rouen
will soon be completely purged of them.

Therefore, because of the services which the two companies render
daily to His Majesty and to the public, and for those which they can provide on future occasions, may it please His Majesty to allow them to
exercise this right of *franc salé*. . . .

(Depping, vol. I, pp. 845–9)

73. Colbert to the mayor of Paris

TOURNAI, *8 June 1671*

As the King has heard on every side that the instigators of all the disorders which have taken place in Paris are seeking refuge in the Luxembourg palace . . ., His Majesty wishes that you visit Madame de Guise
on his behalf, that you inform her of this, and that you convey to her in
the most civil terms possible that His Majesty wishes her to give permission to arrest them, and in future to prevent a disorder which is as
considerable as this one, and which is contrary to His Majesty's vigorous
attempts to chase out of the city all the thieves, swindlers and other
rogues. . . .

(Depping, vol. I, p. 837)

74. Colbert to Braque[1]

ATH, *18 June 1671*

I have already told the King of the decision taken by Madame de Guise, to expel from the Luxembourg palace all the men suspected of crimes who had taken refuge there, and to prevent it happening in the future. His Majesty is very pleased with the decision taken by Her Royal Highness. . . .

(Depping, vol. I, p. 838)

75. Pontchartrain, secretary of state, to the cardinal de Furstenberg

VERSAILLES, *23 January 1703*

You have been informed of the complaints which have been made, for some years past, by the officers of the Paris police about the difficulties which they encounter when they wish to make an inspection and to do their duty with reference to the workmen and others who live in the new houses and shops which you have had constructed in the forecourt of your abbatial palace. They say, in support of their action, that in 1674 all the justice exercised by different lords, and above all by a large number of religious communities, within the limits of the city of Paris, and notably that of your abbey of Saint-Germain-des-Prés, was united in the hands of the Paris police and judicial administration; that the King reserved to the abbey the right of high, ordinary and low justice inside the walls of the monastery and the abbatial palace and buildings occupied by the abbot, the religious and their servants; it was not intended to include a large number of craftsmen who occupy your new buildings, and who claim to be independent of the authority of the King's officers and free from inspection by the police. . . .

(Depping, vol. I, pp. 924–5)

76. La Galissonière, intendant in Normandy, to Colbert

LE HAVRE, *1 October 1670*

Yesterday I at last finalised the regulations for cleaning the town of Le Havre. . . . I have accepted a tender for the right to undertake this task,

[1] A household official of Madame de Guise.

which will be carried out daily with two carts, for 700 *livres* a year. I had even allocated it at 50 *livres* below that sum; but the man who had secured the contract claimed the right to dispose of the refuse himself, which the consuls pointed out to me as being very harmful to the citizens, because the people from the surrounding country would come and collect it as manure for their lands; I therefore thought it right to increase the payment to the contractor by 50 *livres* per year, which is not excessive if he does the job well. For he is obliged to send two carts through the town at the following times: after Easter, from 7 until 11 in the morning and from 2 to 7 in the afternoon; from 1 October to Easter, from 8 to 11 in the morning and from 2 until 5 in the afternoon.

I have also auctioned a contract for providing six common cesspits, each 24 feet long and 6 feet wide . . . without which, until the time when there are such facilities in every house, and that will not be in the near future, it would be impossible to keep the town clean, not to mention the fact that a large number of men are away from their homes almost all the day; it is therefore an indispensable necessity that there be public facilities in various parts of the town. . . .

(Depping, vol. I, pp. 838–41)

77. Arnoul, intendant of the galleys, to Colbert

MARSEILLE, *4 December 1668*

. . . Monsieur Benat is the only one of the ordinary *bourgeois* and lesser merchants of this town whom I have so far found to be open and sincere, a man of spirit and honour, and one who is always offering me good advice which will be of service to the King. It is he who began the improvement of the town, from which His Majesty will receive 100,000 *livres*, and is hated and shunned like a leper as a result. He owns lands which were used as refuse dumps; he collected the sewage of the town which would otherwise have been lost into the sea, and which is considerable in quantity and was thought to be utterly useless. He diverted it through his lands, building canals, reservoirs, boilers and houses for washing linen and woollens, and to such an extent that he derives 1500 *livres* of revenue from them.... The consuls, 7 or 8 days ago, redirected these waters away from his property, letting them flow into the sea, and damaged the channels down which they had flowed, all of this being prompted by simple jealousy, because he had served the King and had proved himself more capable than anyone else of serving him well. Such behaviour is contrary to Christianity and to Christian charity, not to mention the public interest. . . . It is more important here than elsewhere to give strength and support to men of goodwill who wish to serve the King. . . .

(Depping, vol. I, pp. 791–2)

78. Colbert to Tubeuf, intendant at Tours

FONTAINEBLEAU, *2 October 1679*

I am sending you a copy of the council's decree for which you sent me a draft with your letter of 18 September, to order an immediate start on the construction of a new road in the city of Tours, to run from the canal at the end of the rue Traversine to the moat of the new town, in accordance with the estimate and the route which have been drawn up; and that the proprietors of the houses and lands which stand in the way shall be reimbursed at their rightful value by the inhabitants of the rues Traversine and de La Cellerie, and by those who live near the new road, in proportion to the use they will make of it as shown on a list which you will draw up for this purpose.

(Clément, vol. IV, p. 134)

16 May 1680

I have received the three letters you have written me about the auction of the right to collect the new town dues at Tours, both the duty to finance the extension of the new road and that to provide poor relief, and I am keen to remind you that this kind of tax must be levied only with the universal agreement of the citizens; and it has scarcely ever been the practice to charge them, whether for charitable works or for the improvement of their town, without their unanimous consent. That is why you must work to unite everyone and must disperse any opposition, because it is the King's intention that one should not risk an uprising in a town over a matter of this nature, which is probably of no consequence for the state.

(Depping, vol. I, p. 878)

79. Pellot, first president of the *parlement* at Rouen, to Colbert

ROUEN, *10 March 1676*

. . . Two or three days ago, I called together a general assembly of this town, in accordance with the requirement of a decree of the council which was made, Monsieur, at your suggestion, to find the means of maintaining the hospital for the able-bodied poor. It was unanimously decided to ask His Majesty to permit the imposition of a levy on cloven-hooved animals entering the town, which would yield about 50,000 *livres* annually and would be sufficient for our purposes, taking into account the alms and revenues which the said hospital already receives. . . .

This tax is one of extreme necessity . . . for gifts of alms have declined considerably and the burden has increased, seeing that this poorhouse gives relief each week to almost 1900 families, and provides work for more than 600 or 700 paupers who live there, in addition to dispensing aid to others in need. . . .

(Depping, vol. I, pp. 849–50)

80. Colbert to the cardinal de Bonzi, archbishop of Narbonne

VERSAILLES, *2 September 1672*

I thank Your Eminence for the care you have taken to advise me of the fire which broke out in the suburbs of the city of Toulouse, and I deeply regret that a town of such importance should have suffered a substantial blow of this nature. But, with regard to your suggestion about seeking some assistance from the King for those men who have been most seriously affected by this conflagration, I must point out to you that the city of Toulouse contributes nothing to the great expenses of the state, unlike others in the kingdom, and it therefore seems that the consuls and the town council must rather search out the means of helping those citizens who have been involved in this destruction, and not have recourse to His Majesty. . . .

(Depping, vol. I, p. 859)

5 TAXATION AND FINANCE

Adequate and justly assessed taxation was the key to successful central government, in seventeenth-century France as elsewhere. Without sufficient revenues the plans of Colbert for the reform of the administration could not hope to succeed. Yet the French fiscal system was in the hands of officials who were frequently more concerned with their own interests than with the needs of the royal treasury, and who could not easily be dislodged and replaced by a more efficient alternative. Furthermore the policies which many of these taxes were intended to finance were unappealing or positively objectionable to the taxpayers, collectors and privileged orders in the provinces. Colbert could not hope drastically to reform the whole procedure of collecting revenue. He could reduce the number of officials by suppressing some of their offices, although it was an expensive process to remove and reimburse administrators who had purchased their posts and had the right to pass them on to their heirs, and he could keep a close watch on the rest through his intendants, taking action in cases of flagrant corruption. Also he could seek out and enquire into the legality of the innumerable grants of exemption which removed individuals and groups from the ranks of the contributors to direct taxation, remedying this situation either by punishing those who could be proved to have usurped this privilege, or by the inflammatory step of limiting the categories of exemption, or by imposing new indirect taxes. These extra levies would fall on men who escaped direct taxation, especially on the rich officials and the business men in the towns, but would also add to the load of the hard-pressed peasant and humble townsman, doubly so because the members of the local élites would try to shift their new burden on to the poorer levels of rural and urban society by exploiting them in novel ways. The agents who collected these funds caused much bad feeling through their greed and corruption, and Colbert often preferred to entrust the collection of indirect taxes to tax-farmers rather than to royal officials because the former were less secure and easier to bully. It was therefore these dues, not the direct taxes, which provided the motivation and occasion for many of the revolts against the royal ministers, and Colbert increased them only when other methods—reclamation of the royal domain and abolition of the *rentes*, for example—had proved insufficient. In addition the intendant, who was to scrutinise every aspect of the fiscal system in his generality, was so laden with work that he could not carry out any task with the speed and thoroughness which Colbert would have liked.

The peasants, who paid the bulk of the direct taxes, were in no position to have their obligations increased. Having to overcome the effects of bad harvests, plague, seigneurial dues, the maintenance of troops in peacetime and war, the cruel profiteering of financiers who exploited their indebtedness, and improper levies added to the tax burden by unscrupulous officials and tax-farmers, the peasantry were in perpetual danger of destitution, starvation and death.

Moreover, with no effective representative institutions at national level, this principal taxpaying class had no way of voicing its views save by rebellion. Although Colbert and other ministers were not noticeably overcome by pity for these wretches, they at least knew that the survival of the peasant must be given high priority if the number of taxpayers were not to be drastically depleted, and that the provision of the bare means of subsistence would be enough to quell the spirit of revolt.

The early years of the personal rule of Louis XIV saw a thorough examination of the fiscal machinery, and the beginnings of reform. There was no all-embracing plan. The royal agents enquired searchingly into every level of the financial structure, and the council authorised major and minor adjustments when time, privilege and treasury funds permitted. Yet this, the first serious attempt for many years at putting the French finances on a sound footing, was doomed to failure once the king embarked upon a series of expensive wars. Mazarin had not been idle in this field, of course, but he had had to cope with a lengthy and costly international conflict and with extensive internal disturbances. He had tried to curtail luxury, office-holding and *rentes*, to uncover false nobles, to reform the *tailles* and to resume control of the alienated parts of the royal domain, but it was only in the peaceful years after his death that the crown had the leisure to take general stock of the situation. This respite was short-lived, and in 1672 an expensive war began against the Dutch. Colbert hated the cost and disruptive effects of wars, but made an exception on this occasion, eagerly awaiting a quick victory over a commercial rival. Instead the conflict was protracted, large-scale financial reform slipped from his grasp and emergency methods of raising revenue were resumed. While the provincial Estates and towns were borrowing money in order to pay their taxes, the royal treasury was compelled to do the same and to anticipate the revenues of future years. In the 1660s Colbert was the architect of a judicious reform of the finances, to be implemented slowly, piece by piece. From the early 1670s the needs of war gave the supporters of local privileges a weapon by which to repel these encroachments on their extensive rights. Furthermore the champions of provincial liberties were learning to use more subtle means of thwarting the ministers, avoiding the overt confrontations which reminded the king of the Frondeur spirit of his minority.

The first step towards reform had to be taken at the centre. A new supreme body was needed to direct and coordinate the disparate activities of the various branches into which the fiscal bureaucracy was divided, to enable the government accurately to budget for its forthcoming expenditure and to end the scandalous diversion of large sums into the pockets of royal ministers of whom Fouquet was simply the most notorious example among many. After that, the existing system would have to be reformed so that conflicting jurisdictions within the administration were reconciled; there were many occasions when two groups of officials, each obeying their instructions and acting according to their legal rights, claimed cognisance of the same area of local government and therefore undermined each other's work. Thirdly there was the urgent task of investigating innumerable breaches of fiscal regulations which looked impressive on paper but which were not being put regularly into practice. Only when the existing system had been made to work properly by these methods would the central government be in a sufficiently strong financial position to contemplate effective long-term reform, although plans were being drawn up ready for that day. In its propaganda the crown did frequently claim that such projects were already being realised, and some historians have unwisely accepted these statements at face value. The reality of Colbertian reform was less spectacular.

A. Control at the centre: Success and failure

The new royal council of the finances, which was established a mere ten days after the arrest of Fouquet, was to be at the core of the reorganised financial structure (*81*),[1] and Colbert was able to describe with some confidence its first steps towards solvency and prosperity (*82*). However, the balance sheet in 1680 reveals that there had been reversals as well as advances in fiscal and economic policy during the first two decades of the new régime (*83–4*).

81. Decree establishing the royal council of the finances, whose decisions shall be drawn up in the form of ordinances and signed by the King

FONTAINEBLEAU, *25 September 1661*

. . . His Majesty has suppressed for all time the commission of the superintendent of the finances and the functions which were associated with it.

His said Majesty, knowing that he could give no greater sign of the love which he bears for his people than to take into his own care the administration·of his finances, in order to strike out the abuses which have been creeping in until this moment, has resolved to summon a Council, composed of men whose ability and virtue are recognised, on whose advice he will act in all matters which were formerly decided and implemented by the superintendent alone.

The said council shall be called the royal council of the finances, and shall consist of a president . . . and three councillors of whom one shall be an intendant of the finances, His Majesty reserving to himself the right to summon the Chancellor to attend when he deems it necessary, in which case he would be accorded the rank and precedence due to him in his capacity as president of all the royal councils.

[1] See p. 6.

His said Majesty reserves to himself alone the right to sign all ordinances authorising ordinary and extraordinary expenditure, both secret[1] and otherwise. . . .

The said intendant shall present the accounts for all the tax-farms . . . and other fiscal returns to the council, and they shall be inspected and signed by His Majesty and then by every member of the royal council. . . .

The letters patent announcing the sum to be collected for the *taille* shall be authorised in like manner.

Every decree imposing taxes on the people, no matter of what kind or quality, shall be referred to the said council before it is dispatched. . . .

No reduction in taxation may be granted . . ., no matter what kind it may be, except in the presence of His Majesty in the said royal council. . . .

The various councils of finance shall continue to meet as before, save that they shall not discuss any of the aforementioned subjects which are reserved for the royal council of the finances.

In all these councils, the president of the royal council shall occupy the place which the superintendent of the finances was accustomed to take. . . .

(Clément, vol. II(ii), pp. 749–50)

82. Jean-Baptiste Colbert: Memoirs on the financial affairs of France, in the form of a history (1663)

Chapter IV

. . . The vesting of sovereign authority over financial affairs in one or two persons had been found to be undesirable. . . .

His Majesty therefore declared that he was suppressing the office and functions of the superintendent, and that he himself would normally sign all the documents, whether concerned with money received or with expenditure.

At the same time he instituted a council composed of five people, which he called the royal council of the finances, and appears in person

---

[1] See pp. 6–7, including note 1 on p. 6. If there was now a closer check on these *ordonnances de comptant*, which prevented their abuse by ministers, the king himself signed many more than Colbert would have wished. The average annual outlay on these secret grants was 7,840,000 *livres*, in the years 1662–83, reaching a peak of 12,049,000 in 1673.

at its regular, thrice-weekly meetings. These five men propose the matters for discussion, and His Majesty resolves them. He has ordered one of the five, the intendant of the finances, to keep a register of receipts and expenses.

At the first meeting of the council he declared that he wished to apply himself to the increase of his ordinary revenues, and to the abolition of extraordinary duties, sincerely hoping to bring relief to his subjects.

His Majesty has established as one of the inviolable maxims of his administration that there shall be no alienation of revenues and furthermore that unceasing attempts shall be made to regain those which have been lost by this means. . . .

Chapter VII

. . . Before going on to the year 1663, it is perhaps desirable to draw a parallel, with reference to all those matters in which finance plays a part, between the state of the realm in September 1661 and that in December 1662, which is to say sixteen months after the King began to direct business of this kind.

September 1661	*December 1662*
1. The finances were managed by the superintendent alone, from whose sovereign authority sprang every kind of abuse.	1. The King suppressed this office and took the duties upon himself, burdening himself by doing so with three hours labour each day on average, which task he has discharged admirably.
2. The rules for conducting the finances were those of endless creation and annulment, neglect of ordinary revenues and extension of extraordinary dues.	2. The King suppressed all these extraordinary taxes, and has prodigiously increased his ordinary revenues.
3. The *tailles* and other taxes imposed on the people had been increased at every opportunity.	3. The King has reduced the *tailles* by 8,000,000 *livres* in the two years 1662 and 1663.
4. The superintendents tried only: to impoverish the people by increasing taxation;	4. The King has worked: to enrich the people by reducing taxation;
5. To keep the King short of funds in order to further their own advantage;	5. To enrich himself in order to give favours to others;

6. To enrich themselves, their relations and friends, and some thirty men of business. . . .

6. To return all that has been wrongly taken, and to confine the men of business to the modest way of life which befits them. . . .

10. The revenues had been reduced to 23,000,000 *livres*; also they had been consumed for more than two years in advance.

10. The King has increased his revenues to 50,000,000 *livres* in sixteen months.

11. The navy was entirely ruined and destroyed, both ships and galleys, for during almost the last ten years no galley had been launched, and no more than two ships. . . .

11. The King had launched eighteen ships by June 1662, and six during the rest of the year. . . .

(Clément, vol. II(i), pp. 39–40, 65–6)

83. Jean-Baptiste Colbert: Memoir informing the king of the state of his finances (1680)

Chapter 9: Tailles
. . . Note that in 1657 the *tailles* amounted to 53,400,000 *livres*; that between 1662 and 1679 they have always been between 38,000,000 and 41,000,000; that at present they are 35,000,000. . . .

Chapter 10: Improvements effected
Apart from everything which has been done to improve the organisation of the tax farms and the *tailles*, it is unquestionable that the development of trade and industry has greatly contributed to the welfare of the people.

The forbidding of the seizure of livestock;
The liquidation and repayment of the debts of the communities;
Taxes d'office,[1] release from imprisonment, and a host of other remedies applied on a variety of occasions;

All these things have helped to bring them relief. But, notwithstanding everything which has been achieved, it must be openly admitted that the people are heavily burdened and that, since the beginning of the monarchy, they have never had to bear one half of the taxes which are now

[1] See p. 93, note 3.

imposed upon them; that is to say that the revenues of the state had never exceeded 40,000,000, and that at present they amount to 80,000,000 and more. . . .

Chapter 11: Points at which the taxes could be reduced and improved, if the King resolved to reduce his expenditure
If His Majesty were to decide that expenditure should be curtailed and were to ask me how some relief might be afforded to his people, my opinion would be:

To reduce the *tailles* so that in three or four years they will have fallen to 25,000,000 *livres*;

To reduce the salt tax by one *écu* per *minot*[1]. . . ;

To re-establish, if it be possible, the tariff of 1667;[2]

To reduce the *aides*, and to make them uniform and equal everywhere by revoking all privileges;[3]

To abolish the taxes on tobacco and on stamped paper, which are harmful to the commerce of the kingdom;[4]

To complete the general ordinances for all the tax-farms and for the *tailles*;[5]

To create courts of finances, which would replace the justices of the elections, salt depots and customs offices;

To give them powers similar to those of the presidial courts, of delivering judgment without right of appeal;[6]

To round off the jurisdictions of the elections and the salt depots;[7]

To diminish the number of officials as soon as possible, because they are a burden on the finances, the people and the state;

To reduce them imperceptibly, by suppression and reimbursement, to the number existing in 1600.

The advantages which will result from these actions for the population and for the state are difficult to put into words. . . .

(Clément, vol. II(i), pp. 125–7)

---

[1] A *minot* was about 39 litres.

[2] See pp. 189–90, including note 3 on p. 190, and 200–1.

[3] The *aides* were a group of taxes on the sale of goods, chiefly on wines.

[4] These were the dues which had sparked off a number of revolts—see pp. 234–43, 247 and 251.

[5] See also p. 118.

[6] The presidial courts had this right of ultimate judgment in cases involving a limited amount of money, and were courts of first instance where larger sums were at issue.

[7] See pp. 118–19.

84. Jean-Baptiste Colbert: Summary of the king's finances for the year 1680

V. Receipts and expenditure:

Receipts

1	Tax farms[1]	29,318,762
2	*Recettes générales*[2]	23,894,659
3	*Recettes générales* and free gifts from the *pays d'états*	7,369,411
4	Woods and forests	865,736
5	Extraordinary sums[3]	13,961,374
6	Anticipation of receipts for the year 1681	16,349,414
	Total[4] receipts for the year 1680	91,759,356

Expenditure

The King's household	763,338
Victualling account	1,917,413
Extraordinary household expenses	2,246,803
Butchery account	398,510
Royal mews	817,489
Purchase of horses	12,000
Treasurer of the Offertory	88,437
Justice of the household	61,050
Royal guard	187,335
Swiss guard	69,303
Hunting and falconry	342,044
Wolf hunting	34,293
The Queen's household	1,381,128
Madame la Dauphine's household	867,498

[1] This includes the salt tax and customs dues.

[2] Direct taxes from the *pays d'élections*.

[3] A variety of miscellaneous debts from individuals and official bodies, and the income from the sale of the newly created *rentes* of 1679 (see pp. 127–8).

[4] This figure, the correct total, does not correspond to the figure in the manuscript, which M. Clément notes is incorrect; nor does it agree with that of M. Clément, who has himself made a small error. These, and other small inaccuracies, are explained by the fact that this was not a working document, but was simply a brief digest which had to be light enough for the king to carry it in his pocket. Important decisions would be taken on the basis of much fuller and more accurate statistics.

Monsieur's household[1]	1,198,000
Madame's household	252,000
Favours and rewards	193,366
Ready cash for the King's personal use	2,030,092
Building and maintenance of royal houses	8,513,804
Swiss regiment	262,000
Garrisons	2,345,269
Military supplies	1,509,502
Bread ration	86,571
Extraordinary military expenses	31,233,986
Bounties to commanders of troops	825,616
Navy	4,928,773
Galleys	2,869,223
Fortifications	4,603,386
Embassies	810,100
The Bastille	189,330
Salaries	1,215,700
Emoluments of officials	2,302,427
Emoluments of marshals of France	276,150
Ordonnances de comptant[2] for rewards	2,176,988
Ordonnances de comptant for secret business	2,224,969
Other emoluments	491,400
Roads and bridges	300,364
Paving of Paris	58,258
Payment of back-interest on government bonds (*rentes*)	1,182,013
Reimbursements	10,792,927
Commerce	324,281
Interest on loans and expenses of tax-collection	2,389,200
Small gifts paid by ordinance	784,813
Travel	406,892
Total	96,318,016[3]
Deficit for the year 1680	4,558,660

[1] 'Monsieur' was the courtesy title of the king's brother, the duc d'Orléans.
[2] See p. 6, note 1, and p. 86, note 1.
[3] This is not the total of the preceding sums, as one item has apparently been omitted from the list in the original compilation of the document.

VI. Table of revenues and expenditure from 1662 until 1680

Year	Receipts	Expenditure	Surplus[1]	Deficit[1]
1662	75,568,750	74,826,456	742,294	
1663	48,053,826	46,826,576	1,227,250	
1664	63,602,796	63,071,008	531,738	
1665	90,883,973	90,871,856	12,117	
1666	67,459,001	66,611,895	847,106	
1667	72,520,925	72,090,744	430,181	
1668	70,875,374	70,875,381		7
1669	76,468,967	76,283,149	185,818	
1670	73,900,755	77,209,879		3,309,124
1671	87,501,077	83,875,723	3,625,354	
1672	87,067,787	87,928,561		860,774
1673	96,971,302	98,242,773		1,271,471
1674	105,738,044	106,803,861		1,065,817
1675	112,133,054	111,866,488	266,566	
1676	110,936,796	110,132,622	804,174	
1677	116,315,294	115,819,462	495,832	
1678	106,705,242	106,910,519		205,277
1679	126,132,816	128,235,300		2,102,484
1680	91,759,460[2]	96,318,016		4,558,556

During the period 1662–80, expenditure exceeded receipts by 4,205,030 *livres*.

(Clément, vol. II(ii), pp. 774–83)

B. The punishment of corrupt officials and the problem of conflicting jurisdictions

Although a new supervisory council had been created at the centre, Colbert was still confronted by the deficiencies in the existing financial system. There were three things to be done. The first was to prevent officials from misusing their powers and to punish those who had been guilty of this offence in the past. Secondly he had to reconcile conflicts in the administration where different jurisdictions overlapped. Thirdly he needed to add to the bureaucracy to meet novel situations. The first task was to be carried out on the grandest scale by the institution of a Chamber of Justice, which would punish some offenders and frighten others into an honest way of life (*85*). Officials and financiers were already apprehensive because of the arrest of Fouquet, and this new threat seemed a serious

---

[1] The surplus and deficit figures were added by Clément.
[2] The correct figures for 1680 have been given in section V above.

one. The financiers in particular were very unpopular and would have few defenders. Yet the chamber was ultimately to fail (*86*), after which such reforms had to be carried out piecemeal. The problem of conflicting jurisdictions had arisen largely because more and more machinery had been added to the administration over the years, without sufficient attention to the definition of the exact responsibilities of the old and new bodies. As time passed, controversial issues arose which led one group to assert its powers against another. At the heart of a number of these disputes were the *cours des aides*. These courts, situated in Paris and in nine provincial centres, delivered judgment without right of appeal on many fiscal claims, and frequently undermined the work of other financial officials. In his Memoirs,[1] Louis XIV designated the *cour des aides* in Paris as one of the most dangerously independent tribunals in his kingdom and quickly removed some of its most outspoken members. But such measures were of short-term effect. A redefinition of its powers was essential. The worst clashes of all occurred between the *cours des aides* and the intendants over taxation. Colbert insisted that the intendants should cooperate with these courts in so far as this was possible (*87*),[2] but he was meanwhile considering how to limit their ability to negate the *taxes d'office*[3] by which the intendants sought to remedy deficiencies in the allocation of taxes (*88*). Yet it was not easy to apply the ideal remedy of curtailing the authority of the court, because both parties to the disagreement were acting with perfect legality and attacks on privileges always brought a storm of opposition against the royal ministers. It was better to avoid repetitions by trying instead to solve the underlying problem—how to allocate the taxes more justly (*89–90*). At the same time, the intendant was to spend part of his busy life in examining all the judgments of the *cours des aides* so that they might be persuaded to exercise their authority more wisely (*91*). Once again Colbert realised that caution was the only course.

85. Royal edict establishing a Chamber of Justice, to investigate abuses and malpractices in the finances since 1635

FONTAINEBLEAU, *November 1661*

. . . We recognise that the disorders and malpractices which have marred the running of our finances for many years past are responsible for all the evils with which our subjects have been burdened, and have caused the

[1] See p. 5.
[2] See also p. 25.
[3] The intendant had the right to impose these temporary taxes in order to adjust apparently low tax assessments, but the taxpayer could then appeal to the *cour des aides*. The courts, who detested this power of the intendants, usually found reasons for allowing the appeal.

extraordinary surcharges which have been unavoidably laid upon them as a means of defraying the urgent needs of the state, while a small number of men, profiting from this maladministration, have . . . accumulated rapid and prodigious fortunes. . . .

Now that our attention is no longer directed elsewhere, as it was during the war . . ., we have resolved, both in the interests of justice and to demonstrate to our people our hatred of those men who have subjected them to such violence and corruption, as well as to prevent a repetition in the future, that we shall impose severe and exemplary punishments on everyone who is found guilty of financial malfeasance. . . .

To this end . . . we have established a Chamber of Justice, composed of officers from our sovereign courts. . . .

It is our wish and intention that its judgments shall rank in force and quality with those of our sovereign courts.[1] . . .

(Clément, vol. II(ii), pp. 751–2)

86. Royal edict suppressing the Chamber of Justice

SAINT-GERMAIN-EN-LAYE, *August 1669*

. . . By a general amnesty contained in our edict of July 1665, we converted into monetary payments the penalties which had been incurred according to the letter of our ordinances by the authors of these financial disorders and their accomplices.

The execution of this edict has not been as prompt as we would have wished. The whole process has had its delays and difficulties; these were increased by the resistance of the debtors, against whom, after all kinds of threats, the full force of law and justice has been used.

But, despite the advantages which we could have promised ourselves if the chamber had continued, as the whole of France wished that it should, the dread of these investigations kept many families in a state of perpetual disquiet through uncertainty about the state of their property and fortunes; we have therefore resolved to suppress it, concentrating our efforts on sharing with our subjects the fruits which we have received from it. . . .

It is our wish that, on the day this edict is published, all prosecutions against tax debtors and all sentences passed by the Chamber of Justice shall cease. . . .

(Clément, vol. II(ii), pp. 764–6)

[1] See p. 130, note 2.

87. Colbert to Bercy, intendant at Riom

PARIS, *15 April 1683*

. . . It is right for you to know that the *cour des aides* at Clermont complains strongly about your every action; and while you can rest assured that if you act wisely, the King will always support you, I feel I should tell you nevertheless that you ought to proceed with a great deal of moderation and that, in carrying out the orders you receive from His Majesty, you must always base your conduct on his ordinances and regulations. It would also be judicious and would be agreeable to the King if, when the *cour des aides* wishes to confer with you, whether through the first president or through the public prosecutor and other officials, you were to explain to them the reasons behind your actions, yet never departing, no matter what the circumstances, from the King's intention that you should labour unceasingly to speed up law cases and to prevent his subjects from ruining themselves by the expense of judicial procedures—all this to be done without taking away their liberty to appeal when they do not share your view.

(Clément, vol. II(i), pp. 218–19)

88. Colbert to all intendants

SCEAUX, *6 October 1673*

I have learned, from some of the letters sent me by the intendants, that the *taxes d'office* imposed by them, which are absolutely vital if the *tailles* are to be collected easily, are being cancelled—with scarcely any attention to the circumstances of each case—by the *cour des aides*, simply because the taxes are the work of the said intendants.

As nothing is more harmful to the interests of His Majesty nor more burdensome to the community than these annulments, especially as they increase the impudence of the 'cocks of the parish' who escape from the *taille* by all kinds of ruses, heap a further burden on the poor and lay upon the community the expenses incurred through these legal procedures, His Majesty has instructed me to tell you that he wishes you to enquire into these annulments and send me the details; if he feels, because of the number of instances which are reported to him, that the said court is too easily persuaded to quash *taxes d'office*, he will completely remove its power to hear such cases. . . .

(Clément, vol. II(i), pp. 294–5)

89. Colbert to Le Bret, intendant at Limoges

PARIS, *28 January 1682*

In your letter of 16 January, you have informed me very fully of the *taxes d'office* which you have levied. As these taxes are authorised by special powers and stand apart from the normal method of collecting the *tailles*, you should not become accustomed to regard them as a firm and lasting remedy for the evils which have obliged you to levy so many on this occasion. You must find some alternative solution, which the collectors themselves can be compelled to implement. . . .

(Clément, vol. II(i), p. 175)

90. Colbert to all intendants

PARIS, *6 November 1681*

In my letter of 12 April last, I wrote that the King wished you to investigate thoroughly: (i) all the difficulties which have arisen in the nomination of tax collectors, and the number of legal disputes which have been taken to the election courts and, by the lodging of appeals, to the *cours des aides* as a result of these nominations; including the abuses caused by the power given to the *élus* to nominate them *ex officio* when the inhabitants of the parishes have not done so within the time prescribed in the regulations; (ii) if the institution of a rota of collectors, as is the practice in Normandy, would partially remedy this disorder, which is all the more important because in that province we have seen a reduction in this kind of corruption; if you consider that such a method should be adopted, His Majesty could include it in the ordinance for the regulation of the *tailles* on which he is at present working.

It is appropriate that you should note what one intendant has written about the use of this sort of rota which, being established in a parish within his generality, has given rise to an evil practice of some magnitude, namely that the collectors, spontaneously or by agreement, reduce the contribution to the *taille* of the men whom they know to be their successors. . . .

(Clément, vol. II(i), pp. 170–1)

91. Colbert to Le Blanc, intendant at Rouen

SAINT-GERMAIN-EN-LAYE, *5 August 1678*

I have seen the draft decree you have sent me about the *cour des aides* at Rouen. It is undoubtedly true that this court has always been accused of many malpractices in the administration of the judicial matters which are entrusted to it; and although such decrees are valuable as a means of telling them the maxims and principles they should observe and even of showing them the way they should behave if they are to prevent the continuation of the evil habits into which they have fallen, I must frankly admit to you that I do not think this to be the best course of action. It would be better instead to scrutinise all the decisions which the court has made, in order to single out those which are contrary to the ordinances, and in such a case to annul them and to demand the name of the judge concerned; and when a judge is found to have given three or four wrong decisions, to suspend him and to make him give up his office. I can assure you that this is the best and the quickest method of all. . . .

(Clément, vol. II(i), pp. 381–2)

C. The plight of the peasant taxpayer

While Colbert was trying to introduce harmony into the conflicting groups of the financial hierarchy, he was always concerned with the position of the humble taxpayers. The life of the peasant was so precarious that he might well have starved to death long before the fruits of a reformed tax system reached him. It was clear from the failure of the Chamber of Justice that corrupt officials would still profit from the collection of taxes, whether the rules for raising revenue were reformed or not. Surveillance was too difficult and punishment too haphazard. It was therefore vital to ensure that the peasantry—the principal taxpaying class— survived the cruel oppression of officials, seigneurs and financiers. (If a peasant did become more prosperous, he would often send his sons to the nearest privileged town, so that they might acquire the status of 'bourgeois' and henceforward be free from paying the *taille*.)

There were three priorities to be observed in supervising tax collection (*92*), and the intendants were reminded of them over and over again, year after year, as the central government saw that its orders were being only partly carried out. It was essential that the peasant should not be deprived of his means of livelihood (*93*), although even this provision had to be waived at times when the demands of war pressed too heavily on royal resources. In more normal circumstances, Colbert frequently condemned the use of troops as an aid to tax collection (*94*) and always emphasised that no constraints should be put on the peasantry during the

97

crucial farming seasons (95). When allocating taxes, account should be taken of the damage caused by natural disasters, although one should beware of exaggerated descriptions of these additional hardships which the people (96) and even the intendants were wont to give (97). As these attempts to relieve the burden on the taxpayer failed to produce the desired result, the minister began to accept that sheer poverty, not corruption, was the real cause of this inability to pay taxes. Towards the end of his ministry, in a mood of increasing cynicism about all the kinds of men with whom he had dealings, he started to believe that there was one further reason—that the peasants were often simply lazy (98). Whatever the cause, extreme penury remained widespread, especially in the countryside where poor-relief was non-existent (99).

92. Colbert to La Galissonnière, intendant at Rouen

SAINT-GERMAIN-EN-LAYE, *12 September 1670*

I have received the two letters which you took the trouble to write to me on 6 and 8 September. You can understand, from the disorder which you have found at Gisors, why these tours of the elections are vital and bring ever greater advantage to the people. I would have been happier had you let me know the number of prisoners you discovered at Gisors, or even had you sent me an exact record of the expenses incurred in each election since the beginning of the year, for there is nothing more crucial in bringing relief to the people than to work unceasingly at these three tasks: firstly to reduce the costs of tax collection; secondly to prevent the imprisonment of the collectors; and thirdly to stop the seizing of livestock.

(Clément, vol. II(i), p. 73)

93. A royal declaration renewing the prohibition on the seizure of livestock

PARIS, *25 January 1671*

. . . As there is nothing more useful to agriculture nor anything which contributes more to the fertility of the soil than livestock, we have deemed it necessary to deliver them for a time from all forms of seizure and distraint, and in this way to give exhausted lands a period of rest in which to restore themselves, by making the means of increasing fertility more easily available, or even to bring new land under cultivation in the areas where this is desirable.

That is why, in our edict of April 1667, we forbade all sergeants-at-arms and other officers of justice, during the next four years, to use the methods of seizure and distraint against any kind and species of animal whatsoever which is used to fertilise or to till the soil, whether it be to meet the debts of communities or of individuals, and this order was to be carried out without exception.

But as this period of relief has almost expired, and as we have learned that it has been of great benefit to the people, we have resolved to prolong it, knowing that the success which we had hoped for would be incomplete unless it were extended for a few more years. . . .

For these reasons . . . we are forbidding all sergeants, during the next six years (beginning on the date of expiry of our edict of April 1667), to seize or sell livestock, whether to meet the debts of communities or of individuals, on pain of forfeiting their office and of paying a 3000 *livres* fine. . . .

(Clément, vol. IV, p. 578)

PARIS, *3 October 1681*

As the King has learned that in some provinces of the kingdom the declaration which His Majesty issued in 1678, forbidding the seizure of livestock in payment of individual debts, has not been carried out, His Majesty has ordered Monsieur the attorney general to present to the *parlement* the decree of which you will find a copy enclosed, together with the declaration. His Majesty has instructed me to send you these documents, in order that you may watch closely to see that they are carried out promptly throughout the length and breadth of your generality. His Majesty also wishes that you should prevent, wherever possible, the receivers and collectors of the *tailles* from seizing livestock as payment of these taxes, although you should not stop them from doing so when every other method has failed to yield up His Majesty's dues.

(Clément, vol. II(i), p. 168)

94. Colbert to Poncet, intendant at Limoges

FONTAINEBLEAU, *12 August 1683*

I have received, together with your letter of 27 July, the new memoir about your tour of the generality. You must prevent the collectors of Tonnay-Charente from sending soldiers to Brouage to facilitate the collection of the *taille*, because this method is too violent and is utterly contrary to the intentions of the King. You must use every possible means to end this constraint through billeting, in all areas of your generality. Let me know if there are some elections where this practice has become established and, in such cases, try hard to stamp it out and replace it by the use of sergeants-at-arms where possible; if not, discover how many brigades there are in each election, how many men each contains, how much pay they receive, and ascertain thoroughly both the abuses which are committed by using this method of collection and the means of uprooting them.   (Clément, vol. II(i), p. 224)

95. Colbert to La Barre, intendant at Riom

11 July 1662

The King has received a number of complaints that, during the weeks of the harvest, troops have been used to aid the collection of taxes in your generality, thus causing widespread disorder and bringing great hardship to the people, who have already suffered a bad year.

I have firmly assured His Majesty that you will quickly remedy this situation, and that, in the months of July and August, you will not allow anyone to exert pressure of any kind on the parishes, because it is only reasonable to give them time to bring in the harvest so that they may afterwards be in a position to acquit themselves of their obligations; I beg you to keep a close watch on these things.

(Clément, vol. II(i), pp. 226–7)

96. Colbert to Bazin de Bezons, intendant at Orléans

SCEAUX, *18 June 1682*

I have just received two of your letters, dated 15 and 16 June, to which I am now replying. With reference to the parishes which have suffered severe hailstorms, you must follow the customary procedure, which is to give them relief in proportion to what they have lost, but without reducing the total yield of the tax. Yet you must remember that the fuss which is made about these storms is often greater than their actual effect. Thus, one must wait for three weeks or a month before trying to assess the harm caused by the hailstones, as the destruction always seems worse initially;

but, when the fruit begins to swell and new leaves and shoots appear, the damage—or most of it—will have repaired itself. . . .

(Clément, vol. II(i), p. 192)

97. Colbert to Morant, intendant at Aix

SAINT-GERMAIN-EN-LAYE, 18 December 1680

In reply to your letter of 11 December . . ., I feel I should tell you for your ears alone that His Majesty has not been persuaded of the extreme misery of this province, and that all the obvious overstatements contained in every letter which has reached here have not been accorded a great deal of credence, His Majesty knowing only too well how much money he sends each year into this province and how little he draws from it.

I am saying this simply to advise you that you should avoid writing these exaggerated phrases yourself, for they are very frequently used and the King sees them year after year.

I would go further and say that, if you wish to decide honestly and for your own benefit whether or not there is hardship in the province, you should consider whether the urban population is decreasing, if commerce and marriages are declining, if offices, lands and property are reduced in price or not. These are the safest ways to judge the state of a province; and assuredly you will find through such a study that the province is nowhere near as miserable as you had let yourself be persuaded. . . .

(Clément, vol. IV, pp. 141–2)

98. Colbert to Bazin de Bezons, intendant at Orléans

SAINT-GERMAIN-EN-LAYE, 21 November 1681

There is good reason to be very surprised that the collection of the *tailles* is as difficult as you say, because you yourself must know how greatly it has been reduced since 1659.[1] It seems that these obstacles must stem from the laziness of the people; for it appears that the considerable favour

---

[1] See pp. 88 and 120–1.

which the King has shown them, forbidding the seizure of their animals, and many similar kindnesses, should enable them more easily to pay their taxes. . . .

(Clément, vol. II(i), p. 172)

99. The duc de Lesdiguières, governor of Dauphiné, to Colbert

GRENOBLE, *29 May 1675*

I can no longer hide from you the miserable state to which I have seen this province reduced. Commerce has completely ceased, and from all parts men have come to me, begging me to make known to the King that it is impossible for them to pay their dues. This is assuredly true, Monsieur, and I must tell you, in order that you be properly informed about the situation, that the greater part of the population in this province has survived the winter only by eating acorns and roots, and can be seen at the moment munching grass from the meadows and the bark of trees. I feel I am obliged to represent things to you as they are, if the orders I shall give are to be pleasing to His Majesty. . . .

(Depping, vol. III, p. 265)

D. The tax officials: Rivalries, corruption, real and feigned poverty

If Colbert was determined that the peasant should not be penalised when his inability to pay taxes lay beyond his control, so too he felt that the frequent failure of the tax-collector to bring the requisite revenues to his superiors was not always his fault, and that it was therefore unfair to punish him. The imprisonment of tax-collectors was one of the three evils condemned most strongly and regularly by the minister (*92*), and it is true that in some generalities this problem was slowly being solved (*100*); in other areas the situation was much worse and remained virtually unaltered during a period of ten years in which the central government tried to improve it (*101–2*). Colbert was determined to protect these humble agents from noble interference (*103*) and from domination by other, more powerful, royal financial officials (*104*), who were guilty at times of extreme cruelty. The troops too, who could sometimes aid the tax-collectors in exploiting the peasants (*94–5*), might in turn become enemies of the collectors, for the army was impartial in its tyranny (*105*).

The intendant, in accordance with his general instructions[1] was to examine the whole fiscal system thoroughly (*106*)—a task which took a great deal of time

[1] See pp. 18–21.

and could never be fully completed—in order to find the real culprits. They were usually to be discovered among the office-holders and the *noblesse*, rather than among the collectors, while those who administered the *tailles* seem to have been less corrupt than those who were concerned with other forms of taxation, notably with the salt tax. At the beginning of the personal rule of Louis XIV, Colbert expressed his intention to reduce the number of office-holders (*107*), and was still seeking ways to do so twenty years later (*108*). There was of course no suggestion that these officials be replaced altogether, not only because there was no alternative system but because the office-holding process yielded considerable revenue from a wealthy stratum of society which would otherwise have avoided much of the fiscal burden. If such men would not voluntarily invest their profits in the commercial and industrial schemes proposed by the minister, they must at least support the finances of the state. It was just the excessive number of officials, devouring too large a share of the fruits of administration, which alarmed Colbert, and his concern therefore was simply to suppress surplus posts whenever possible and to ensure that the holders of those which remained were encouraged to carry out their duties personally and well (*109*). Nevertheless the abuses often survived these ministerial attacks (*110–11*), and were made worse when one group of local officials tried to whip up popular feeling against another; such confrontations, as Colbert told the intendants many times,[1] brought discredit on the whole bureaucracy. Yet certain of the complaints from these tax officials were genuine, and it was the business of the sometimes reluctant intendant to find remedies for them as well (*112*), if the system were to continue to function. A final point, and one which provides a link with the next group of documents, is the extent to which the tax officials were in league with the local *noblesse d'épée*, and were helping to preserve their interests (*113*).

Thus, as the wealth of the nobles, privileged towns and institutions, the church and other social groups who were exempt from some or most taxes was preserved almost intact, untouched by the fiscal officials, and as seigneurial dues further reduced the ability of the peasant to pay large sums to the state, the revenues which the treasury could legitimately hope to raise were already limited. Of those, a sizable part went illegally into the pockets of the army of officials and collectors, whose ability to profit personally from their duties gave them a vested interest in the administration and prompted them to procrastinate, deceive and even openly oppose the royal ministers.

100. Colbert to Le Camus, intendant at Riom

SAINT-GERMAIN-EN-LAYE, *18 July 1670*

I have not delayed in making known to the King the substance of the letter you sent me on 10 July. His Majesty has been well pleased to learn

[1] See p. 24.

that there are so few collectors in the prisons of your generality, and that the collection of the taxes is going so smoothly. . . .

(Clément, vol. II(i), pp. 70–1)

101. Colbert to Voysin de la Noiraye, intendant at Tours

SAINT-GERMAIN-EN-LAYE, *1 August 1670*

I have received your letter of 29 July. I was extremely surprised to discover the number of tax-collectors who have been imprisoned throughout the length and breadth of your generality since the beginning of the present year, and also the number who are at this moment in prison. I can assure you that, judging from the lists which I have received from Messieurs the intendants, in all the generalities taken together there are not so many as in that of Tours alone. Because this is without doubt highly prejudicial to the King's subjects, seeing that, while these men are in prison, their work is completely halted, His Majesty wishes that you set to work, with all the care and precision of which you are capable, to unearth the root causes of such a widespread evil, which assuredly arises only through the inequalities in the allocation of the *tailles* and the costs incurred in collecting it; and while doing this, you must be making an effort to remedy this situation. . . .

(Clément, vol. II(i), p. 71)

102. Colbert to Tubeuf, intendant at Tours

SCEAUX, *1 August 1680*

In replying to your letter of 23 July, I must say that I was surprised to learn the number of tax-collectors who are detained in the gaols of the generality of Tours in connection with the *tailles* and the salt tax, seeing that I have discovered 102 for the *taille* and 14 for the salt tax in the prisons of Angers[1] alone, and moreover that the number of prisoners throughout the entire generality adds up to nearly 400. As there is nothing more important, with this method of tax collection, than to avoid such imprisonment, it is desirable that you should examine the problem in detail, to ascertain whether this disorder is the fault of the

[1] Angers was one of the elections in the generality of Tours.

receivers or of the people. There is little evidence that the people are responsible, in view of the large reductions in the *tailles* which the King has granted to them, and this reinforces my belief that blame lies rather with the receivers. If I am right, it will be necessary to deprive some of them of their powers for this next year, to serve as a warning for others; there being nothing to which Messieurs the intendants could more profitably devote their attention than the eradication of this abuse, because the imprisonment of a man takes away from him his ability to work and provide food for his family, who will thus indubitably sink into beggary. . . .

(Clément, vol. II(i), p. 137)

103. Jean-Baptiste Colbert: Memoirs on the financial affairs of France, in the form of a history (1663)

Chapter VII
. . . During the month of March (1663), His Majesty performed two important actions which made France fully aware that he could be at one and the same time severe and just in protecting the poor from oppression by the powerful. A valet of the marquis de La Châtre, governor of Bapaume, had come to Berry, where he had cut off the nose and ears of a collector of the *tailles*, after which he returned to Bapaume; the King sent a squad of his guards to seize the man in the very room of his master, and to deliver him into the hands of justice in order that he might receive an exemplary punishment.

At the same time, a similar outrage occurred in the election of Astarac, one of the distant parts of the kingdom; His Majesty gave orders for the imposition of a comparable punishment. . . .

(Clément, vol. II(i), p. 67)

104. Colbert to all intendants

FONTAINEBLEAU, *6 October 1679*
I have been informed that, in a great many generalities, the collectors of the *tailles* are but rarely nominated by the inhabitants of the parishes, as is required in the regulations, and that nearly always they are appointed

by the *élus*.[1] Because this is an abuse of some magnitude, and gives the assessment of the *tailles* almost entirely into the hands of the *élus*, the King has instructed me to tell you that, while you are dividing the *taille personelle*[2] among the elections of the generality of————————, you should take great care to discover the number of parishes which are contained in each of them, those where the collectors are appointed by the people, and those where they are chosen by the *élus* ex officio, thus, by a thorough study of this disorder, you will be able to apply the remedies you deem necessary. Should you need some help from the council in doing this, I will not delay in sending it as soon as you inform me.

(Clément, vol. II(i), pp. 118–19)

105. The *trésoriers de France* at Soissons to Colbert

SOISSONS, *29 December 1664*

. . . It is of the utmost importance that the garrison be not too powerful in this town, and especially so because the poverty of the place and the evil effects of the weather have allowed the greater part of the city walls to fall into the moat, so that one may pass easily through the breaches, which are numerous; the soldiers, leaving the city during the night by this route, can ambush collectors on their way to the receiver's office, and receivers on the way to the office of the receiver general, of which behaviour we have had a number of examples recently. . . .

(Depping, vol. III, p. 133)

106. Decree of the council of state, authorising the inspection of accounts

PARIS, *25 April 1669*

The King, wishing to be informed regularly of the state of the accounts of the receivers general of the finances and of the receivers of the *tailles*, in

[1] The *élus*, chiefly a judicial official, was concerned also with the collection of the *tailles*. He had the right to appoint collectors, but only when the parish had failed to elect them. It is suggested here that appointments are being made without a prior attempt at allowing the parish to elect these men.

[2] The *taille personelle*, collected in the *pays d'élections*, was a tax on the resources of the individual, as arbitrarily assessed by the collector. The *taille réelle*, in the *pays d'états*, was based on property and was more fairly allocated. See pp. 123–4.

order that he may give the necessary instructions for speeding the collection and assuring the safety of His Majesty's revenues, and for preventing their retention and misappropriation:

Having heard the report of Monsieur Colbert, counsellor in the royal council and controller general of the finances, His Majesty, in his council, has ordered and orders the intendants sent out into the eighteen generalities of the *pays d'élections* to visit the offices of the receivers general and of the local receivers every three months, and to inspect their daily registers and those containing the copies of the receipts issued by the receivers; to ensure that they have been drawn up and signed in accordance with the regulations; to calculate the amounts received; to examine the receipts for payments, together with His Majesty's accounts and those of the receivers, duly attested as prescribed by ordinance; to investigate the legal proceedings which have been taken against each parish—that is to say those measures which have been instituted for use in cases of negligence; to give instructions that funds should be transported and paid out according to the purpose for which they are intended; and in general terms to take any action which will help to hasten and secure the collection of these same revenues, in order that the said intendants may draw up their official reports and send them to the said council, with their recommendations as to what steps they think appropriate for furthering the best interests and the service of His Majesty[1]. . . .

(Clément, vol. II(ii), p. 762)

107. Jean-Baptiste Colbert: Memoirs on the financial affairs of France, in the form of a history (1663)

Chapter VII

. . . Since the beginning of the year 1662, and considering that there was then nothing more prejudicial to His Majesty's subjects than the multiplication of officials in the elections of the kingdom, who numbered as many as twenty-two or twenty-three in each election, and not only lived at the expense of the population by the exercise of this kind of administrative power, but who also caused innumerable troubles in the parishes by the exemptions and relief which they gave to the richest people for a

---

[1] See also pp. 18–21. In the *pays d'états*, such direct investigations were impossible, and the central government had to inspect these accounts through the agency of the Estates—see pp. 35–6.

variety of interested motives, His Majesty wished that the edict which authorised their suppression, and which was registered at the *cour des aides* in the presence of Monsieur during August of last year, be punctually enforced. . . .

But as this edict also included the suppression of the officers of the salt tax in the kingdom, and as His Majesty felt that, were this edict to be carried out in respect of these men, he would be burdened with such heavy costs of reimbursement that it would be impossible to meet them; considering moreover that a total suppression would deprive him for ever of the opportunity to re-establish them, a course of action that the necessities of some war which might occur during his reign could well commend to him, he resolved that these offices should not be subject to the *paulette*[1] and that there should be a heavy surcharge on them when they fell vacant, in the hope that he could by this means deliver his people in three or four years from the burdens which a large body of officials of this kind imposed upon them, that he would acquire their emoluments and rights when they died, would be spared the cost of their reimbursement, and would gain considerable sums through the *parties casuelles*[2] from the prices of the vacated posts, all of which could be used in time of need. . . .

(Clément, vol. II(i), pp. 60–1)

108. Colbert to Ménars, intendant at Paris

FONTAINEBLEAU, *4 August 1681*

Since 29 August 1679, I have written, at the instruction of the King, to the intendants in the generalities which are subject to the levy of the salt tax that His Majesty wishes them to examine most carefully, during the visits they pay to their elections, the number of officials who compose each of the salt depots, to send an exact list of them, and to make thorough enquiries about the good or bad reputation which each of these officials has acquired in the exercise of his duties; His Majesty's intention being to suppress those who have discharged their obligations most unsatisfactorily, and to amalgamate the ablest with the officers of the elections, thus creating a single body which will become, by this means, more impressive. . . . Be sure, if you will, that the estimate which you are

---

[1] The tax by which an office-holder acquired the right to bequeath his office to his heirs.
[2] The *parties casuelles* was the royal administrative department which dealt with the financial aspects of office-holding as they affected the crown.

to send to His Majesty of the good and bad qualities of these officials is utterly just, in order that he does not err in the choice he must make, which is always aimed at bringing relief to his subjects.

(Clément, vol. II(i), pp. 163–4)

109. Declaration of the king, concerning the residential obligations of officers of the finances, waters and forests, elections, salt depots, police and others, and requiring them to discharge their duties. . . .

PARIS, *29 December 1663*

Although the ordinances promulgated by the Kings our predecessors require the officers of the finances, the waters and forests, the elections, the salt depots, the police and others to reside in the town where they work; nevertheless many of them have dispensed themselves from this said obligation of residence, from which it follows that justice is not meted out to our subjects in the way we would have wished, and the collection of our revenues is not effected with sufficient speed to provide funds for the expenses of the state; the majority of our official receivers have arranged for their work to be delegated to agents who, in order to turn their position to account, impose additional burdens on the taxpayers . . .; over and above all these abuses and shortcomings, there is yet another which is highly prejudicial to our interests, namely that most of these said receivers are some years in arrears with their accounts, and they should not be allowed to carry out the responsibilities of their office until their handling of affairs in the past has been assessed. . . .

We therefore, by these letters signed with our hand, have announced and decreed, and announce and decree that we wish all the officers of our finances, waters and forests, elections and salt depots, police and others to go to their place of work and reside there from the moment these letters are made public; failing which they will be deprived of their tax exemptions, their salary and the percentage they receive of the funds they collect, which will revert to the treasury. We shall enjoin our prosecutors in the said jurisdictions to keep a register of the periods of residence of these said officers in their town of work, and to send copies of this document, authenticated by them, both to the intendant in the province and to the clerk of the records at the local finance office, in order that they be sent to our council and to our public prosecutors in our *chambres des comptes*.[1] We forbid the receivers to pay salaries, or to make any payment whatsoever, to an officer who has not resided and served as prescribed, on pain of dismissal. . . .

(Clément, vol. II(ii), pp. 753–4)

110. Colbert to Le Blanc, intendant at Rouen

SCEAUX, *17 June 1678*

I must inform you that I have never received such a complaint as that which you have lodged against the farmers of the wine dues, which is that they demand payment on the basis of a rate of two *sous* per *pinte*[2], when the wine in fact sells at only one *sou*; and I find it very difficult to believe that in Normandy the people pay double the sum they ought to be paying, without appealing either to the *élus* or to the *cour des aides*, as I have never heard tell, in any province of the kingdom, of any pretension so fanciful and unfounded as this one.

Summon the tax-farmers and their agents, if you will, find out the truth of this matter, and discover on what this claim is based; . . . it will be necessary to take legal action against those farmers who have taken part in this trickery.

(Clément, vol. II(i), p. 381)

111. Colbert to all intendants

VERSAILLES, *8 May 1682*

The King has received many complaints from the provinces and generalities about the general farm of the salt-tax, concerning the ways in which the agents of the tax-farmers are using the *prêt du sel*.[3] These complaints are that the agents encourage the people, by every sort of means, to take

[1] The *chambres des comptes* in Paris and in certain provincial centres were the courts with supreme responsibility for supervising the accounting of the taxes and for searching out abuses in the process of collection.

[2] The *pinte* was a French liquid measure nearly as large as the English quart.

[3] The *prêt du sel* permitted the sale of salt on a credit basis, in order to increase the final price. However it was considered that a *minot* was a sufficient year's supply 'for pot and salt-cellar' for 14 people. It was thus scandalous to persuade men, as in this letter, to divide a *minot* among four or six.

away salt on credit, at the rate of one *minot* for every four or six persons; that they make these men liable, either collectively or each for his own share, and immediately condemn them to payment of the sum due or to interest on it; they then send out sergeants with orders demanding settlement, or in default of this to seize chattels and livestock; and after they have been paid the interest and perhaps some extra sum as a gratuity, they allow them a few weeks respite, after which new writs are issued, with further attempts at coercion and seizure of livestock. Thus, by repeating these pressures again and again, they extract from the population three or four times the original price of the salt they had delivered to them. . . .

(Clément, vol. II(i), pp. 183–4)

112. Colbert to Miromesnil, intendant at Châlons

SAINT-GERMAIN-EN-LAYE, *15 December 1673*
I see that the receivers of the finances, the farmers of the wine and stamp duties, and in general all those who have to collect taxes, whether ordinary or extraordinary, in the generality of Châlons, have begun to complain and to put forward demands for considerable reductions in the sums to be collected, some of them even wishing to give up their positions as farmers and collectors.

As it is of the utmost importance that these revenues be maintained, and that you should give this matter your attention above all others, it is necessary for you, if you will, to ask all the receivers general and receivers of the *tailles* and the farmers of the wine and stamp duties, who are authorised to collect them, to call on you regularly, so that you may consider with them all the difficulties which they are encountering and the claims that the taxes should be reduced, giving them every assistance which is within the power granted you by the King to relieve them of these problems and to maintain the collection of the dues. Although I am not persuaded that you will need any other powers or commission from the King apart from those which His Majesty has already accorded you, nevertheless should you require some particular authority and send me word, I will not delay in forwarding it to you. . . .

(Clément, vol. II(i), pp. 312–13)

113. Caumartin, intendant at Châlons, to Colbert

CHÂLONS, *14 April 1669*

I tried today in the presidial court of Châlons the case against the royal judge of Barbonne, whom I found guilty of much misappropriation of funds, of using violence and of other malpractices. . . . The intendants have never been able to make his parish pay the *tailles*, he ridicules all the obligations of his office, and exempts his relations from taxes as well; he auctioned to himself, using assumed names, the right to collect the double tithe in his parish; he has imposed considerable levies during the past fifteen or sixteen years, which he has not reported to the community, and although he received nearly 2500 *livres* in revenue, he has lived so well that he owes more than 10,000 *écus*. Beyond that he has committed a thousand other deceits; but he has made himself so pliant and amiable towards the local nobility that there is not one of them who has not spoken on his behalf. Many people from the court have also written to me in his favour. That has not prevented him from being condemned to make a public apology for his crimes, to be banished for nine years from Champagne and Brie, to give up his office, and to pay a fine of 4000 *livres* of which a large part will be used to pay the *taille* of his parish, and to repair the market-hall, the gates and the walls of the town. I have also fined one of his relations who has held back money for supplying the troops, and I am also bringing actions against some other members of his cabal in their absence. I hope that an example of this magnitude will be a strong incentive to all judges and other officers of justice in the province to keep strictly to the law.

(Depping, vol. III, pp. 168–73)

E. Unfair tax allocation, aristocratic clientage, seigneurial dues and 'false nobles'

The preceding document has shown that it was sometimes possible for an intendant to discover sufficient evidence against a corrupt official that he could be tried and punished for his crimes, in which case his fate might encourage others to take their responsibilities more seriously. The relatively small number of successful trials—and the royal council would never have risked the disruptive effects of a law suit of this kind whose outcome was dubious—reflects the difficulties involved in ferreting out proof of these misdemeanours. The rival claims on the time of the hard-pressed intendant were partly responsible, but more important was the way in which the privileged groups in the localities drew closer together and obstructed his investigations. The local nobility and certain other substantial citizens frequently aided suspect officials or acted on their own in a common attempt to advance personal interests and to frustrate the purposes of the central government. This next group of extracts deals with their role in the allocation and collection of taxes, illustrating some of the different situations in which important men either influenced the allotment by favouring their own dependents and clients, or were at least allocated an unfairly light burden of their own (*114–5*). At times an aristocrat might even have to be asked if he would give the order for certain villages to pay perfectly legitimate dues, so strong was his influence over his territories (*116*). An additional burden was the series of fiscal levies which the nobles were themselves able to impose on the peasantry and which therefore rivalled the royal taxes as suitors for the peasant's meagre resources, especially when these seigneurial rights were also abused and exploited (*117*). Yet, although the crown heavily penalised the abuses, it did not try to stamp out these time-honoured seigneurial dues as such, knowing them to be so highly treasured by the nobles that their abrogation would have caused widespread disorder. There was no point in costly provocation.[1]

One problem which the central ministers never ceased to combat and were unsuccessful in mastering was that of the 'false nobles', men who claimed a title of nobility which was not rightfully theirs in order to gain exemption from the worst burdens of taxation (*118*). Like the Chamber of Justice,[2] this enquiry provoked excessive discontent and was abandoned (*119*), while the corruption which it had attempted to root out could flower again unimpeded (*120*). Finally there is a letter which describes some other methods of deceit to which unwilling taxpayers resorted (*121*).

114. Colbert to all intendants

VERSAILLES, *28 May 1681*

The King has instructed me to write to you about two very important matters which were omitted from the letter which I wrote to you on the order of His Majesty on 12 April last, concerning the tour which you are to make of your generality. These two matters are as follows:

The first, that His Majesty has received a variety of reports from every province to the effect that nearly all, or at least a considerable number, of the nobles, officials and other powerful men are arranging for the allocation of the *tailles* to be decided at their houses in town or in the country, or on their orders.

---

[1] When the crown did attack the excessive seigneurial rights of the Breton nobles, it helped to provoke a serious revolt—see pp. 54, 58 and 238.
[2] See pp. 92–4.

The second, that in almost every parish the principal inhabitants and the wealthy find it easy to discharge themselves of their obligation to pay the *tailles* and add their share to the burden of the humble and the poor; and even that the poor acquiesce in these evasions by the rich, because it is the rich who provide them with the opportunity for work and thus furnish them with the means of meeting their needs. . . .

His Majesty instructs me to leave you in no doubt that he wishes you to investigate these two problems with the utmost care; that you should discover, especially in the places where you are spending some time, if they are true or not; and with regard to the first one, that you should not only use all the authority of your position to prevent the continuation of such an abuse, but that, if the corruption is of so great a magnitude that you think an example should be made, you should inform His Majesty of it, in which case he intends to send you power to judge the culprits without the right of appeal. . . .

On the second point, His Majesty wishes you to remedy this situation by *taxes d'office*[1] and by the other means at your disposal. . . .

(Clément, vol. II(i), pp. 154–5)

115. Colbert to Hachette, *trésorier de France*, at Paris

PARIS, *16 October 1670*

I have received reports from three or four places in the election of Dreux, where it seems that a large number of parishes have had their burden of taxation lightened because they belong to a person of quality in Paris or to a local noble, and because the *élus* own land there. Do not fail to discover most carefully if there is some truth in these charges, and to apply the appropriate remedies, as nothing is more contrary to the intentions of the King, and nothing is more worthy of your fullest attention, than that one parish be oppressed in order that another may be given relief. . . .

(Clément, vol. II(i), p. 75)

116. Colbert to the duc d'Arpajon, lieutenant of the king in Languedoc

8 July 1662

The receivers general of the finances at Montauban have sent me a list of taxes still outstanding in that generality, and I have noticed that the

[1] See p. 93, note 3.

majority of those in the elections of Rodez and Millau are owed by parishes which belong to you. When I asked the reason for this, I was told that your villagers did not begin to think about paying their dues unless they were strongly pressed to do so by you, and that you would not wish them to be constrained to pay through the use of troops. To which end, Monseigneur, I am compelled to write you these lines, begging you most humbly to give the necessary orders throughout your lands, so that the people will comply with the demands which have been made of them; otherwise it will not be in my power to prevent these complaints from reaching the ear of the King, and I know you would wish to avoid that.

(Clément, vol. II(i), p. 226)

117. Colbert to Le Bret, intendant at Limoges

SAINT-GERMAIN-EN-LAYE, 20 February 1681

I am only too keen to bring to your notice the accusation which is commonly made that the nobles and other powerful men in the generality inflict a considerable number of impositions on the people, pretending that they are *péages, corvées, vinages,* double *tailles,* increases in the seigneurial rights of the 'double' and 'triple',[1] or in short by innumerable other means which are burdensome to the ordinary man. As you can do nothing which would be more beneficial to the King's service than to find out everything which relates to this subject, so that you can send a report to His Majesty who will then make his intentions known to you and will issue his orders, it is essential that, during your various tours of inspection, you never cease to seek out this information, compiling memoirs about your findings and sending them to me; because, as these are matters for the local civil cᵣ irts, His Majesty wishes you to estimate whether these disorders are so widespread or of such magnitude that it will be necessary to invoke some extraordinary authority, which might mean that you would be given the power to investigate these abuses, bring the culprits to court, and sit in judgment upon them.

(Clément, vol. IV, pp. 143–4)

---

[1] These are some of the numerous seigneurial dues which still survived in seventeenth-century France. The *péages* were tolls on roads, bridges and rivers; the *corvées* were labour dues; the *vinages,* duties which were levied chiefly on wines, were often used for the maintenance of road and river routes.

118. Declaration of the king against usurpers of nobility, in order to interpret the declaration of 8 February 1661. . . .

FONTAINEBLEAU, *22 June 1664*

The difficulties which have been encountered in the implementation of our declarations against the usurpers of nobility, among others that of 8 February 1661, have constrained us to examine the methods necessary for ensuring their prompt execution, in order to end this kind of usurpation within our realm, which is prejudicial to the honour of the true nobility and to the good of our subjects who contribute to the *tailles*. . . .

We have commanded that a general commission shall be sent out to investigate these said usurpers, under the terms of which all usurpers of the rank of noble or gentleman, or those who have been improperly exempted from the *tailles*, shall present, within reasonable time and allowing for the distance they have to travel, the originals of the letters of their pretended nobility; failing which . . . they will be declared commoners. . . .

(Clément, vol. II(ii), p. 754)

119. Colbert to all intendants

PARIS, *1 December 1670*

As the King daily receives complaints about the vexations and malpractices which are committed during the quest for usurpers of nobility, His Majesty has resolved to end these investigations. In consequence of which he has instructed me to tell you that he wishes you to serve no further writs on any individual, nor to proceed with cases which are already before you as a result of these enquiries. . . .

(Clément, vol. II(i), pp. 77–8)

120. Colbert to Tubeuf, intendant at Bourges and Moulins

SAINT-GERMAIN-EN-LAYE, *1 December 1673*

In your letter of 25 November, you tell me that the investigations into the usurpers of nobility which were undertaken throughout the two generalities of Bourges and Moulins have been almost useless, because you have not even glimpsed the fruit which the King chiefly wished to procure for his subjects when he ordered these enquiries, which was the imposition of the *taille* on all those who were declared to be usurpers; and moreover that, whether because of the reason given by you that the richest have arranged for themselves to be exempted by a decision of the council, or because you have no knowledge of those who were found guilty by Monsieur d'Herbigny,[1] or because those whom you have yourself convicted have managed to prolong the exemption which they had usurped through their false titles, you find that these pursuits have brought no relief whatsoever to the King's subjects. It is therefore most important that you devote all your efforts to this matter, and you must search out, in every election, those who are in this position so that the *taille* may be imposed upon them next year without fail. I do not believe that, if you do this carefully, you will find many who have been discharged by decisions of the council without good grounds, and I suspect that, if you make only the smallest effort, you will recover the memoirs about all the men who were convicted by Monsieur d'Herbigny.

With regard to those whom you have yourself judged and condemned, I trust that you will not fail to impose upon them the amount of *taille* due since the day they were convicted. . . .

(Clément, vol. II(i), pp. 304–5)

121. Dugué, intendant at Lyon and Grenoble, to Colbert

LYON, *30 November 1666*

The tours of inspection which I have been required to make through the elections of the generalities of Dauphiné and the Lyonnais for the administration of the *taille*, and the effort which I have been compelled to devote to it, have deprived me of the honour of writing to you as often as I would have wished. I have noticed . . . that, as soon as a man becomes wealthy and comes to possess property of some worth, and if he has children, he arranges that one will enter the church and become a priest, and then hands over all his fortune to him by deed of gift, thereby freeing it from the *taille*, and although he continues to enjoy the fruits of it under the cover of his son's name, he does it so secretly that it would be impossible to produce any proof of it. The second, which is no less prejudicial to the collection of His Majesty's revenues, is that the

[1] Tubeuf's predecessor as intendant.

head of a family, who sees that his life is nearing its end and leaves most of his possessions in trust for his children, gives his wife the freedom to choose any one of them as his heir; after a family council, she never fails to select the youngest, because she can be assured that, as long as he is under age, he will not have his name inscribed on the tax rolls of the parish. . . .

(Depping, vol. III, pp. 165–6)

F. Fiscal reform: Rationalisation and simplification; indirect versus direct taxes; concessions and incentives

Although the central government often had to punish the misdeeds already committed by its officials, instead of being able to produce reforms which would prevent similar abuses of power in the future, it could at least attempt some improvement in the position of the ordinary taxpayer by systematising conflicting provincial practices and by rationalising the structure of the bureaucracy. In doing so, Colbert tried to concentrate on aspects of administration which were not intimately linked with the private interests of the privileged and the office-holders, hoping to avoid yet another confrontation with them. Firstly the boundaries of the tax districts were to be made more logical (*122*), and the rates of assessment unified (*123*). This second letter raises the important point that the generality was very much a self-contained unit and that the intendant, although aware of the variations within his own district, might be ignorant of discrepancies between his generality and that immediately adjacent. It was equally vital to promulgate ordinances which regulated the tax-farms and reconciled a host of conflicting judicial decisions, although these royal decrees, as on so many other occasions, looked impressive on paper but failed to change prevailing practice in the localities. These attempts at reform came very late in the ministry of Colbert, not until after the end of the Dutch War in fact, and little had therefore been achieved at the time of his death.

The circumstances of costly wars and a privileged society dictated the character of financial policy, and Colbert frequently had to pursue the short-term advantage. Nevertheless it is possible to discern a number of principles which underlay his whole strategy of fiscal reform. Taxes on necessities should be decreased and others increased (*124*), while indirect taxation should rise and direct taxation should be reduced.[1] The *taille* should be lowered in general, although it should be raised in the relatively undertaxed *pays d'états*; also the more fairly calculated *taille réelle* of the *pays d'états* should replace the *taille personnelle* in the *pays d'élections*. This double revision of the *taille*, one of the dearest dreams of the minister, was not so easy to realise (*125–6*). Yet some reductions were possible from time to time, although these concessions were never made at a moment when it

[1] See also pp. 234–5.

might appear that the government was responding to popular pressure. That might encourage the people to try the same tactics at a later date. Those remissions which were granted were immediately used as royal propaganda (*127–8*), both to convince the peasant that the king had his welfare at heart and was shifting the burden on to the shoulders of the privileged who paid only indirect taxes, but also to persuade foreigners that the country was obviously becoming more stable and was safe to invest in.[1]

Another belief of Colbert and other ministers was that the sheer size of population was connected with prosperity, and fiscal concessions were therefore made to encourage early marriage and large families (*129*), in these days of high mortality. Once again, corruption crept in (*130*).

122. Colbert to all intendants

PARIS, *20 July 1679*

One of the plans for these years of peace, and one which concerns the royal finances, is the correction of a disorder which has grown to considerable size and is burdensome to the people, namely that there are many parishes within an election or a salt tax district which are much nearer to the town where the offices of the adjacent election or salt district are situated, so that the inhabitants of these parishes are sometimes obliged to travel two or three times as far when transporting their taxes to the receiver of the *tailles* or when petitioning the officials of the election, which would be unnecessary if the area of competence of each election had been more carefully delineated at the outset. It is therefore the King's intention that you should compile an accurate map of the generality of —————, on which the parishes in each election will be marked, together with their exact distance from each collection office, so that from these maps, and with your advice, the King can redistribute the parishes among the said elections and salt districts in order to ensure that each will be responsible for the parishes which are nearest to it. His Majesty also wishes that the elections and salt districts be made conterminate. His Majesty accordingly intends that you apply yourself diligently to this task throughout the rest of this summer and the forthcoming winter; and in case you cannot find anyone to compile these maps within the generality of —————, inform me and I will send you men from Paris who are qualified to undertake this work.

(Clément, vol. II(i), p. 110)

[1] See pp. 127–8.

123. Colbert to Breteuil, intendant at Amiens

FONTAINEBLEAU, *28 October 1682*

. . . The King has instructed me to write to inform you that, with reference to the allocation of the *tailles* in the elections of Beauvais and Clermont (the first of which is in the generality of Paris, and the second in that of Soissons), both of which border on to parishes in the generality of Amiens, it seems that the parishes of these two elections bear a heavier burden than those of your generality in proportion to their area and the wealth of their lands. It is therefore His Majesty's wish that you examine, in consultation with the intendants of these two generalities, whether this is true and, if so, from what comes this discrepancy, because His Majesty regards it as a matter of some consequence as it may readily persuade the inhabitants of parishes in the elections of Beauvais and Clermont to change their abode and take up residence in the parishes of Amiens. . . .

(Clément, vol. II(i), p. 211)

124. Colbert to Miromesnil, intendant at Châlons

. . . Do not forget to take into account the fact that the salt tax, which has been regulated by a single ordinance, has also been reduced considerably because it is a necessity of life; but the same cannot be said of duties on wine, because drinking is not a necessity of life. Thus I have no wish to reduce these tax-farms, if it is possible to avoid doing so. . . .

(Clément, vol. II(i), pp. 169–70)

125. Table showing the yield of the *tailles* in the *pays d'élections*

Year	Livres	Year	Livres
1661	42,028,000	1666	36,084,000
1662	40,969,000	1667	36,699,000
1663	37,991,000	1668	36,033,000
1664	36,233,000	1669	33,832,000
1665	35,295,000	1670	34,019,000

Year	Livres	Year	Livres
1671	33,845,000	1678	40,480,000
1672	34,798,000	1679	34,939,000
1673	36,645,000	1680	32,904,000
1674	37,181,000	1681	33,915,000
1675	38,122,000	1682	35,023,000
1676	40,270,000	1683	37,907,000
1677	40,421,000		

(Clamageran,[1] vol. II, pp. 617–8)

126. Table showing the yield of the *taille*

Year	Pays d'élections	Pays d'états[2]
Average: 1662–83	36,527,000	2,166,000
1683	37,907,000	2,618,000
1684	37,698,000	4,829,000
1685	35,464,000	3,861,000
1686	33,875,000	3,777,000
1687	33,738,000	3,751,000

(Clamageran, vol. III, p. 8)

127. Colbert to Marillac, intendant at Poitiers

VERSAILLES, *31 August 1674*

I do not dispute that the generalities are suffering in a war as widespread and mighty as this one; but you must remember and must make public as often as possible that in the year when the King first took control of the finances the *tailles* stood at 56,000,000 *livres*. His Majesty, in seven or eight years, reduced them to 32,000,000; and moreover that, although they were increased during the war, in 1675 they stood at only 38,000,000. . . . The people must be made to believe that the same spirit which prompted His Majesty to bring them relief in time of peace will still prevail, as soon as he, by his determination and efforts, and by risking his very life at the head of his armies, can once again bestow it upon them. . . .

(Clément, vol. II(i), pp. 349–50)

[1] J.-J. Clamageran, *Histoire de l'impôt*, 3 vol., Paris, 1867–76.
[2] The *pays d'états*, although seeming undertaxed, had extra demands made on their local funds—see p. 33.

128. Colbert to all intendants

SAINT-GERMAIN-EN-LAYE, *17 August 1679*

I am sending you some printed copies of the decree which the King has ordered to be sent out, announcing a reduction of 2,000,000 *livres* in the amount of the *tailles*, and it is important that you should make such generosity widely known so that the people may be reminded that, although His Majesty asked for considerable help from them to maintain the war effort, he knows equally well how to show them his favour and let them taste the fruits of the glorious peace which he has concluded. . . .

(Clément, vol. II(i), p. 114)

129. Edict conceding privileges and exemptions to those who marry before or during their twentieth year, until they reach twenty-five years, and to heads of families who have between ten and twelve children

SAINT-GERMAIN-EN-LAYE, *November 1666*

. . . We can but note with approval that the Romans, those wise states-men . . ., gave recompense to fathers who offered their children to the state . . .; and are moreover aware of the special custom in our province of Burgundy, according to which all men and women who have twelve living children enjoy exemption from all taxation, and we wish to provide for every subject in our realm by extending these same favours and insti-tuting new ones.

To which end we have decreed that from this moment all our taxable subjects who have married before their twenty-first year shall be and shall remain exempt from all contributions to the *tailles*, taxes and other public levies . . ., until they attain and complete their twenty-fifth year. And with reference to those who marry during their twenty-first year, they shall enjoy the same exemption until they have completed their twenty-fourth year.

So too it is our wish and pleasure that every father of a family who has ten living children, born in lawful wedlock, who are not priests or re-ligious,[1] is and shall be exempted from the collection of all *taille* . . . and

[1] Colbert detested the religious orders because they were an idle class, contributing nothing to the state.

other taxes . . ., and from billeting of soldiers . . ., and, if it happens that one of the said children should die bearing arms in our service, he shall be regarded as still living. . . .

And we wish that noblemen and their wives who have ten children living, born in legal wedlock, who are neither priests nor religious, save only if they have died bearing arms in our service, shall enjoy a pension of 1000 *livres* each year, and those who have twelve alive, or deceased as stated above, shall have a 2000 *livres* pension. . . .

(Isambert, vol. XVIII, pp. 90–1)

130. Declaration revoking the edict of November 1666, concerning the privileges of fathers who have between ten and twelve children

VERSAILLES, *13 January 1683*

We have been informed of abuses which have crept into the implementation of our edict of November 1666, in which we granted to fathers of families who had ten living children exemption from the collection of our revenues and all other levies on the people; and to those who had twelve, from the *tailles* and the same dues.[1] But we have learnt that, in contravention of the exact terms of our edict, our *cour des aides* has maintained these privileges for fathers who have ceased to have ten or twelve children, even though they were not killed while bearing arms in our service; and more especially that these abuses have led to the oppression of our other subjects, for whose welfare we are never able to spend too much effort in providing by preserving equality in the allocation of those impositions which are necessary to sustain the expenses we are obliged to incur. . . .

(Isambert, vol. XIX, p. 413)

G. *Tailles réelle* and *personnelle*, redemption of the royal domain, *rentes*

If the *taille réelle* were to replace the *taille personnelle* in the *pays d'élections*, a great deal more information would be needed about those provinces than was at present to hand. In the *pays d'états* the *taille réelle* was assessed on the basis of cadastral

[1] The 1683 declaration does not state the terms of the 1666 edict with complete accuracy.

surveys which, while they were sometimes very out of date, gave the tax officials some guide to a man's landed wealth, and reduced the opportunities for corruption in the allocation of taxes among individuals.[1] The *taille personnelle* was based not on land nor on any statistical survey, but on the total resources of the individual as arbitrarily estimated by the collector. Although the Estates might be uncooperative about the amount of taxes they would pay[2], they were able to collect the agreed dues efficiently and were successful in keeping some kind of cadastral records. The attempt to provide this information for the rest of France, which was an essential preliminary to the establishment of the *taille réelle*, was beyond the means of the officials in the *pays d'élections*, and Colbert's efforts at producing such a nationwide survey were almost as fruitless as those of his predecessor, Mazarin, in 1656. Even the very first stage of this process, the standardisation of the *taille réelle* in the *pays d'états* themselves proved to be an impossible task (*131*). Had this first problem been surmounted, much opposition lay ahead, because the *taille réelle* was levied on actual land, and if a noble purchased commoner land, it remained taxable although its new owner was from a social group which was basically exempt from direct taxation. As the *noblesse de robe* had made many purchases of this kind, whereas the old families of the aristocracy had rarely done so, it was the *robe* of the *pays d'élections* who were eager to prevent such a change in the manner of assessment.

The *taille* therefore remained largely unchanged, and it was the indirect taxes which were expected to yield the extra revenues which were needed more urgently almost every year.[3] Finally Colbert tried to redeem the alienated lands of the royal domain (*132*), and to reduce the extent of investment in government bonds—*rentes*. Success in these two enterprises looked possible in peacetime, but these reforms were too costly to maintain during expensive wars, and much ground which had been gained was lost.

131. Colbert to d'Aguesseau, intendant at Toulouse

SAINT-GERMAIN-EN-LAYE, *20 February 1681*

I am well pleased to learn, from your letter of 11 February, that you are all assembled at Montpellier and are drafting the regulations for the *tailles réelles*. I have read most carefully a proposal which was sent to me

[1] See pp. 112–14.
[2] See pp. 38–59.
[3] For the effect of these taxes on commerce and industry see pp. 234–5, and on the promotion of revolts see pp. 237–43, 247 and 251.

by Monsieur du Mousseau, counsellor at the *cour des comptes* of Montpellier, and which has been drawn up, I imagine, by some officials of that court. As you have a copy in your possession, I assume that you have observed their aim to be neither the reduction of the court's jurisdiction nor the pruning of the causes of law suits within it. You must always be on your guard against such plans. . . .

(Clément, vol. II(i), pp. 149–50)

VERSAILLES, *19 August 1682*
We have carefully examined yet again, Monsieur Pussort[1] and I, the draft regulations for the *tailles réelles*; but I must admit to you that as so many difficulties have come to light, it will be almost impossible to effect a compromise between the good order and principles worthy of a legislator on the one hand and the customs of Languedoc on the other. . . .

(Clément, vol. II(i), p. 196, note 2)

132. Colbert to Bouchu, intendant in Burgundy

VERSAILLES, *24 April 1682*
As it is the King's intention to make special efforts towards the redemption of the crown domains, and as His Majesty may well wish to begin with those of the province of Burgundy, I ask you to devote yourself particularly to learning the details of all the crown lands which are in this province; the amount which has been alienated, and at what value; and taking both these together, the yield of every estate, and whether or not they could be made more profitable in the hands of the King. But it is essential that you carry out these enquiries without any fuss, and that the whole process be seen simply as curiosity on your part, and not as if you had specific orders from the King.[2]

(Clément, vol. II(i), pp. 182–3)

[1] Henri Pussort, counsellor of state and uncle of Colbert, was one of the men who were given specific responsibility for simplifying complex legal procedures and preparing new ordinances.

[2] The king had first announced this policy in an edict of 1667, but nothing significant had yet been done to implement it.

133. Olivier Lefèvre d'Ormesson: Journal

June 1664

. . . After leaving the chamber, I went with Besnard to see the first president, who took us to dine at Auteuil. He showed us a printed copy of a decree which had been conveyed the day before to the controllers of the *rentes* and posted up in the streets, in which the King, wishing to make reimbursement for the Paris *rentes* at the value at which they stood twenty-five years ago, orders all *rentiers*, within one month, to present their warrants to Messieurs d'Aligre, de Sève and Colbert, counsellors at the royal council, and Marin, intendant of the finances; and during this time the sums will be paid. The decree is dated 24 May. We discussed every aspect of this action, which seemed to us to be highly imprudent.

In the evening, I heard that the *rentiers*, having been advised of this decree, had hurried to the City Hall, and that consternation and despair were in everyone's heart.

The next morning, Friday 6 June, at the Chamber of Justice . . . anxiety was written on every face, because there was no one who was not concerned with the suppression of the *rentes*, whether due to the income they would lose, or because there was no other way for them to invest their money. . . .

On Saturday 7 June, at the Chamber of Justice, Monsieur Voisin[2] told me that on the preceding day there had been a crowd of *rentiers* at the City Hall, making a great deal of noise; that he had addressed them, and that he would go to Fontainebleau.

I noticed that discontent about the *rentes* was growing rapidly; but no one dared to speak of it. I do not know what will be the outcome of this affair; but it is feared that there will be angry scenes; because many men are in despair, believing that they will be ruined, and having no other assets. . . .

Monday 9 June, Monsieur Voisin told me that he had been to Fontainebleau, and that the King wished the decree to be implemented. . . .

Tuesday 10 June, at the chamber . . . I learned from Monsieur Voisin that, on the preceding day, there had been an uproar at the City Hall, with men demanding a meeting; and that there were many present who were not even *rentiers*, and who attended in greater numbers today.

After Monsieur Voisin had left, Monsieur the Chancellor spoke,

[1] Journal d'Oliver Lefèvre d'Ormesson, 'Collection des documents inédits sur l'histoire de France', 2 vol., Paris, 1860–1.
[2] The mayor of Paris.

saying that the King's plans for the *rentes* were perfectly just; that he was
a prince who followed no guide but reason; that to assemble and make
loud protestations was strange indeed; that one had to pay respect to the
majesty of kings . . .; that men who were not *rentiers* were involved, like
the devil in a thunderstorm; that it was known that couriers had been
sent out into the provinces; that one should take care not to cause offence
to the King's majesty. . . .

Then Monsieur Pussort said that it was another Fronde. . . . To this,
no one made a reply. . . .[1]

134. Colbert to all intendants

SAINT-GERMAIN-EN-LAYE, *24 May 1679*

The King has resolved to create 1,000,000 *livres* of *rentes* for the City Hall
of Paris, at $6\frac{1}{4}\%$, and, because this kind of investment is in great demand,
His Majesty has instructed me to send you a copy of this edict, in order
that you may publish it throughout the generality of ——————, so
that if some of the officials and inhabitants wish to take advantage of this
offer, they can do so.

(Clément, vol. II(i), p. 102)

135. Colbert to Cotolandi, French resident in Florence

SAINT-GERMAIN-EN-LAYE, *24 May 1679*

I am sending you some copies of the edict which the King has issued, creating 1,000,000 *livres* of *rentes* for the City Hall of Paris. Use all the skill
and methods at your disposal to persuade the subjects of the Grand Duke
of Florence to invest in them, yet without seeming to be pressing them.
You will be pleased to hear that, in the four days since the issue and registration of the edict, we have already received more than 100,000 *écus*.

(Clément, vol. II(i), p. 102, note 1)

---

[1] In fact it proved impossible for Colbert to take such drastic action, but the
profits of the *rentiers* was nevertheless considerably reduced.

136. Colbert to Compans, French resident in Genoa

28 June 1679

You received the edict announcing 1,000,000 *livres* of *rentes* rather too late, because the whole issue was bought up within eighteen days, but the King has resolved to create a further 1,000,000 at $5\frac{1}{2}\%$. . . .

(Clément, vol. II(i), p. 102, note 1)

6 JUSTICE

The legal powers of the king in France were theoretically strong and all-embracing. He could issue whatever laws he chose, unhampered by any codes of common or customary law, free from binding obligations to uphold the ordinances of his predecessors, and unrestricted by the tradition of consulting the representatives of his subjects. The restraining force of the 'fundamental laws of the kingdom' was a weapon more appropriate for political theorists than for practical politicians. The monarch was thus the unique initiator of law, and he was in that sense 'absolute'. Yet his legislative authority was in reality much more limited, chiefly by the judicial bureaucracy which had been appointed by the crown to register and execute its ordinances and edicts, but which could be as obstructive in dispensing royal justice as it was in running the finances[1] and other areas of administration. The reform and close supervision of these vast ranks of hereditary officials was as essential to the extension of an effective judicial system as were the rationalisation and the codification of the laws themselves. There was no feasible alternative to the existing hierarchy of courts; the only possibility was to increase their efficiency, and this was to be no easy task. Lower down the scale there was an unsatisfactory vacuum, because the agents deputed to carry out the decisions of the judges were also unreliable—whether it was the sergeants and tipstaffs of the courts, who were frequently as dishonest as they were brutal; or the inadequate municipal police and militia, often more concerned with their privileges than with their duties;[2] or the soldiery, underpaid, ill-disciplined and disruptive. Although all these groups of men could be persuaded to make arrests, it was not within the power of the Paris ministers to guarantee that they apprehended the men in greatest need of judicial correction. The serious criminals were likely to be in league with the provincial judges and to be the financial benefactors of the men who were sent to arrest them.

On paper, the reform of law was in some ways the high point of the achievement of Colbert. Although abuses remained in the daily practice of justice and the central government had continually to compromise with local interests, there was published during his ministry a series of ordinances which united the disparate traditions of provincial courts into a national legal code. He was thus able to create in jurisprudence the uniform framework which eluded him in his attempts to bring order into taxation, commerce and industry,[3] and he bequeathed to his

[1] See Chapter 5, especially pp. 92–100, 102–14. One contemporary source discloses that in 1664 there were 45,780 judicial and financial officials in France, 5,149 in Paris alone.

[2] The enforcement of law in the towns, the corruption of consuls, private jurisdictions etc. are also discussed in Chapter 4, especially pp. 67, 76–9.

[3] See Chapter 5, pp. 118–20, 123–5, and Chapter 7, pp. 195–205, 210–18, 228–30.

successors a corpus of legal rules which was to be consulted in later reigns and to be put into effect more extensively than in the years of his own life. During the personal rule of Louis XIV, the ideas and pronouncements of royal ministers remained far removed from the daily practices of officials in the localities.

Commercial, industrial and fiscal reforms had to be attempted partly by overhauling the existing bureaucratic apparatus and partly by introducing wholly new policies based on novel theories—e.g. new definitions of class privileges, *dirigiste* approaches to economics. In the field of justice there was no such controversial theorising about the nature of law. The central government was able to concern itself solely with the machinery of legal administration, although the reconciliation of conflicting procedures and the purging of corruption were considerable challenges to the skill and tenacity of Colbert. His methods were similar to those used in tackling financial reform—a new conciliar organisation at the centre; commissions sent out into every province, gathering volumes of information, with the long-term aim of systematising the processes of law and stamping out local variations; short-term measures to eradicate the most blatant abuses, with special tribunals meting out severe and exemplary punishments to flagrant offenders.[1] Some of these offences have been mentioned above in connection with fiscal law suits—delays in dispensing justice; expensive progresses from one court to another, notably when the various courts, with their overlapping and ill-defined jurisdictions, deliberately undid each other's work in order that the lawyers who composed them might profit from the extra litigation; and sheer neglect of their duties by a significant minority of officials.

Thus the crown uttered threats which were beyond its power to carry out on a national scale, but,which worried its bureaucrats to some extent because any of them might be punished individually as a warning to others. Also, if the officials opposed innovations by the ministers, they had to administer the existing law on a routine daily basis if they were to profit from their offices. It was impossible for there to be a total breakdown of justice as had occurred during the Frondes, because the king was now ruling personally and openly taking the responsibility for general policies. It was sometimes convenient for both sides to blame some specific matter on a minister, but at the core of any more prolonged confrontation would undoubtedly lie the very nature of royal authority. Neither the king nor the sovereign courts[2] dared to risk the consequences of such an encounter. Although there were some real points of legal controversy between the monarch and his judiciary, the principal substance of his complaints was that individuals were corrupt and the whole system was inefficient.

[1] See Chapter 5, especially pp. 83–9, 92–7.

[2] The 'sovereign courts' were those which gave judgment without the right of appeal—the *parlements, cours des aides, chambres des comptes* and the *cour des monnaies.* In a slightly different category, but of similar prestige, was the Grand Council—a most important court which had developed from the legal aspect of the old council of the king, and was often designated incorrectly as a 'sovereign court'.

There was also the complex network of seigneurial justice, which existed beside the lower levels of the royal courts. As with seigneurial taxes,[1] the king preferred not to interfere with those noble jurisdictions which were legitimately established and properly exercised. Such actions simply stirred up ill feeling against the crown with no compensating return. Yet, when these rights were manipulated, as by the unscrupulous Bretons,[2] then stern retribution was authorised. A more worrying problem was the situation in the towns, where the elected officials played a part in dispensing local justice and did so with their customary disdain for honesty and regard for personal advantage.

Faced with this broad topic, the king and his ministers knew that much would remain undone. They wisely chose to concentrate on those areas which were most closely under their control or which would bring them the greatest glory in the eyes of the world.

A. The plan for reform and the great ordinances

There were two immediate priorities in the minds of Louis and his advisers during the early days of the personal rule, the prevention of any challenge to the royal power and the establishment of an efficient central bureaucracy. In finance, which required the instant attention of the government, the dangerous figure of Fouquet was removed even before the new council of the finances was set up.[3] In justice, marginally less pressing, there was not one ogre but many—less dangerous but more difficult to remove. These past challengers of authority, the *parlementaires* and the officers of the other sovereign courts, were the subject of the first instruction of importance on justice in September 1663,[4] and a little time then elapsed before the busy Colbert looked more deeply into the whole problem of judicial reform (*137–9*). Before any concrete results emerged, there were further delays. Not only did it take time to gather and codify all the relevant information, but other aspects of reform were given preference.

Apart from emergency measures, these plans for overhauling the machinery of the state can be divided into distinct phases. Except in periods of war, when such projects had to be totally suspended because of the all-absorbing problem of financing the army, the energies of the central bureaucracy tended to be concentrated at any one time on a single field of administrative reform. Only after Colbert had initiated new policies for the navy and colonial trade and had made an unsuccessful start at reorganising the financial system did he turn his full attention to the improvement of justice. This topic then dominated the later 1660s and early 1670s, years which at first sight seem to have been crowned with great achievement. It was a time when the ministers did not have their usual difficulty in meeting the expenses of government and they could therefore act more independently of the sources of royal revenue, which were also the fount of most oppo-

[1] See pp. 112–13 and 115.
[2] See p. 238.
[3] See pp. 6 and 85–6.
[4] For some of the results of this survey, see pp. 140–1.

sition to the policies of the crown. Thus the great ordinances—the product of years of research by provincial agents—were published as uncompromising declarations of a law which was to apply throughout the lands of the French king. Unfortunately the kingdom was soon to be plunged into the costly Dutch War, and the crown could not implement its new codes as vigorously as it had promulgated them. Many of their provisions remained unobserved for years to come.

The extracts printed here (*140–1*) are taken from the two most important—the Civil Ordinance of 1667, the first one to be published, and the Criminal Ordinance of 1670 which was produced with considerably more difficulty and dispute.[1]

137. Jean-Baptiste Colbert: Memoir for the king

PARIS, *22 October 1664*

My zeal for Your Majesty's glory will, if it please you, serve as my apology, should I sometimes seem to speak my mind rather freely. . . .

Your Majesty must limit the ways by which your subjects make their living, in so far as this is possible, to those callings which further your grand designs.

These are agriculture, commerce, war on land and war at sea.

If Your Majesty could succeed in limiting his peoples to these four occupations, one might say that he could become master of the world. . . .

The two professions which consume the talents of one hundred thousand of your subjects, aimlessly and without adding to your glory, are finance and justice. . . .

Justice has this fault above all, which is that, apart from using up the energies of more than seventy thousand men, it imposes a tyrannical and burdensome yoke, in your name, upon all the rest of your peoples; by its chicanery, it occupies a million men and gnaws away at a million others, reducing them to such misery that they can think about no other profession for the rest of their lives.

If Your Majesty were to consider, should it please him, how much his glory would increase, were so many men to contribute to it, this could indeed be brought about; not in one year of course, nor in two, but perhaps in ten, fifteen or twenty. To reach such a goal it is necessary to start at once, and to follow a sure and steady path, without letting anyone see Your Majesty's plans. Secrecy is vital to the success of grand designs, not only in order to avoid obstacles which would be great and even insur-

---

[1] The Commercial Ordinance is included in the chapter on Commerce, pp. 195–9.

mountable if such intentions were made public, but also to foster the reputation which Your Majesty will acquire as not just the most powerful, but also the most virtuous prince in the world, when one will read in the history books not just that you had formulated these plans at a time when usage and custom would have prompted no man to think of them, but that you brought them to fruition unbeknown to the whole population. . . .

(Clément, vol. VI, pp. 3–4)

138. Jean-Baptiste Colbert: Memoir about the reform of justice

SAINT-GERMAIN-EN-LAYE, *15 May 1665*

. . . As His Majesty has informed us that he wishes to reduce to a single corpus of ordinances all those things which are necessary for the establishment of a stable and unquestioned jurisprudence, and to diminish the number of judges—the only methods which have not yet been tried until now as ways of shortening law suits—it remains for us, following the instructions which it has pleased His Majesty to give us, to expound our views on the means which could be used in an attempt to attain these two great goals.

It seems that His Majesty's first step must be to select subjects who are capable of undertaking work of such profound importance; and he appears to have decided to resolve this by ordering all members of his council to send him their opinions, so that he might decide in the fullest knowledge the number of men he wished to employ for this grand design.

At the same time . . . he should choose eight *maîtres des requêtes*[1] who are men of both ability and honour, and send them to serve at this moment in all the *parlements* of the realm, bearing instructions to the first president, the royal advocates and one or two of the most skilful men of goodwill that they should assemble twice weekly at the house of the first president, to examine all the abuses which have slipped into the workings of the courts and suggest remedies for them, sending their views without delay to His Majesty's council.

It will be necessary to draw up a full set of instructions for these said *maîtres des requêtes*.

Having chosen the people who are to compose the special council

[1] The *maîtres des requêtes* were one stratum of judges in the sovereign courts, and tended to be more amenable than others to the king's wishes. It was from their ranks that the intendants were almost invariably selected.

which His Majesty is creating for the reform of justice, it is important that a regular day should be chosen for its meetings, either weekly or fortnightly, and that the topics for investigation be divided up among the members, as follows:

The scrutiny of every ordinance, in order to decide on the changes which should be proposed.

For this task, which is the most crucial and extensive of all, it will be necessary to choose four or six of the ablest councillors of state, who should take with them four or six of the most skilful advocates from the *parlement*, thus forming themselves into a special commission which will meet at the house of the senior councillor of state.

Justice will have to be divided up into civil law, criminal law and police.

Two councillors and two advocates will investigate each of these fields, discussing in the council of twelve what has been decided by each group of four, and finally reporting their conclusions, clearly tabulated, to the royal council. . . .

The six councillors and the six advocates who have been chosen to reduce all these ordinances into a single corpus shall examine every ordinance, old and new, article by article, distinguishing those which have been enforced from those which have not, weighing carefully those which need change or correction; and they shall note all the variations which are encountered in the jurisprudence of the different courts. . . .

Consider the discipline and regulations of the courts, both internally, between their various chambers, and between one court and another, in order to make them as uniform as possible. . . .

Examine everything connected with criminal justice in the kingdom, as the highest priority, uprooting all chicanery, and taking care to work out infallible plans for protecting the innocent and for punishing criminals promptly. . . .

Having promoted these reforms, perhaps His Majesty will decide to extend this enquiry to cover the whole range of his ordinances, and will instigate a similar examination of those which concern the crown domains, the finances, the rivers and forests, the admiralty, the army, the functions of every office-holder in the kingdom, from the Chancellor and the Constable to the humblest official of the army, justice or whatever else, and at the same time include the jurisdictions of the Grand Council, *chambres des comptes, cours des aides, cour des monnaies, trésoriers de France,* elections, salt depots and the rest, in order to produce a body of laws as complete as that of Justinian for Roman law.

The second point of His Majesty's design concerns the diminution of the excessive number of officers of justice in the realm, on which depends the realisation of the first part of the plan, granted that it is impossible to dispense pure justice if one does not reduce the ranks of those men who corrupt it daily. . . .[1]

(Clément, vol. VI, pp. 5–11)

139. Deliberations of the council for the reform of justice

PARIS, *11 October 1665*

. . . Monsieur Hotman . . . said that criminal jurisdiction had too few laws and regulations, whereas its civil equivalent sinned by an excess in the opposite direction. . . .

PARIS, *25 October 1665*

. . . Monsieur de Verthamont said . . . that it had been established that it was the sovereignty of the King alone which could issue laws in the kingdom, and that the sovereign courts and others were simply to be numbered among his subjects, whose job it was to obey. . . . The verification of edicts was not some kind of confirmation which the ordinances and the wishes of kings had to receive before they could be carried out, but was simply a way of making them known to the people. . . .

Monsieur de Verthamont said . . . that the word 'sovereign' signified not independence, but only superiority. . . .

(Clément, vol. VI, pp. 369–79)

140. The Civil Ordinance, concerning the reform of justice

SAINT-GERMAIN-EN-LAYE, *April 1667*

As justice is the most solid foundation for the survival of a state . . ., and as we have learnt from men of wide experience that the ordinances which were so wisely established by the kings our predecessors, in order to curtail the number and length of law suits, have been changed by time and by the malice of litigants; that they are even differently interpreted in

---

[1] In 1680 Colbert was still giving priority to this as yet unfulfilled plan for reducing the number of officials—see p. 89.

many of our courts, which brings ruin on families through the multiplicity of hearings, the costs of the actions and the variety of judgments; and that it is necessary to attend to these matters and expedite the business of the courts, making them simpler and safer by the avoidance of many delays and useless litigation, and by establishing uniformity of procedure in all our courts . . ., we therefore order and declare that which follows.

Section I—On the observance of ordinances

1. We wish that this present ordinance, together with all the edicts and proclamations which we shall issue in the future, be obeyed and enforced by all our courts . . ., and by all our other subjects, including those who are members of the clergy.

2. Our courts of *parlement* and our other courts shall take care to proceed immediately with the publication and registration of our ordinances, declarations, edicts and other letters, as soon as they shall have received them, without permitting any delay, and meanwhile all other business in the court shall cease. . . .

3. It is not our intention, however, should the course of time, usage or experience reveal that some of the articles of the present ordinance be contrary to the convenience and best interests of the public, or be in need of explanation or moderation, that our courts should not make known to us at all times those points which they deem to be appropriate, but simply that this should not be a pretext for delaying the execution of the ordinance.

4. The ordinances, edicts, declarations and letters patent which are published in our presence, or by our express command, and conveyed by persons to whom we have assigned them, shall be obeyed and enforced from the day on which they are published.

5. With reference to these ordinances, edicts, declarations and letters patent which we send to our courts in order that they may be registered, it is for our courts to present to us anything which they deem to be appropriate within six days of their decision having been made, in the case of those courts which are with us in our place of residence; and within six weeks for those which are further away. After this time has elapsed these ordinances etc. will be deemed to have been published, and will therefore be enforced. . . .

6. We wish that all our ordinances, edicts, declarations and letters patent be obeyed, both in the judgments given by courts of law as elsewhere, without any contravention thereof; neither on the pretext of equity, the public good, the acceleration of justice, nor for those reasons

which our courts have reported to us, may they or any other judge dispense from or modify their provisions, no matter what the circumstances, no matter what the reason.

7. If, in the judgment of a case which is pending in our *parlements* and in our other courts, there arises some doubt or difficulty about the implementation of certain articles within our ordinances, edicts, declarations and letters patent, we forbid them to offer an interpretation, but wish them in such a case to refer the matter to us, in order to learn what is our will. . . .

(Other sections, all concerned with the expedition of justice, and with reducing the cost of legal action, dealt with:

Summonses and subpoenas (II–III); briefing of counsel (IV); acquittal and default (V); dismissal of cases (VI); days of grace for preparing evidence (VII); guarantors (VIII); days of grace and procedure in the courts of *parlement*, Grand Council and *cours des aides*, in cases of first instance and in appeals (XI);[1] regulations for ordering the inspection of documents (XII); court procedure (XIV); procedure when benefices are involved (XV); procedure in commercial courts (XVI); summary proceedings (XVII); restitution (XVIII); sequestration (XIX); admissibility of evidence (XX); inspection of the scenes of crimes (XXI); courts of enquiry (XXII); challenging of witnesses (XXIII) and of judges (XXIV);[2] suing for denial of justice (XXV); the giving (XXVI) and the carrying out (XXVII) of judgments; collection of bail (XXVIII) and fines (XXIX); restitution of the fruits of the land in the form of cash (XXX); legal costs (XXXI); damages (XXXII); seizure and sale of goods (XXXIII); imprisonment for debt (XXXIV); remedies for miscarriages of justice (XXXV).)

(Isambert, vol. XVIII, pp. 103–80)

141. The Criminal Ordinance

SAINT-GERMAIN-EN-LAYE, *August 1670*

The great benefits which our subjects have received from the careful methods we have employed to reform civil justice in our ordinances of

[1] Although this section was designed to reduce delays, it still permitted up to two months grace for the serving of a summons, according to the distance from the seat of the court.

[2] In sections XXII–XXIV, as in certain others, a major concern was to eliminate vagueness; evidence was to be carefully substantiated and recorded, while challenging of witnesses and judges was to be permitted only if specific reasons were given in detail.

April 1667 and August 1669 have prompted us to devote equal attention to a code of criminal law. . . .

(Sections concerning:
The competence of the various kinds of judges (I–II); indictment and notice of trial (III); reports of the whole proceedings to be kept by the judge (IV); reports of doctors and surgeons (V); witnesses and preliminary investigations (VI); use of ecclesiastical letters to compel the faithful to reveal information (VII); the verification of handwriting and signatures in criminal cases (VIII); forgery (IX); issuing of warrants of arrest (X); granting permission to an accused to be absent from the court (XI); provisional damages (XII); prisons, their registrars, gaolers and turnkeys (XIII); interrogation of prisoners (XIV); presenting the accused with the testimonies of, and confrontation by, witnesses (XV); letters of reprieve, remission and pardon (XVI); defaulters (XVII); the deaf and dumb, and those who refuse to reply (XVIII).)

Section XIX—Condemnation to torture and reports thereon
1. If there is a considerable weight of evidence against a man accused of a crime which is punishable by the death penalty, and which seems to be proved, any judge may order him to be put on the rack, in case the evidence turns out to be insufficiently conclusive. . . .
3. When condemned to death, a man may be ordered beforehand to be put on the rack, in order to reveal his accomplices. . . .
7. Condemnations to torture shall be implemented only after they have been confirmed by a decree of our courts. . . .
9. The rack shall be used only in the presence of commissioners, who shall compile a record of the state of the rack and the replies, confessions, denials and changes of answers at each stage of the interrogation. . . .

(Conversion of civil cases into criminal ones (XX); the method of hearing cases involving whole communities of towns and villages, corporate bodies and courts (XXI); bringing of cases against the dead (XXII); judgment and sentence (XXV); appeals (XXVI).)

(Isambert, vol. XVIII, pp. 371–423)

B. Reform of the sovereign courts

The great ordinances were primarily designed to clarify and systematise legal procedure, rather than to introduce important changes into the judicial system. Innovations were best put forward in small stages, when they were less likely to provoke a widespread reaction. Of the royal courts, the *parlements* posed the greatest potential threat because of the leading role they had played during the Fronde. In those turbulent years the *parlement* of Paris had seemed at times to be the leader of sedition throughout the kingdom. The sovereign courts had often put the safeguarding of their own interests before their duty to the crown, although it must be admitted that these challenges to ministerial policies were frequently supported by other influential groups in French society. The courts were the champions of tradition and stability against the unpopular reforms of the central government.

In answer to the demand from Colbert in September 1663[1] that they should scrutinise the sovereign courts in their generality, the intendants sent in portraits of every official within them (*142*). Some of these tribunals were obviously in need of drastic purification,[2] although many undesirables escaped punishment and the quality of the judges and lawyers remained imperfect, if improved, throughout Colbert's ministry. The minister rejected violent methods of reform (*143*), preferring legislation which would provide better officials in the future (*144*) to witch-hunts against existing members of the bureaucracy in the present. Yet, as with the great ordinances themselves, edicts of this kind were not scrupulously observed by the courts and their provisions had to be reiterated again and again in further edicts (*145–6*).

The hardest blow which the crown delivered to the sovereign courts was the abolition of their right to send remonstrances to the king before they registered his edicts, asking him to amend certain of the clauses contained in them. Since the 1667 ordinance[3] registration was to be an automatic process, and remonstrances could only follow afterwards. Six years later it was necessary to reiterate this regulation more forcefully (*147*). It is more than coincidence that many of these novel assaults by the crown on the privileges of social groups and institutions took place in time of war, when opposition was likely to be a little more muted, and it is probable that the ministers did not have high hopes of maintaining their advance when peace returned. Certainly their complaints about the behaviour of the sovereign courts did not cease with the publication of these new strictures (*148–9*), although the judiciary was taking steps to make its opposition less controversial. Like other institutions who were confronted by powerful reassertions of royal authority, the courts decided that it was wiser to avoid the bitter conflicts which arose when they openly defied the king, and to oppose him instead on the lower level of routine judicial administration. It was better to register the edicts and then find reasons for dispensing litigants from their provisions in individual cases.[4] Thus a slow war of attrition was waged against the courts by their royal master, who was careful to clothe the struggle in a cloak of

---

[1] See p. 131.

[2] Especially the *cours des aides*; see pp. 5, 92–3 and 95–7.

[3] Section I, articles 2 and 5—see p. 136.

[4] This same attitude—of delaying the execution of royal orders rather than of objecting to them outright—became characteristic of many social groups and administrative bodies. For example the provincial Estates ceased to dispute so vigorously the amount of the 'free gift' which the king demanded of them, and preferred instead to default on payment of the sum they had agreed. See pp. 40 and 46.

legality. He tried to find justifications for every innovation, and was scrupulous in observing the rules as they stood at any given moment. For example he insisted on maintaining the right of the sovereign courts to remonstrate after they had registered edicts (*150*).

142. Secret notes on the personnel of all the *parlements* and *cours des comptes* of the kingdom, sent by the intendants to Colbert at his request (1663)

Parlement *of Paris*
  Grand chamber: presidents and lay counsellors

Lamoignon—underneath a veneer of great honesty and integrity, he hides a strong ambition, to which end he maintains firm links with all zealots, no matter what party or cabal they may belong to; evincing a wish for the reformation of justice which has not won him the esteem of the gentlemen of the grand chamber. Of indifferent wealth, which has been acquired solely by legitimate means. His friends are Messieurs Feneton, d'Albon and Pelletier; he is tutor to Messieurs de Bouillon, and this tutelage brings him into close association with Monsieur le maréchal de Turenne; possesses the *aides* of Châteaudun, worth 26,000 *livres*.

De Nesmond—becomes deeply interested, works quickly; married the sister of Monsieur the first president, is ruled by her, places great trust in Monsieur the first president, as well as in the *abbé* his son. Monsieur Jamant, deputy attorney general, has considerable credit with and influence over him; has a number of friends within the *parlement*, because of his aptitude in tackling all kinds of matters. Will always take a lot of trouble for small returns. Monsieur his son has acquired the reversion of his office; possesses the *aides* of Courtray. . . .

Potier de Novion—is a man of immense presumption but of poor judgment, selfish and timid when under pressure, quite cunning in the palace of justice, having a cabal made up of his relations and friends. . . .

De Coigneux—a violent man, proud and affecting a love of justice in order to acquire respect, but nevertheless ill thought of by the lawyers because of some maltreatment of counsel; little inclined towards the humanities, he prefers to pursue his own advantage and to be entertained. . . .

Sevin—cunning man, trustworthy when he gives his word, selfish, commanding no respect in court, loves debauchery. . . .

Menardeau-Sampré—very capable, resolute, obstinate, trustworthy, self-seeking and dedicated to serving the court; is ruled by a lady of the rue Saint-Martin, whom he supports, and by Violot, *trésorier de France* at Moulins; his clerk advises him, Monsieur le comte de Nogent and Aimé Jean have power over him. . . .

Parlement *of Metz*
    Presidents[1]

De Bretagne—first president, a man of very fine appearance, who enunciates clearly and does not speak badly in public; but has little insight and commands no respect in the court.

Le Vayer—a man of a somewhat fiery spirit, but insane and strongly motivated by self-interest.

De Maupeou—rather a worldly man, good at his profession because he learnt it at the Châtelet;[2] in addition, he is carried away by his enthusiasm for appeals.

De Loynes—great reciter of nothing, undertaking much but achieving little, nevertheless commanding some respect with the younger members of the court, although more because of his nephew than of himself.

Vignier—no longer serves, and has been declared insane.

Fremin—skilful and of high reputation in his court, motivated to some extent by selfishness. . . .

De Gallichon de Courchans—less than nothing, and presumptuous with it. . . .
                                                    (Depping, vol. II, pp. 33–98)

---

[1] Not all these reports nor their authors were of equal merit. The remarks sent by this intendant were so brief that the King had to send for further information.
[2] This principal court of the Paris municipality had functions which gave it a national role in judicial administration.

143.   Jean-Baptiste Colbert: Means to employ for returning the *parlement* to its natural state; and to deprive it for ever of the maxims on which this court has based its intention to disrupt the state by wishing to play a part in the administration of it

October 1665

It has been proposed to His Majesty that he should extend the 'annual'[1] for four more years, and then should abolish it;

Should insist that all officers be thirty years old;

Should drastically reduce the meetings of courts by rescinding their right to hear appeals;

Should arrange to have struck from the registers all that happened during the time of troubles;

Should issue a declaration, forbidding them ever to take cognisance of matters of state.

It seems to me that all these suggestions are too vigorous, and will not produce the result which His Majesty desires. . . .

Such things can be done only with time and patience, free from all haste. . . .

(Clément, vol. VI, pp. 15–16)

144.   Edict to determine the price of offices in the higher courts

PARIS, *December 1665*

. . . Although we are aware that in the interests of justice and of our subjects we should reduce the large number of our officials . . ., we have nevertheless been pleased to consider the position of the individual families of these office-holders, and taking into account the fact that the greater part of their wealth frequently consists in the yield of the offices in their possession, and preferring on this occasion the well-being of indi-

---

[1] The *annuel* or *paulette* was the yearly payment by which an official assured his descendants of the right to succeed to his office. This privilege was renewed on a national basis, every few years. Although some reformers dreamed of abolishing it, and opening offices to those who merited them, the financial yield of the *annuel* and the social pressures for its retention were too strong.

viduals to that of the public, have granted a extension of the 'annual' for a few years; but despite this, we cannot conceal the considerable harm which is done to our subjects by the excessive levels to which the prices of judicial offices have risen, and, seeing that it is our duty to halt the infinite disorders which have resulted and to facilitate the entry into these posts of men who merit them but who are excluded from them by a price which knows no limits, we have resolved to bring them within their reach by fixing a scale of appropriate charges . . .; also it is essential that in these matters we should conform to the wisdom of ancient ordinances, which have prescribed an age of greater maturity as a qualification for admission to courts which judge without the right of appeal than the less rigorous requirements which are contained in more recent edicts . . .; we therefore wish and order that the prices of the offices named below shall be fixed, regulated and curbed as follows. . . .

(Isambert, vol. XVIII, pp. 66–7)

145. Edict to determine the price of judicial offices, and the age and experience of the officers

SAINT-GERMAIN-EN-LAYE, *August 1669*

. . . As the best laws may be put to bad use, and as all their force depends on the judges who administer them, we have therefore decided that the prime reformation of justice should be concerned with the judges themselves. . . . Accordingly we have thought it wise to issue a solemn edict, to be observed in all the courts of our realm, which prescribes the ages necessary for admission to the various levels of the judicature, as required by the ancient ordinances; also to list the degrees of kinship which render incompatible the holding of offices within the same seat of justice; to fix the price of offices on a proportionate basis, and to stamp out alien titles and privileges which the passage of time has sanctioned at the expense of the principal advantages and rightful prestige of the old and veritable magistrature.

For these reasons etc., we have ordered that the regulation issued by us, concerning the requisite ages for entry into judicial offices, and contained in our edict of December 1665, shall be implemented according to the clauses and conditions expounded hereafter: that no one from this moment shall be appointed or admitted to the office of president in any of our courts which judge without right of appeal, unless he shall have attained the age of forty; to that of *maître des requêtes* . . . unless he be thirty-seven; to that of counsel or public prosecutor unless he be thirty; and to other offices of the courts unless he be twenty-seven. . . . All of these rules must be observed on pain of annulment of the letters of appointment and admission, and the forfeiture of the office; also that relatives of the first, second and third degrees, which is to say father and son, brother, uncle and nephew, together with relatives by marriage to the second degree, which includes father-in-law, son-in-law and brother-in-law, shall not be permitted to hold office conjointly. . . .

It is also our intention that the offices of our said courts shall have an unchanging and stated price, and that an end be made of the abuse which has arisen in the execution of our edict of December 1665 as a result of the stabilisation of these prices; it is our wish and pleasure that the prices of the said offices shall henceforward remain fixed and moderate, in accordance with the rules laid down in our edict of December 1665, and shall not be increased . . . for any reason whatsoever. . . .

(Isambert, vol. XVIII, pp. 325–7)

146. Edict to determine the age and service requirements for judicial offices. . . .

SAINT-GERMAIN-EN-LAYE, *February 1672*

As the most important reform of justice depends particularly on that of the judges who distribute it to our subjects . . .; and as abuses easily gain superiority over the best laws; and although care was taken in ancient ordinances, confirmed by our edicts of December 1665 and July 1669, to prescribe exactly the age, length of service and other qualities necessary for the leading magistrates, nevertheless some have managed to avoid obeying them. It is thus vital to attack this problem, and to use the severity of the penalties as a means of restraining those who, forgetting their duty, wish to indulge in such activities.

For these reasons etc., it is our wish and pleasure that our edicts of the months of December 1665 and July 1669 be implemented according to their terms and provisions. . . .

(Isambert, vol. XIX, pp. 1–2)

147. Letters patent to regulate the registration in the superior courts of edicts, declarations and letters patent concerned with matters affecting state finance and justice, sent out by the King of his own accord

VERSAILLES, *24 February 1673*

As it is vital to our service and to the well-being of our state that our ordinances, edicts, declarations and letters patent concerning affairs of state, issued on our authority and at our wish, be registered at once in our courts, that they may be published and put into effect, we ordered..., in articles 2 and 5 of section I of our edict of April 1667,[1] that our courts which were with us in our place of residence should have a week after registration in which to comment on the contents of ordinances, edicts, declarations and letters patent; and that those courts which were further away should have six weeks, after which they would be deemed to have been registered and published; but as the different interpretations which have been given to these articles could be harmful to our interests and those of our realm, because of the delays in carrying out our orders, we have thought it wise to explain our intentions. . . .

We forbid our courts to permit any opposition to the registration of our letters patent . . ., on pain of suspension from office, no matter from whom the objection should emanate. . . .

We intend that our courts shall register our letters patent as they stand, without making any modification, reservation or addition which could delay or prevent their wholesale implementation; and if our courts, when discussing these said letters, should nevertheless wish to send us their remonstrances about their contents, the register shall record the fact, and the appropriate document shall be drawn up, but only, however, after the decree of registration without alteration has been issued separately . . .; if these remonstrances seem to us to be well founded, and we feel that it is proper to accede to them in whole or in part, we shall send a declaration to this effect to the courts, and this also will be treated in the manner described above . . ., save that no officer can speak against it, and no court can compile any further remonstrances about either our first or our second letters on pain of suspension from office of those responsible. . . .

(Isambert, vol. XIX, pp. 70–2)

[1] See p. 136.

148. Bouchu, intendant in Burgundy, to Colbert

DIJON, *14 July 1669*

You will find attached my report, together with my views on the establishment of a poorhouse in this town, which is most sorely needed but which will never come about unless you give the plan your personal support, because of the opposition of the *parlement* which takes every opportunity to thwart all the good which men wish to do. Its members are so intoxicated with their sovereign powers that they believe themselves to have the sole right to authorise actions, and that the orders coming from the council are usurpations, although I have tried to disabuse them and with your help and protection have made good progress, until I have now fully re-established the King's authority among those who did not show regard for it. I must assure you, however, that I have not destroyed their desire to restore their former greatness, and they lose no opportunity to say loudly and often that they look forward to better times. . . . Considering the minimal respect and deference they show towards His Majesty's orders, one wonders what they will actually do when these eagerly awaited better times arrive. . . .

(Depping, vol. II, pp. 29–30)

149. The chancellor Le Tellier to the first president of the *parlement* of Toulouse

SAINT-GERMAIN-EN-LAYE, *28 December 1679*

We are continually receiving complaints at the royal council that the *parlement* of Toulouse has delivered judgments which interpret, correct or rescind others, despite the section on extraordinary procedures against miscarriage of justice in the edict of 1667 and a special declaration on this point of 21 April 1671,[1] both of which were registered by the said *parlement*. . . . These frequent irregularities give me all the more pain because one is obliged not only to annul these judgments, although some contain good points, and thus to burden the litigants with further expense, but also to censure those who presided over the meetings when these verdicts were issued and those counsellors on whose information they were

[1] Both these ordinances had prescribed that the only way to appeal against a judgment of the sovereign courts was to obtain letters of *requête civile*, on the grounds that there had been a miscarriage of justice. Otherwise, there was no way of modifying a judgment.

based. I urge you, as strongly as I can, to use all the authority at your disposal to prevent these improper practices. . . .

(Depping, vol. II, p. 224)

150. The chancellor Le Tellier to Marin, first president of the *parlement* of Paris

VERSAILLES, *16 June 1682*

In addition to my letter of today, I am sending you this to inform you that you should not prevent the *parlement* from debating with a view to selecting delegates who are to draw up remonstrances. . . . You are aware that the ordinance permits courts to produce remonstrances only after the registration of letters patent, and it is very right to maintain their freedom to exercise this privilege. . . .

(Depping, vol. II, pp. 240–1)

C. Continuing abuses in the sovereign courts

Confronted with the Civil and Criminal Ordinances, and the restrictions on their right of remonstrance, the sovereign courts decided to avoid direct clashes with the power of the crown and oppose it instead at the local level. It was better to fail in implementing an edict than to refuse registration at the outset. The courts dared not mount against the personal rule of Louis XIV the vigorous opposition which they had shown to Mazarin. Then they had been able to claim that the king was a victim of evil counsel. Now the king made it clear that he was directly responsible for his policies. Similarly the crown wished to avoid a total rift with the judiciary because, although they might disagree at times, each needed to co-operate with the other—the former because it was the only way to maintain any effective justice in the kingdom, the latter because the support of the monarch was essential if the legal profession were to survive as a profitable way of life.

It was thus in their daily routine as courts of justice that the *parlements* and other sovereign tribunals began to concentrate their opposition to the central government, although this misuse of authority was nothing new in itself. The ministers attempted to prevent these abuses, but they were only partially successful. The *parlements* exceeded the limits of their jurisdiction by interfering with the workings of other courts and officials (*151*);[1] authorised actions which were outside their competence (*152*); tried to impose taxes without having the right to do so (*153*); wasted time on endless questions of precedence and rank, and sometimes simply found excuses for delaying all business. It was far from uncommon for the best interests of justice to be sacrificed to the jealousies which preoccupied

[1] See also pp. 92–3 and 95–7, about the irregular proceedings of the *cours des aides*, and about their relations with the intendants.

147

and divided the various levels of judges, magistrates and lawyers (*154*), giving the whole profession a bad public image. It is not surprising that this selfish behaviour, together with the heavy expenses and lengthy processes of litigation, prompted the people to rebel from time to time (*155*), or even to set up their own illegal courts as a desperate alternative (*156*). Cases could drag on for many years, especially when a court official was one of the parties in the dispute; if this kind of situation came to light, the royal ministers could intervene in the cause of justice (*156*), but many such instances obviously escaped their notice. In moments of really serious provincial disobedience, it was possible to use extraordinary weapons which it would have been too disruptive to employ regularly— the exile to another region of individual members or even of whole courts.[1]

151. The chancellor Le Tellier to the *parlement* of Grenoble

SAINT-GERMAIN-EN-LAYE, *9 September 1679*

The King has learnt that the *parlement* of Dauphiné has had a number of skirmishes with the provost general of the province or his lieutenants,[2] by interfering in the jurisdiction which has been assigned to them by edicts and ordinances. . . . His Majesty has ordered me to write you this letter on his behalf, telling you that not only is it incumbent upon you neither to receive appeals and complaints which are brought to you against the decisions of the provost, nor to forbid them to continue with an action and transfer it to your court, but also that it is not for you to judge the limits of their competence, whether it be to accord or to deprive them of the cognisance of a case. . . .

(Depping, vol. II, p. 217)

152. The chancellor Le Tellier to Pellot, first president of the *parlement* of Rouen

FONTAINEBLEAU, *4 October 1678*

Two books have appeared in Paris, which are printed in Rouen with an

---

[1] See pp. 5, 51–2, 56 and 252–3, for examples of these tactics.

[2] The *prévôts généraux* or *prévôts des maréchaux* were primarily military judges, who also dealt with matters such as highway robbery and vagabondage. They must not be confused with the prévôt or provost, who was the lowest of the three levels of royal local justices—see p. 65, note 1.

imprimatur granted by the *parlement* of that city.[1] . . . The King has been surprised to learn that your court has granted such permission. . . . I am sending you these lines to point out to you that it is not for the *parlement* to take action of this kind, and that it must abstain from doing so in future. In addition I feel myself obliged to tell you that we often see judgments from the said *parlement* which contravene the rules of justice; I am utterly convinced that you have no part in them, but I must nevertheless bring the matter to your notice because there is no one who is more concerned than you with the reputation of your court; I have no doubt that you will make every effort to prevent it from declining further.

(Depping, vol. II, p. 210)

153. Colbert to Pellot

SAINT-GERMAIN-EN-LAYE, *18 May 1679*

I have reported to the King about the draft decree which you have sent me, and which is to be issued by the *parlement*. As His Majesty noticed that this decree would lead to the imposition of a tax, whether on property or on individuals, he has instructed me to tell you that the situation is not sufficiently serious for recourse to such an unusual expedient and one so infrequently used by *parlements*; and that, although this course was adopted in 1661, it was not to be regarded as establishing a right belonging to your court, which has never had the power to authorise any general levy on the people, no matter what the reason.[2] Accordingly, His Majesty does not wish the decree to be published in this form.

(Depping, vol. II, p. 193)

154. The *chambre des comptes* of Dijon to Colbert

DIJON, *8 February 1665*

The public prosecutor in the *chambre des comptes* of Burgundy and Bresse had become aware that Bernardin Monot, receiver of the taxes in the election of Bourg, had abandoned his place of residence, taking with him the revenues which he had received and which were not accounted for during the years 1656–61, and on the strength of this the court ordered

[1] Censorship was uniquely the prerogative of censors appointed by and directly responsible to the chancellor.

[2] See p. 86, where the king prohibited all such increases in taxation.

his arrest. . . . A number of individuals joined the said Monot in pursuing a course of violence and revolt against the implementation of this order, so that the sergeant-at-arms who was to serve the warrant was in danger of being assassinated by these accomplices who wished Monot to escape; when the court was informed of this, it issued warrants for their arrest, and the public prosecutor wanted those carried out which referred to Monot and to La Palue, his partner in the crime of rebellion; however the *parlement* of Dijon, in a manner which is a great affront to the authority of these ordinances, has accepted the appeal which was lodged by Monsieur La Palue, and has forbidden the execution of the warrant of arrest issued by our court; as this decision is directly opposed to the interests of His Majesty and to the jurisdiction of our court, we have felt obliged to send as our representative Monsieur Troai, master of accounts, our colleague, to convey our complaints to His Majesty. . . .

(Depping, vol. II, pp. 145–6)

155. L'Amirault, president of the *cour des aides* of Bordeaux, to Colbert

BORDEAUX, *27 January 1665*

. . . Last Saturday there appeared before our palace of justice a crowd of more than three hundred people, whose extraordinary insolence obliged the litigants, prosecutors, counsels and clerks to withdraw into the building, to escape stones and snowballs. Not content with achieving this, they threw a large number at the windows of the palace and made such a tumultuous noise that I, as president, was forced to adjourn the court, to the disgust of the lawyers. Wishing to remedy this situation, we decided to send for the city consuls who, by their very presence, would cause the assembled crowd to disperse; but we were most surprised to learn, when our clerk of the court returned, that they had refused to come.[1] This has prompted the court to instruct me to seek justice from you on its behalf, and to beg you to represent to His Majesty the importance of making the consuls obey our orders, and come to our palace to receive them on matters affecting the King and the people. . . .

(Depping, vol. II, pp. 144–5)

[1] For another example of hostility between the consuls and the forces of law, see p. 67.

156. Colbert to Harlay, attorney general at the *parlement* of Paris

SAINT-GERMAIN-EN-LAYE, *16 March 1671*

The King has been advised that there are being held in Paris assemblies of individuals known as 'courts of mighty works' which, although animated by zeal and by good intentions, are nevertheless contrary to the laws of the kingdom and could be used as a pretext for introducing, on various occasions which might arise, ideas which would not conform to the views of those who compose these assemblies at the moment; His Majesty has instructed me to tell you of this and at the same time to ask that you make careful enquiries as to whether these assemblies really exist, in which case you should inform the men who compose them that His Majesty wishes them to hold no meetings whatever without his express authority and permission.

(Clément, vol. VI, pp. 32–3)

22 March 1676

His Majesty has instructed me to tell you that he wishes you to take pains to arrange for a trial of the case which Guillaume Lambert, priest, and Gilles and Jean Lambert, inhabitants of Vire, generality of Caen, brought to the *parlement* of Paris sixteen years ago, and to ensure that Monsieur Fournet, one of your deputies, who has had all the evidence for three years, now announces his findings.

(Clément, vol. VI, p. 37, note 2)

SAINT-GERMAIN-EN-LAYE, *12 December 1671*

The abbot and community of Saint-Antoine-de-Viennois in Dauphiné have presented a petition to the King, in which they complain that they have had a law suit outstanding against Monsieur de Chevrières, president of the *parlement* of Grenoble, which is pending in one of the courts of first instance; and, according to Monsieur Fraguier, a counsellor, they have not been able to obtain a verdict during the twenty-three years in which they have pursued their cause, it having always been prevented by the prestige of Monsieur de Chevrières.

On which matter His Majesty has instructed me to inform you that he wishes you to employ every means, together with your habitual diligence, to bring the case to a conclusion as quickly as possible, and to advise me when this has been done, if you please, in order that I may tell His Majesty.

(Clément, vol. VI, pp. 36–7)

D. Methods of punishment: Excessive and insufficient penalties

The malaise which afflicted French justice could not entirely be blamed on the shortcomings of the legal profession. The law itself was inadequately codified, the civil law suffering from an excess, the criminal from a dearth, of regulations.[1] The great ordinances[2] went part of the way towards remedying this deficiency, but the problem remained. In particular, penalties for crimes continued to be severe, crude and callously carried out, except when an official was involved (*157*), and torture was still habitually used, even if the 1670 ordinance had standardised the ways in which it might be administered.[3] The king could always intervene, through the right of remission which was uniquely his, and quash or commute some of the cruellest sentences, provided that the information reached him in time (*158*).[4] Although the crown insisted on the death penalty when it was specifically prescribed by ordinance (*157*), on the whole it was the local courts who favoured the wider use of capital punishment whereas the royal ministers believed that convicted criminals were of more use in the galleys (*159*). Legislation about galley-slaves suggests that the victims regarded their life on board these ships as slightly preferable to death (*160*), though the disadvantages of either fate must often have seemed little different from perpetual imprisonment or from life in the countryside during a year of bad harvest. To the poor, conditions were always hard. The central government had little opportunity or inclination to show concern for these wretches, although it did insist on a more enlightened approach to matters of superstition, such as witchcraft (*158*).

Some men never reached the stage of being punished. They might be held without trial, unless some higher authority came to hear of their plight (*161*), while others went unpunished—either because their high rank dissuaded the courts from carrying out the sentence or because the local administration could not afford the expense of doing so (*162–3*). Insufficient funds undermined the efforts of those who sought to mete out better justice, just as they prevented the improvement of the financial system.

[1] See p. 135.
[2] Pp. 131–2 and 135–8.
[3] See p. 138.
[4] Equally he could order the imprisonment of someone simply by issuing *lettres de cachet* and without having to prove a case against him.

157. Robert, public prosecutor at the Châtelet, to Colbert

PARIS, *16 September 1677*

This morning we tried the case of Monsieur de Maupeou, (counsellor) at the Châtelet, and although the charge seemed very clearly proven, and although he was declared guilty of making and circulating money, he was only condemned to the galleys for life, and this judgment was delivered by four officers of the Châtelet, two of whom were not even in the criminal courts. Attempts were made to convey to the judges that the ordinance was precise on this point,[1] and the importance of making an example to impress the public; mention was even made of the specific instructions we had received from the King about the hearing of this case, and that there was to be no dispensation from the rigorous penalties prescribed in the ordinance. . . . It is with displeasure, Monseigneur, that I take the liberty of telling you something which brings no credit to the court of which I am an officer, all the more so because this error is irremediable; but perhaps, Monseigneur, you will decide that it would be not without benefit if you were to have a word, on behalf of the King, with the chief officials of the Châtelet, in order that they may in future follow the rules of justice more exactly.

(Depping, vol. II, p. 207)

158. Pellot, first president of the *parlement* of Rouen, to Colbert

ROUEN, *19 July 1670*

The order which I have received from His Majesty, reprieving the four people condemned to death by the *parlement* for witchcraft, has arrived in the nick of time; for we sent a courier to Carentan, where they had been taken for execution, and he reached that town on the very day when the sentence was to be carried out. The order also suspended judgment on more than twenty others who were confined in our prisons for the same reason.

Thus, His Majesty will have all the time he needs for drawing up regulations about this kind of sentence, about which there is much corrup-

[1] The crime of counterfeiting was to be punished by death, and it had also been decreed that no pardon could be issued to those so convicted.

tion, because the judges impose these penalties either through ignorance, prejudice, or to make themselves feared and respected.

(Depping, vol. II, pp. 184–5)

159. The chancellor Le Tellier to Maisons, president at the *parlement* of Paris

VERSAILLES, *21 November 1682*

Having reported to the King the substance of the decision of the vacation court of the *parlement* which you have given me, in which His Majesty is beseeched to issue a declaration establishing the death penalty for bigamists, His Majesty has instructed me to tell you that, if he had to promulgate a law on the subject, he would consider perpetual confinement in the galleys to be more appropriate, estimating that this would bring more benefit to his service than the other would give satisfaction to the public.

(Depping, vol. II, p. 241)

160. Declaration about galley-slaves who mutilate themselves

FONTAINEBLEAU, *4 September 1677*

... We have been informed that a number of criminals, who have been condemned to serve in our galleys as slaves, have been carried by their madness to such extremes that they have mutilated their own limbs to avoid being chained up, thereby putting themselves into a state where they cannot be subjected to the penalties suited to their crimes; and this is of greater significance because, as long as this abuse is tolerated, it provides an easy method of escaping from the prescriptions of our laws and means that crimes which are not subject to the death penalty cannot be punished; considering moreover that these excesses of madness offend equally against human and divine law, we have thought it necessary and just to announce severe penalties for those men who fall into such blind error.

For these reasons ... we therefore order and wish that criminals who have been condemned to serve in our galleys as slaves, and who, after they have been sentenced, mutilate themselves or have themselves mutilated, shall be put to death as reparation for their crimes.

(Clément, vol. VI, p. 406)

161. The marquis de Louvois to Charles Colbert, intendant in Alsace

18 February 1669

... His Majesty was very surprised to learn that a man has been kept in prison for three years, without having been brought to trial. And at the same time he commands me to tell you that he wishes you to send him the reason for this gentleman's confinement, so that, if he be guilty, he can be tried, and if not, can be given his freedom.

(Depping, vol. II, p. 182)

162. Pontac, public prosecutor at the *parlement* of Bordeaux, to Colbert

BORDEAUX, *8 February 1664*

I feel obliged to inform you that in those places which belong to the royal domain, it is impossible to compel the receivers and the tax-farmers to furnish the sums needed to finance the punishment of criminals, and to hear their appeals. They say that they have no funds, so that a number of major crimes remain unpunished, which is surely contrary to His Majesty's intentions . . .; I hope that it may please you to apply the appropriate remedy for this evil, which requires an authority no less powerful and benevolent than yours. That is why we have condemned no one to the galleys, and that is why there are at present only five men in prison, and two at Sarlat. . . .

(Depping, vol. II, p. 133)

163. Colbert to Tubeuf, intendant at Tours

SAINT-GERMAIN-EN-LAYE, *13 October 1679*

I am sending you a letter from the King's prosecutor in the *maréchaussée*[1] of Laval, from which you will see that the executioner in this place has refused to execute a man who has been condemned to death by the military court, unless he is paid first. . . .

(Clément, vol. VI, p. 59)

---

[1] The area of jurisdiction of a *prévôt général*—see p. 148, note 2.

E. The nobility and the perversion of justice, the Grand Assize of Auvergne, laws against duelling

At all levels of society, the reform of justice encountered the same obstacles which had curtailed the overhaul of the fiscal system. Thus, while financial and judicial officials alike ignored the rules governing their duties which had been issued by a king to whom they were allegedly loyal, the local nobility flouted the law and disrupted the work of the courts in the same way as they hampered the tax-collectors[1] (*164*). The most dramatic way of dealing with such lawlessness would be to send out a special tribunal of great prestige and power—the *Grand-Jours* or Grand Assize. To be really effective, these courts would need large supporting staffs, and it was therefore possible to create only a few and for a limited time. The plan was to assign them to the areas of greatest corruption, in the hope that their reputation for severity and ruthlessness would spread throughout neighbouring lands and bring a reduction in crime. Although the king threatened to institute them in a number of provinces (*165*), it proved impossible to establish Grand Assizes outside the jurisdiction of the *parlement* of Paris because the provincial *parlements* were successfully uncooperative. Fortunately for the central government, the most disorderly province lay within the Paris jurisdiction, and it was thus in Auvergne that the *Grands-Jours* were to acquire their terrifying reputation (*166–8*). Even so lawlessness and revenge were not slow to return after the court had departed (*169*). The idea of such a tribunal was not novel. A number of them had sat during the sixteenth century, and Richelieu had planned one in 1625. Colbert had always been in favour of these sudden assaults on corruption, as seen in his Chamber of Justice which sent waves of fear through the financial officials at the beginning of the personal rule.[2]

The royal attack on duelling had an equally long history, although the edicts of Henri IV, Louis XIII and Mazarin against this crime were conspicuous by their failure. The controversy about duels epitomised the central conflict of the *ancien régime*—the duty to obey the king versus the right to uphold the privileges of one's social group or institution. At the peak of the social hierarchy, the noble cherished his right to wear the sword and to fight for his honour. The king, for his part, insisted that he was the fount of justice, and that his courts alone could decide cases. To decide a dispute by the sword was, *ipso facto*, to deny the universal nature of royal justice. Yet the sheer prestige and the usefulness of the aristocracy restrained the ministers from taking drastic action against duellists, even though they did pursue, often without success, those noble combatants whose grievances seemed particularly insubstantial. Not until after the end of the Dutch War was there a sufficient breathing-space, and the edict was duly published, this time putting the emphasis on alternative means of arbitration (*170*). The crown appealed to the bishops and other men of influence for

[1] See pp. 112–17. See also pp. 76 and 78–9 for the problem posed by private noble jurisdictions within towns, and p. 65 for a bishop who tried to thwart the local court.

[2] See pp. 92–4.

help in enforcing it, but this traditional method of deciding questions of honour could not be eradicated. It was yet another of the theatrical gestures made by the monarch, as a reminder to the privileged that their independence would be undermined whenever the opportunities presented themselves.[1]

As reforming ordinances failed to work, and as conflicting provincial procedures prevented the formulation of national codes of fiscal,[2] judicial and commercial[3] practice, Colbert at least determined to produce a more highly trained and professional judiciary for future generations by reviving the academic study of the law at the university of Paris. Even though he would not see the fruits of this plan, he could hope that his schemes for uniting France would thus be realised one day. Concentrating meanwhile on separating conflicting jurisdictions and pruning superfluous litigation, Colbert appointed a number of special commissioners who were to roam the country, seeking out areas of legal practice which were ripe for reform. Yet many of their suggestions came to nothing because their work was carried out in the second decade of his ministry, and was therefore doomed to be superseded by that other matter which came to dominate legislation and the attention of the king—the persecution of the Huguenots.

164. Pomereu, intendant at Riom and Moulins, to Colbert

AURILLAC, *2 October 1663*

I have noticed that for some time Monsieur le duc de Bouillon, governor of this province, has strongly taken up the cause of Monsieur de Massiat d'Espinchal whom everyone knows to be blackened by crime. All the nobles of the province are proclaiming that he will intercede with the King on his behalf to obtain a pardon, and I myself know that the agents of my said Lord de Bouillon have, for about the last six weeks, accompanied the said Espinchal almost as far as his estates at Massiat, in order to verify certain facts which he has put forward in his own defence. During this time he rode at the head of forty horsemen, and I was scandalised by such bragging; but what shocked me even more was that there arrived, a fortnight ago, an officer of the court of the royal household,[1]

[1] When the nobility became so corrupt that the king could no longer ignore their behaviour, as in Brittany, the crown was prepared to risk a revolt (see p. 238), but it was more usual for the royal ministers to avoid open confrontations with these upper levels of society.

[2] See pp. 123–5.

[3] See pp. 195–205 and 210–17.

[4] Although the *prévôte de l'hôtel* was really concerned with judicial cases at and around the court, its officers did undertake tasks in the provinces in cooperation with the intendants.

with five or six guards, who showed me a decree from the council, ordering the seizure and removal of all the revenues of the said Espinchal from
his entire lands . . .; at the same time Monsieur de Bouillon wrote to the
inhabitants of Massiat, ordering them to guard the revenues of the said
lord, that he would hold them responsible for doing so, and that when he
arrived they should give him an account of them. . . . You may judge for
yourself the bad effect this action has produced. . . .

(Depping, vol. II, pp. 18–19)

165. Colbert to Fieubet, first president of the *parlement* of Toulouse

18 July 1662

As the King has not yet taken the decision to send the Grand Assize into
the Comminges, the county of Foix and other places within the jurisdiction of the *parlement* of Toulouse, I cannot give a precise reply to the last
letter which you have done me the honour of writing to me.

I can only say to you that as it can produce nothing but a great many
benefits, both in re-establishing justice and in bringing relief to the
people who are oppressed by the violence of the nobility, His Majesty
will not take long in giving his orders about the proposals which you
have submitted. As for the moment that one should choose, it seems
to me that there is none more appropriate than the vacation, because
the ordinary courts will not then be interrupted. . . .

(Clément, vol. VI, p. 1)

166. The president de Novion to Colbert

24 November (1665)

. . . You have done me the honour, Monsieur, in your last letter, of
listing for me the three principal functions of the Grand Assize: the
chastisement of culprits in general, the punishment of judges for
maladministration of justice, and finally the injection of new vigour
into good officers and the re-establishment of the authority of law and
the courts.

As for the first, it occupies our attention daily, and if we are not
successful, it is undoubtedly this praiseworthy devotion which the
King continually shows towards the running of his state, and the
singular wisdom with which His Majesty governs, making him feared
and respected, which have caused criminals to flee from the lands which

owe him allegiance, and have forced them to escape his justice and seek safety elsewhere.

To achieve the second goal on your list, we are holding many judicial officials in our prisons; their cases are under investigation and I shall neglect nothing in fulfilling a task which I know to be of the utmost urgency. . . .

(Depping, vol. II, pp. 165–7)

167. Fortia, intendant at Riom, to Colbert

25 September 1665

. . . Monsieur the president de Novion arrived on the 23rd of this month, and Messieurs the commissioners of the Grand Assize were all here on the 24th. Today they left for Clermont. . . . As they wished to make an example of a man of high birth, they selected from the records of legal proceedings the name of Monsieur le vicomte de La Mothe-Canillac, who had been charged with killing a man some years ago. I had not been able to arrest him, because he had obtained a court order forbidding it. These gentlemen lifted the ban, and he was taken prisoner. . . .

I must tell you, Monsieur, that, with reference to the order given to the provost general to arrest Monsieur de La Mothe-Canillac, that officer has done his duty: for this man is his best friend, and had just dined at his house. . . . I am sure that the imprisonment of Monsieur de Canillac will cause the departure from the province of all those whose conscience is heavy.

(Depping, vol. II, pp. 160–2)

168. Esprit Fléchier, bishop of Nîmes: Memoirs on the Grand Assize of Auvergne in 1665

. . . I noticed that throughout the countryside and in Clermont itself, there was general terror. All the nobles were taking flight, and there was not a single gentleman who had not examined his conscience, gone over in his mind all the unsavoury aspects of his past life, and tried to make reparation for the wrongs he had committed against his subjects in order to anticipate and deflect the complaints which might be made. . . . Those who had been the tyrants of the poor now became their supplicants. . . . The imprisonment of Monsieur La Mothe de Canillac was the chief source of their fear.

Scarcely had we arrived, after 25 September, when Monsieur the president and Monsieur Talon together decided to order the arrest of Monsieur le vicomte de La Mothe de Canillac, highly respected in the province for his distinguished birth, and in the opinion of everybody the most guiltless of all the Canillac. . . .

Different explanations have been put forward of the conduct of these gentlemen, who arrested him so suddenly. Some believe that Monsieur the president wished to show how blindly he promoted the best interests of royal justice, and that he had therefore put aside all other considerations which might have influenced him by first arresting a man who was related to him by marriage; others imagine that he wished to begin by making an example which would shake every other noble, by bringing to trial a man of high birth, and one who seemed the most guiltless of his family. Yet others thought the name of Canillac to be so discredited at the court, that there was no better way to magnify the authority of the Grand Assize in the eyes of the King than to arrest a nobleman of this name, even though he was not one of the most criminal. . . . Everyone agrees that this first captive is a good catch for the judge, but not for justice. . . .

On 23 October, sentence was passed in the case of Monsieur le vicomte de La Mothe-Canillac, and he was executed four hours later . . ., condemned for a crime which could not have been proved, had he not himself admitted it . . ., claiming that he had been defending himself against an enemy who was the aggressor. . . . But witnesses testified that the *vicomte* was accompanied by thirteen or fourteen horsemen, and his opponent by only five. . . .

A singular fact about this trial, and one which could only be encountered in a province as full of crime as this one, is that the prosecutor, the man who had investigated the case, and the witnesses were all greater criminals than the defendant himself. The first had been accused by his own father of killing his brother, of attempted parricide and a hundred other crimes; the second was an acknowledged forger, and had been condemned for betraying the trust of the public; while the rest, for a variety of crimes, had been consigned either to the galleys or to perpetual banishment, and were in fact fugitives. . . .

On 6th November they executed an unfortunate who had committed adultery and incest simultaneously, having violated the honour of a woman who was both his sister-in-law and his daughter-in-law, he and his son having married two sisters. . . .

On the 7th the vicar of Saint-Babel was condemned to death. . . . He was particularly discredited because of his love affairs . . ., and for inspiring in his parishioners a love other than the love of God. . . .

On the 13th, the court heard the case of a woman who had given birth to a child by someone other than her husband, and had killed it. Her father, her husband and her sisters gave evidence against her, and her whole family denounced her as an adultress and a murderess. . . .

One noticed during these trials that the peasants were very outspoken, and that they willingly lodged complaints against the nobles, now that they were not restrained by fear. If one failed to speak to them respectfully or to greet them civilly, they would appeal to the Grand Assize. . . . A lady from the country complained that all her peasants had bought themselves gloves, and thought that they were no longer obliged to work. . . . Thus much do the people hope for from the Grand Assize, and thus too do the nobles fear it . . . !

It would be difficult to describe all the criminal cases which were decided before the end of the Grand Assize. . . . Suffice to say that assassination, murder, kidnapping and oppression were frequent subjects of sentence,[1] and there were so many men convicted that one day about thirty were hanged in effigy. . . . This technique was invented by the courts as a means of defaming those whom they could not punish, and of castigating the crime when they had not captured the perpetrator. . . .

169. Harlay, attorney general at the *parlement* of Paris, to Colbert

26 May 1667

. . . Violence has broken out again with some force in Auvergne, and chiefly around Aurillac. That is why I beg that you may see fit to write to Monsieur de Fortia, telling him to use all his authority to protect the officials of this province and the people who have served as witnesses in law cases from the harassment which they are beginning to suffer.

(Depping, vol. II, pp. 176–7)

170. Edict containing general regulations for the suppression of the duel

SAINT-GERMAIN-EN-LAYE, *August 1679*

As we recognise that one of the greatest gifts which we have received of

[1] Also sorcery and improper conduct by professed religious and priests.

God, for the government and direction of our realm, consists in the resolution he has been pleased to give us to uphold the prohibition of duels and combat between individuals, and severely to punish those who contravene a law which is both just and essential to our aristocracy; we have the firm intention carefully to nurse this precious gift, which gives us hope that during our reign we may achieve the abolition of this crime, after the unsuccessful attempts made by the Kings our predecessors. Therefore we have applied ourselves afresh to examine most closely all the edicts and regulations made against duels, and everything which has occurred in consequence, to which we have deemed it necessary to add various provisions. . . .

3. We declare that all those who are present at, or who come across by chance, places where these affronts to honour are being committed . . . shall afterwards be obliged to inform our cousins the marshals of France. . . . And in order that we may be better informed in future of all the duels and combats which occur in our provinces, we enjoin the governors general and the lieutenants general who are in charge of them to tell the appropriate secretary of state about every such confrontation which has taken place within their jurisdictions. . . . We further order all our subjects to inform us, by whatever means seems best to them, of duels which arise in the provinces, promising to reward them for details and proof of those about which we have not already received word.

10. Although the care which we show for the honour of our nobility can be clearly seen from the preceding articles, and from the meticulous examination made by us of the most suitable means of extinguishing such quarrels in their infancy, laying upon those who have offended the blame and dishonour they have merited; nevertheless, knowing that there will still be men who are sufficiently daring to contravene our wishes which have been so expressly stated, and who claim to have reason for seeking revenge, we wish and order that those who, believing they have been wronged, issue a challenge to someone, shall perpetually forfeit the right to receive satisfaction for the offence which they claim to have suffered, and shall be held prisoner for two years and be condemned to a fine which shall be paid to the poorhouse of the town which lies nearest to their place of residence, this to be not less than half the annual revenue from their property, and moreover that they shall be suspended from all their offices and deprived of the income therefrom during the period of three years. We permit our judges to increase these penalties, according to the rank of those involved and the reasons for the quarrel. . . . If the person challenged, instead of rejecting the challenge and informing our cousins the marshals of France . . ., should come to the place appointed

for the combat . . ., he shall be punished in the same degree as the challenger. . . .

15. Although we hope that our prohibitions and penalties so justly prescribed against duels will henceforward restrain our subjects from falling into this error, nevertheless, if anyone is found to be brazen enough to oppose our wishes, not only by accepting a challenge himself, but in addition by involving seconds, thirds or an even larger number of people in his quarrel and resentment . . ., we wish that those who are found to be guilty of such a criminal and dastardly breach of our present edict, shall be sentenced to death without remission, no matter whether or not anyone was wounded, let alone killed, in these confrontations; that their wealth shall be seized in the manner described above; that they shall be deprived of their nobility and declared commoners, incapable of holding any office in future; that their coats of arms be blackened and publicly destroyed. . . . And as no punishment is severe enough to chastise those who involve themselves so capriciously and criminally in the taking of revenge for an offence which in no way concerned them, when they ought rather to have been seeking to reconcile the parties.. . ., we therefore wish that those who are guilty of the crime of being seconds, thirds or other supporters, shall be punished by the same penalties which we have invoked against the men who employed them. . . .

(Isambert, vol. XIX, pp. 209–13)

F. Paris: The regulation of its daily life and privileges; police and order; the poor-law

The administration of Paris, unlike that of many other large towns and cities, concerned the royal ministers closely. Although the officials who ran the capital were rather more skilful and efficient than their provincial counterparts, the central position of Paris in the life of the state and its tendency to attract seditious elements necessitated a higher standard of control and order.[1] In the municipalities the function of maintaining order was divided up among a number of different kinds of officials, and Colbert determined that in the chief city of the kingdom it must be in the hands of a single senior official, appointed by the crown (*171*). He also confirmed the considerable privileges of the citizens and the city council (*172*), restating in addition all the regulations about the administration of the capital (*173*), so that there might be no room for disputes about the various jurisdictions and responsibilities.

[1] For the problem of private jurisdictions, where criminals might seek sanctuary from the Paris authorities, see pp. 76 and 78–9.

The next group of documents illustrates the kind of supervision which the Paris police had to undertake in the cause of good order (*174–6*), adding further to the list of detailed points with which Colbert dealt personally. The poor were of particular concern here, because the great city was a magnet for the vagabonds, criminals and riff-raff of the whole realm.[1] The attack on such idlers and trouble-makers was mounted both inside the walls of Paris (*177–8*) and throughout the kingdom, but these continual assaults could never solve the problem. As a result, the life of the ordinary Frenchman, in town as in the country, was fraught with insecurity.

171. Edict creating a lieutenant of police for Paris

SAINT-GERMAIN-EN-LAYE, *March 1667*

As our great city of Paris is the capital of our realm and our usual place of residence, which must therefore serve as an example for all the other towns of our kingdom, we have estimated that nothing is more worthy of our efforts than the regulation of justice and the police within it. . . . But as it is essential that the reforms which we have carried out be supported by the judges; and as the functions of the law and of the police are often at variance with each other and are of too great magnitude to be exercised properly by a single officer in Paris, we have resolved to divide them. . . . Therefore we suppress and abolish the office of civil lieutenant of our chief justice of Paris . . ., and we create two posts of lieutenant of our chief justice of Paris, of which one shall be called and styled our counsellor and civil lieutenant, and the other our counsellor and lieutenant for the police, which two charges are to be filled and carried out by two different officers . . .; the lieutenant of police shall be responsible for the security of the city . . ., the carrying of weapons which have been forbidden by ordinance, the cleaning of streets and public places, together with adjacent buildings, the giving of the necessary orders in time of fire or flood; equally for supervision of all the goods needed for the sustenance of the city . . .; for inspecting the covered and open markets and fairs, hostelries, inns, lodging houses, gambling dens, smoking-saloons and places of ill fame; for dealing with illicit gatherings, riots, revolts and disorders . . .; for standardising the weights and scales of all communities in the city and its suburbs, to the exclusion of all other judges; for hearing cases

---

[1] Poor relief in the towns had to be financed out of charitable gifts, municipal taxes and certain legal fines (see pp. 82 and 162), while in the countryside it was usually provided informally by the local communities who succoured their own needy members.

arising from contravention of the ordinances, statutes and regulations
about printing and printers. . . .

(Isambert, vol. XVIII, pp. 100–2)

172. Edict confirming and resuming the privileges of the mayor, consuls and citizens of Paris

PARIS, *March 1669*

As the power of states and the grandeur of sovereigns is to be seen chiefly
in the capital cities which are the hub of their empires . . ., thus the Kings
our predecessors wished to express their affection and their royal munifi-
cence by the privileges and immunities which they took pleasure in heap-
ing upon our great city of Paris . . .; the officers of this city have taken
care to obtain confirmation of them, from time to time, from the Kings
our predecessors and to register the letters by which he accorded it; it is
this which has obliged our much loved and trusted subjects, the mayor
and consuls of the said city, to beg us humbly to grant them confirmation
of the same letters. . . . To which end. . . .

(Isambert, vol. XVIII, p. 210)

173. Edict confirming the privileges, ordinances and regulations about the police of the City Hall of Paris, and rules about the jurisdiction of the mayor and consuls

VERSAILLES, *December 1672*

Because of the singular affection we feel for our loyal subjects, the citizens and inhabitants of our great city of Paris..., we have rewritten all
the ordinances, customs, statutes and regulations of the mayor and consuls of the said city, concerning its government and administration, and
the control of the sale of all goods which arrive by river, and are distributed on the quays, in the squares and in the markets; which seemed
to us to be even more necessary to the said city because the ancient ordinances dated back as far as 1415, had not been revised or reformed and
were in many ways out of date. . . .

165

(Sections concerning:
The maintenance of the river and its banks (I) and the rules for navigation upon it (II), the landing, unloading and sale of merchandise (III), the duties of the various port and river officials (IV), public transport on the river (V), the sale of grain (VI), of wines and cider (VIII), fish (XV), hay (XVI), timber (XVII), coal and charcoal (XXI), and a section on the duties of the city officials (XXXIII).)

(Isambert, vol. XIX, pp. 25–66)

174. Colbert to La Reynie, lieutenant of police in Paris

VERSAILLES, *12 November 1678*
The King, wishing to issue regulations to deal with the continual disputes which break out between the members of the corporations of merchants and artisans of Paris and those artisans who are under the special protection of the judge of the royal household and the Grand Council itself . . ., has ordered me to instruct you to compile, with the help of the King's prosecutors, all the memoirs which you think necessary for the drafting of these regulations. . . .

(Depping, vol. II, p. 211)

175. The marquis de Seignelay[1] to La Reynie

SAINT-GERMAIN-EN-LAYE, *12 February 1676*
As the King has learned that lackeys have begun once again to carry swords at night, His Majesty instructs me to tell you that he wishes you to ensure that the ordinances on this matter are promptly executed, and that it is one of the duties of the police to which you must devote the utmost attention. . . .

(Clément, vol. VI, p. 43)

---

[1] Colbert's son, who was already associated with some areas of his father's administrative responsibilities.

166

176. Ordinance for the policing of theatres[1]

9 January 1674

It is forbidden for all kinds of people, no matter what their birth, condition or profession, to assemble in front of or around places where plays are being presented; to carry firearms, to attempt to force entry, to draw the sword and to commit any act of violence or to excite any tumult, whether it be inside or outside, on pain of their lives and of extraordinary proceedings being taken against them as disrupters of the peace and of public safety.

(Clément, vol. VI, p. 406)

177. Colbert to Harlay, attorney general at the *parlement* of Paris

VERSAILLES, *27 July 1677*

The King has told me to say to you that he hears many complaints about the large number of beggars who are to be found in the streets of Paris, and about the freedom which the directors of the General Poorhouse allow them, not only by failing to make an exact survey of the said beggars, in order to shut them up in the Poorhouse, as they are required to do, but also by setting free those who have already been taken there. . . .

He instructs me to say to you that the sure way to multiply the number of beggars without limit is to let them know that they have some hope of leaving the Poorhouse once they are locked up within it. . . .

(Clément, vol. VI, p. 47)

178. Regulations for the administration of the General Poorhouse of Paris

SAINT-GERMAIN-EN-LAYE, *23 March 1680*

As there were no general poorhouses for shutting up the poor and for punishing able-bodied but idle beggars, at the time when that in our great city of Paris was established in 1656, and as those which have since

---

[1] This was not the first attempt at dealing with the far from infrequent attacks on theatres and their patrons by the lackeys and pages who troubled Parisian social life.

been created in other towns on our orders were not instituted until some years later, the Paris house has received a large number of paupers from other towns and provinces who presented themselves at its gates; but as there are at the moment general poorhouses in almost every considerable town in the kingdom; and as the ordinances of the Kings our predecessors have stated that each town should succour its own poor, and as we have been informed that the penalties contained in our edict of April 1656 against able-bodied but idle beggars have not been sufficiently rigorous to abolish this disorder altogether, and as there is no more effective remedy than to shut them up in the institutions designed for the purpose, in order to punish them by the loss of their liberty, by the kind of food which they are given, and by the essential work which they are compelled to do:

We have therefore thought it reasonable to regulate on the one hand the kinds of people who must be received and looked after charitably inside this Poorhouse, and on the other to create new penalties which will make a rather stronger impact on these vagabonds. . . .

To this end we order that there shall be freely received into this Poorhouse of our great city of Paris all poor children and the aged of either sex, those suffering from epilepsy, fits and other ills of this nature, provided that they were born or have lived for a number of years in the said city of Paris, its suburbs or environs, and are unable to subsist without the aid of the said Poorhouse. . . .

We further order that all able-bodied persons of either sex, and over sixteen years old, who have the necessary strength to gain their own livelihood, and who are found begging in the city, suburbs and environs of Paris, and at Saint-Germain-en-Laye or at Versailles when we reside there, or on the roads leading thereto, shall be confined in separate buildings for each sex, for a fortnight or any other length of time which the directors shall determine, where they shall be given only what is absolutely necessary for their existence, and shall be employed on the harshest work which their bodies will support; if such people are found begging a second time, they shall be confined in the same place for three months; if a third time, for a year, and if a fourth time, we order that they shall be confined for the rest of their lives, never going out, no matter what the pretext, even in case of illness. . . .

To ensure that this present regulation, those which have already been issued and those which will be published in the future, are obeyed to the letter . . ., we shall appoint every year six directors who will visit these poorhouses at least once in each month, and make a report on their findings. . . . (Isambert, vol. XIX, pp. 232–5)

7 COMMERCE AND INDUSTRY

Colbert has been remembered, above all else in his long and varied ministerial life, for his attempts to bring order to the French economy, whose revival he felt to be an essential precondition of a powerful kingdom in an internationally aggressive age. Yet once again the declared aims and policies of the central government consciously exceeded its ability to put them into practice. Although the crown could promulgate impressive codes of industrial and commercial regulations, its attempts to awaken the profit motive in its subjects was less successful.

Economic reform was, of course, intimately linked with many of the topics already discussed above. An excessively large and costly bureaucracy, the petty privileges of local bodies and individuals, the apparently insoluble indebtedness of the towns, the multiplicity of jurisdictions, the delays in legal procedures—all hampered its progress, as did natural disasters like poor harvests and plague, and the man-made catastrophe of war. Yet there was one factor which outweighed these restraints on ministerial planning—the almost total disinclination of the privileged and powerful groups in society to regard commerce and industry as desirable ways of accumulating wealth. This virtually complete absence of 'middle-class' values thwarted all the seventeenth-century royal advisers who sought an economic revival in France. The Frenchman who had made a respectable small fortune in the world of business was not interested in reinvesting it there, preferring instead to buy an office and land in order to approximate a little more closely to the aristocratic ideal which was the ultimate aim of everyone. Also the ministers were concerned primarily to order the economy along lines which would benefit France at the expense of her enemies, and this led them to encourage certain kinds of industries which were central to international trading and conflict but were not keystones of the French internal economy.

The opposition encountered by Colbert was not new in kind. It appears greater simply because his schemes were more grandiose, more far-reaching and therefore more offensive than those of his predecessors. Once again these opponents must not be dismissed as selfish reactionaries, because there were times when the economic policies of the central government seemed to many Frenchmen to bear little relation to the needs of their own province, which was a much more realistic geographical unit to them than the kingdom of France of which royal edicts perpetually spoke. Colbert would certainly have agreed with this to the extent that there were moments when some areas had to sacrifice their own interests for the good of the state. What the ministers could not do was to convince the localities that such sacrifices were worthwhile.

Colbert was not helped in his task by the complete lack of enthusiasm for commerce and industry of Louis XIV himself, unless the goods being manufactured or transported were relevant to war or to the strength of his armies. Although

Louis gave Colbert extensive freedom to implement his economic schemes, he did not use his considerable personal aura to publicise them, and he was always disinclined to favour measures which would have benefited the treasury but would also have involved some restriction on his military ambitions. The king shared the distaste of his aristocracy for finance and economics, even though he fully realised their importance in the running of the kingdom in peace and war.

A. The glorification of commerce and the first plans for the expansion of trade

The antipathy towards trade which was felt by the sword and robe nobility persisted in the face of endless attempts to change their attitude. Although a host of writers throughout the seventeenth century had designated commerce as the chief means by which the prosperity of the kingdom could be revived, the idea of entering into it remained socially unacceptable to large groups of the population. The nobility had long been forbidden to trade on pain of forfeiting their rights as nobles, and many wealthy merchants preferred to purchase respectability by buying an office, thereby acquiring a passport to nobility for their families, than continue in commercial practice. Some aristocrats, it is true, had always speculated in these fields, and some merchants did so after they had taken steps to enhance their social position by joining the bureaucracy, the authorities failing to detect or at least to penalise these infringements of the law. The majority of established or aspiring nobles, however, respected the theoretical incompatibility between nobility and commerce. The governments of the seventeenth century made many attempts to reconcile the two, but their edicts barely changed the existing situation. As early as 1629 the praises of maritime trade had been sung, and in 1669 they were repeated (*179*), but neither edict prompted many nobles to take up the profession which was officially opened to them by these documents. The investigation of false nobles for tax purposes[1] caused a number of them to be wary of indulging in practices which could lead to the possible loss of their considerable fiscal privileges, for all were ready to suspect a government trick behind every apparent reform.[2] Yet the panegyrists of commerce were keenly convinced that theirs was the unique path to national salvation, and painted it in glowing terms.

The most famous writer in this tradition was Jacques Savary, a man on whose work Colbert relied a great deal, and whose book *Le parfait négociant* was a highly detailed manual for the conduct of national and international trading, describing the resources and advantages of commerce in various parts of the world, the organisation of credit and banking, the regulations for gilds and corporations of merchants, the rules for efficient accounting and the conditions of apprenticeships—all illustrated by specific examples. The extracts reproduced here (*180*) contain some of the general principles underlying his work, most of which would have been accepted as self-evidently true by his contemporaries in the field

[1] See pp. 113 and 116–17
[2] See p. 185.

of economic theory. The final document in this first group is concerned with an overall analysis of the commercial situation at the beginning of the personal rule, and the general strategy for improving the state of trade in France (*181*).

179. Edict permitting the nobility to participate in commerce at sea without loss of rank

SAINT-GERMAIN-EN-LAYE, August 1669

. . . Seeing that commerce, and particularly that which goes by sea, is the fertile source from which states draw their wealth, spreading it among their subjects in proportion to their industry and labour; that there is no more lawful and blameless means of acquiring wealth; and also that it has always been held in high regard by the best ordered nations, and is universally welcomed as one of the most honourable occupations in civil life; and considering that, although the laws and ordinances of our kingdom have quite properly forbidden the nobility to participate in retail trading, to practise the mechanical arts and to exploit the property of others, the penalty for contravening the regulations which have been drawn up on these matters has been only that they be deprived of the privileges of nobility, and not suffer the complete extinction of their rank; so too we, together with the kings our predecessors, have inclined most readily towards freeing our subjects from such loss of rank. Seeing also that the custom of Brittany and the privileges of the city of Lyon state that nobility and wholesale commerce are compatible; and that in addition to this, our edicts of May and August 1664, which established the East and West India Companies, state that all persons, no matter what their rank, may join and participate in the companies, without loss of nobility or prejudice to their privileges; yet, as it is essential for the welfare of our subjects and to our own satisfaction that we entirely erase the remnants of this universally held belief in the incompatibility of seaborne trade and nobility, whose privileges it destroys, we have thought it proper to make known our intentions on this matter, and to declare in a law which is to be published and generally enforced throughout the length and breadth of our realm that seaborne commerce shall not cause the loss of noble rank. To which end, wishing to neglect nothing which might more keenly incite our subjects to engage in trade, and make it more flourishing, we have said and declared, by our own special grace, omnipotence and royal authority, and by these presents signed by our hand we do say and declare that it is our wish and pleasure that all gentlemen be permitted, in person or through a third party, to join com-

171

panies for, and take part in, the building of merchant ships and trading in the goods which they carry, without being censored for so doing and without it being claimed that they have forfeited the status of nobility, provided that they on no occasion participate in retail trading. . . .

(Forbonnais,[1] vol. I. pp. 436–7)

180. Jacques Savary: *The Compleat Merchant*[2]

Chapter One: Of the need for, and usefulness of, trade

By the manner in which Divine Providence has dispersed things throughout the world, it is clear that God wished to create unity and love among all men, because He imposed upon them the state of always having need one of another. He did not choose to permit all the necessities of existence to be found in one place, but rather spread out his gifts, in order that men might have to trade together, and that their mutual desire for each other's help would foster friendship among them: it is this endless exchange of the commodities of life which gives birth to Trade, and it is also Trade which adds sweetness to life; because it is by this means that there is to be found everywhere an abundance of all things.

It was not enough that Trade be necessary; it was also essential that it be profitable, in order to compel some men to devote their energies to it; for there are a number of provinces, in which the plentiful supply of most of the goods needed for everyday life would have given rise to laziness, had not the desire for profit and social advancement been a goad which forced them to enter Trade.

One cannot question its usefulness; firstly, with reference to the individuals who practise commerce, because the largest part of the population makes an honest living by this occupation, and every day one sees wholesale and retail merchants acquiring considerable fortunes, and installing their children in the best offices of the *robe*.[3]

The usefulness of Trade extends also to kingdoms and to the princes who rule them; the more Trade there is within a country, the greater its wealth. There have been states which have gained immense wealth in a short time, but when war has disrupted Trade, their provinces have suffered, have sometimes been unable to pay their taxes, and in the end their fields have lain uncultivated.

[1] François Véron de Forbonnais, *Recherches et considerations sur les finances de France depuis l'année 1595 jusqu'à l'année 1721.* 2 vol., Basel, 1758.
[2] The first edition of *Le parfait négociant* appeared in 1675.
[3] That is to say the upper bureaucracy, the *noblesse de robe*.

The kings can also derive great benefit from Trade; because, apart from the dues which are paid to them on goods entering or leaving the kingdom, it is indeed true that all the ready money which is in the hands of the merchants and the bankers is the source from which the tax-farmers and business men draw the immense sums of which the kings sometimes have need for financing great enterprises.

Chapter Forty-two: Concerning wholesale trade and its pre-eminence
All the world remains in agreement that wholesale trade is more honourable and offers greater scope than retail trade; because the latter is influenced by every kind of person, from the greatest to the humblest, and it is enclosed within the walls of towns where those who pursue this calling have their place of residence.

It is not so with wholesale trade; for those who participate in it have to deal only with two kinds of people, namely the manufacturers to whom they give orders (and, if they ever entreat them, it is simply courteously to require them to carry out their instructions), and the retail merchants to whom they sell their crates, bales and even whole consignments of merchandise.

Wholesale trade is practised as much by nobles as by commoners in many kingdoms and states, which is never true of retail trade; because there is something servile about the latter, whereas there is nothing about wholesale commerce which is not honourable and noble. . . .

181. Jean-Baptiste Colbert: Memoir on commerce presented to the first Council of Commerce held by the king, Sunday 3 August 1664[1]

. . . It is fitting first to examine the state to which commerce had been reduced at the time when His Majesty began to take charge of affairs of state.

Trade from within the kingdom to other countries, and from port to port:

The manufacture of cloth . . . and generally speaking all other manufactures were and are still almost entirely in ruins. . . .

[1] The examination of commerce did not begin until 1664 because Colbert had devoted most of his energies since 1661 to the Fouquet affair and the initial overhaul of the finances.

With regard to seaborne trade, whether from one of our ports to another or between our country and foreign lands, it is certain that, even in connection with the former, as there are in all the ports of the kingdom no more than two or three hundred ships belonging to the King's subjects, the Dutch take annually from this country, according to exact calculations which have been made, some 4,000,000 *livres* for undertaking this carrying trade. . . .

The reasons for the poor state of commerce within the kingdom are:

The debts of the towns and communities, which have hindered improvements in communications, on which all the commercial activities of the King's subjects, from province to province and from town to town, are founded;[1]

The chicanery which these debts have produced in the towns, consuming the energies and resources of the inhabitants;

The number of tolls which have been established on road and river routes; the decayed condition of public highways;

The horrifying multiplicity of office-holders;

The excessive taxes levied on all commodities;

The tariffs of the *cinq grosses fermes*[2] which are exorbitant and have been badly drawn up;

The piracy which has been responsible for the loss of innumerable ships;

And, in a single phrase, the want of application on the part of the King and his council, which has led to a similar neglect by all the lesser officials who are responsible for policing, and therefore for the maintenance and augmentation of all manufactures. . . .

Having briefly described the state of commerce within the kingdom and with the outside world, it will not perhaps be thought irrelevant if I say in a few words what are the advantages of commerce.

It is my belief that we shall easily remain in agreement on this principle, which is that it is the abundance of money in a state which makes a difference to its grandeur and its power. . . .

In addition to the advantages produced by the entry into the realm of a greater amount of ready money, it is certain that, by means of the manufacturing industries, a million people who languish in idleness could gain a livelihood;

That a further considerable number could make a living on board ship or in the sea ports;

That an almost unlimited multiplication of the number of ships would

[1] See pp. 68–73.

[2] See p. 190, note 1.

174

in the same way multiply the glory and power of the state.

Those, to my mind, are the ends towards which the King should bend his efforts, his goodness and his love for his peoples.

In order to achieve them, the following methods are suggested:

To make it known to all people, by a decree of the council, issued in His Majesty's presence, together with circular letters, the resolution which His Majesty has taken to pursue these goals;

That all those who have the honour to serve him shall speak of it and shall publish abroad the advantages which the King's subjects shall receive thereby;

That all the merchants who come to the court shall be accorded particular expressions of protection and goodwill;

That they shall be given help with everything which concerns their trading, and that they shall sometimes be heard at His Majesty's council when they come on an important matter;

That they be invited to depute some of their number to be permanently attached to the King's retinue;

That the Grand Marshal of the Household be ordered to reserve for them at all times a fitting lodging in the royal apartments;

That, if they fail to appoint deputies, one man be invested with the authority to correspond with them, to receive all their dispatches and complaints, to act as their representative at court in all things, and to inform them of everything which has been resolved for their greater good and advantage;

To renew all the regulations for the police within the kingdom, which are concerned with the re-establishment of industries;

To examine all the tariffs on goods entering or leaving the realm, to exempt the import of materials which are to be manufactured and the export of goods which have been manufactured, to exempt the manufacturers and to reduce the dues by between 1,200,000 and 1,500,000 *livres* every year;

To spend every year a considerable sum on the re-establishment of industry and the promotion of commerce, in accordance with decisions which are taken in the council;[1]

Idem for navigation, with bonuses for those who buy or build new vessels, or who undertake voyages of great length;

To repair the public highways and to continue removing the tolls levied on river routes;

[1] In 1664, this was to be 1,000,000 *livres*, apart from royal investment in the colonial companies.

To begin all over again the task of paying off the debts of the communities;

To labour unceasingly at making navigable those rivers in the kingdom which are not so;

To study carefully possible communications between the various seas, by way of Guyenne and Burgundy;

Strongly to support the companies of the East and West Indies;

To inspire everyone to enter them;

To have reports delivered in the King's presence about every instance where merchants have invested in them;

To send a general dispatch to all the sovereign law courts of the realm, their first presidents and public prosecutors, telling them of the resolution which the King has made, and ordering them on behalf of His Majesty to take particular care with everything which is relevant to it;

Idem to all the governors of provinces and towns, and to all the mayors and consuls, in order that they too may be informed, and to instruct them to summon the merchants before them and read it aloud to them.

In addition to all this, it is important at each meeting of the council to discuss one field of commercial life in detail; which is to say one of the following:

Trade with the Levant . . .;

Everything affecting the companies of the East and West Indies;

Trade with the North, Archangel, Moscow and the Baltic, and Norway;

The tolls within the realm;

The repaying of the debts of the communities;

The public highways;

The navigation of rivers and seas;

Industries;

The inspection of seaports, and the problems involved.

(Clément, vol. II(i), pp. cclxiii–cclxxii)

B. The encouragement of trading: Incentives preferred to regulations

The principles which formed the foundation of the economic policies evolved by Colbert and his advisers are sufficiently familiar that they are often oversimplified. Colbert was never blinded by theory—he was a practical politician who used his extensive powers in accordance with certain rules which he regarded as guides rather than as masters. It is true that he subscribed in general terms to many 'mercantilist' ideas: a prohibition on the export of precious metals and raw materials, and on the import of manufactured goods; the creation of national

customs boundaries and the abolition of internal customs dues. But on the freedom of trade, his views are a little more complex. The underlying principles,
which were often to be repeated in his letters, were to be the greatest possible
liberty in commerce (*182*), the minimum of pressure on individuals (*183*) and the
encouragement of the use of French resources and shipping in preference to all
others (*184–5*). The minister believed that the volume of world commerce was
unchanging, was indeed fixed in the natural order of things and needed a fleet of
20,000 ships to carry it. Each state should move towards its natural share, 'natural' in relation to its area, population, power and length of coastline. Thus the
existing situation in which the Dutch had 15–16,000 ships and France only 5–600
seemed intolerable both for practical and for quasi-philosophical reasons.

182. Colbert to Herbigny, intendant on a special mission[1]

PARIS, *1 September 1671*[2]

In reply to your letter of 30 August, having read and examined the two
ordinances which you have sent me, I cannot but tell you that, if you continue to draft similar ordinances, you will of necessity compel the King to
remove you from your post, especially so because they cannot be given
approval in any way. For ten whole years His Majesty has worked to establish throughout his realm a complete freedom in trading, and to open
his ports to all nations in order that it may increase; and there is not a
word in these ordinances which does not seek to limit this liberty which is
the very soul of commerce, and without which it cannot survive. The
spirit of your instructions is to extend this freedom, by delivering everyone who sails and brings trade into the ports of this kingdom from all the
annoyances they have to suffer at the hands of the justices. . . .

(Clément, vol. II(ii), p. 632)

183. Colbert to d'Argouges, first president of the *parlement* of Rennes

PARIS, *13 November 1670*

. . . It would be of very great benefit if the merchants of Saint-Malo were
to acquire a taste for commerce with Guinea, which is assuredly the most
considerable and advantageous trade that they could undertake . . .; but

[1] This was a special mission to investigate abuses in naval justice.
[2] Depping dates this letter as 4 September 1671.

177

I know only too well that merchants do not like to be in any way pressed; therefore I am leaving them complete freedom of choice. I simply point out that they should be given what help they require, and should be awakened to these opportunities for their advancement.

(Depping, vol. III, pp. 532–3)

184. Edict reducing entry and exit duties on foodstuffs and merchandise. . . .

. . . Because we had discovered that, for a long time now, foreigners had made themselves masters of all seaborne commerce, including that from one port to another along the coast of our kingdom, and having also learnt that the few vessels our subjects still possessed throughout all our seas were being captured daily, right up to our very shores, and as much in the Atlantic as in the Mediterranean, by the Barbary pirates, we have therefore established a duty of 30 *sous* on every ton of freight in all foreign ships, from which burden we are exempting our subjects in order that, by showing them this favour, we may make them feel obliged to use their own vessels, and to build a sufficient number for carrying trade between French ports; and at the same time we shall put a naval force to sea, composed of both warships and galleys, whose strength will be so great that the Barbary pirates will be obliged to remain in their hiding places. . . .

(Clément, vol. II(ii), pp. 787–9)

185. Colbert to d'Aguesseau, intendant at Bordeaux

SAINT-GERMAIN-EN-LAYE, *12 February 1672*
. . . With reference to the clause contained in the decree issued on behalf of the gild of merchants of Bordeaux, in which the King grants the right of citizenship to those who possess a vessel of their own, I do not believe that anything could be more important than this provision, so long as it is not abused. Thus it is necessary, not to annul it, but simply to avoid its misuse. For example an explanatory decree could be issued, in which it could be stated that all merchants who have a ship of their own, between 200 and 300 tons, should enjoy the privilege of citizenship, but that this

right should be abrogated in a case where they sell the vessel before a date at which they would have kept it at sea for the span of twenty years; thus all seaborne trade would multiply greatly, without any increase in the privilege of citizenship. . . .

It is essential . . . to remedy the corruption which has crept in, as it is certain that one could easily take advantage of the King's good intentions in this matter, by acquiring a vessel and selling it as quickly as possible to someone else. . . .

(Clément, vol. II(ii), pp. 645–6)

C. Colonial companies

Colonial companies were created in many countries of seventeenth-century Europe, some more successfully than others, and attempts had been made to establish them in the France of Henri IV and Louis XIII. The schemes of Sully and Richelieu had all foundered on the inertia of the French people, who preferred the social status of office and the more honourable way of making a living by cultivation of landed estates. Colbert hoped that he might be able to defeat such opposition, and made bold claims for his new East India Company in 1664, quoting the success of similar experiments by other nations and alleging that numerous Frenchmen were enthusiastically waiting to join in this kind of scheme. In the same year he re-established the defunct West India Company, although this second venture was declared to be so sturdy in its growth that by 1674 it was deemed to be no longer necessary and was dissolved. It was in fact its weakness rather than its strength which led to its dissolution, but it seems clear that this company was not regarded as permanent.[1] It was meant to initiate and encourage commerce on a regular basis between the colonies and the motherland, wresting it from the merchants of other states and consigning it into the hands of the French. During the later 1660s, Colbert decided that individuals, provided that they were Frenchmen, could participate in the West Indies trade without joining the Company, and many preferred to do this because the company was considerably in debt and investors feared that they might lose their capital. Thus it soon became a redundant institution.[2] The East India Company, in contrast to this, preserved its monopoly for many more years and was still in existence at the death of Colbert, although it had passed through some periods in which its survival was in doubt.

The history of these companies and the development of the various colonies is not relevant here, where the debate is concerned with the interaction of French society and government. The important question to be raised in this context is

[1] The failure of this company is clearly traced in S. L. Mims, *Colbert's West India policy*, New Haven, 1912.
[2] A number of people had been compelled to invest in it, e.g. as a fine imposed by the Chamber of Justice investigating financial corruption—see pp. 92–4.

179

why Frenchmen of different social groups felt themselves prompted to join or to oppose these new corporate enterprises. Sometimes the king and Colbert applied mental pressure (*186*), gentle persuasion (*187*) or near compulsion (*188*); or they used the services of influential local dignitaries and were prepared to grant further privileges in return for investment in the companies (*189–91*); sometimes, however, an intendant might be too keen to show his Paris masters that he had tried to promote their new creations (*192*). Many parts of the country nevertheless resisted and refused to participate, while others gave less than had been expected, often because of hostile propaganda manufactured by local élite groups (*193*). The office-holders grumbled, but in fact the king had more power to compel them to contribute than he had over the merchants, who frequently required considerable encouragement before they would subscribe (*194*). Even when a man had finally added his name to the list of investors, he knew that there was many a loophole between this paper commitment, which would earn royal approval, and the moment when he would have to part with actual money.

186. Olivier Lefèvre d'Ormesson: Journal[1]

August 1664

. . . I have forgotten to note down that last Thursday,[2] in the afternoon, there was a meeting of the greater council of finance,[3] during the course of which the King sent for the Chancellor, who returned a little later saying that the King had sent for him to inform him that he felt great affection for the trading company of the East Indies, and that he wished all the members of the council to join it; after the praises of this great plan had been sung at some length, Monsieur Berryer took from his portfolio the list of those who had joined, and Monsieur the Chancellor put himself down for 40,000 *livres*, as did Monsieur le maréchal de Villeroy and all the gentlemen of the finances.

Then it was offered to the gentlemen of the council, which took them by surprise: Monsieur de Verthamont signed for 10,000 *livres*. Monsieur des Hameaux refused at first, saying that the treatment which had been meted out to those who had invested money in the state and had been dispossessed did not give one much hope. Monsieur the Chancellor looked blackly at him, and someone whispered in his ear that he should sign; he did so, muttering to himself. Messieurs the *maîtres des requêtes* enrolled after that, for a variety of sums. Monsieur de Bercy signed for 1000 *livres*.

[1] For the edition used, see p. 126, note 1.
[2] 31 July.
[3] This council, the *conseil de la grande direction*, dealt with the most important financial matters, especially those closely connected with the King's interests.

Monsieur Colbert mocked him, saying that he was not showing much concern for his money, and this made him amend it to 3000; the others then did the same. These sums are payable over three years. I was happy that I was not there; for I am convinced that the East India trade will not prosper. . . .

187. Colbert to the presidents and *trésoriers généraux de France* at the finance office of Bourges

PARIS, *20 November 1664*

The King, the Queens, Monseigneur le Dauphin, the princes of the blood and all the persons of quality in the kingdom, and following their example the sovereign courts, together with innumerable members of all kinds of professions, have acquired an interest in the East India Company, in the certain knowledge that they have each gained a hold on the great rewards which will result; His Majesty does not doubt but that you would profit from this wonderful opportunity which is offered you for earning merit in the eyes of God (the principal motive of this most impressive undertaking being the carrying of the light of the Gospel to these distant lands); of the King, who has contributed so strongly by advancing a million golden crowns and is prepared to write off the whole sum in case that should be necessary in these early days...; and of the public, who will come into contact with the goods which will be imported; so that you will be enhancing both the glory of the state and everyday life within it by participating in this company in proportion to your resources. Speaking as an individual, I am so firmly convinced of all the benefits that I cannot refrain from entreating you earnestly to join.

(Clément, vol. II(ii), pp. 428–9)

188. Colbert to Brulart, first president of the *parlement* of Dijon

SAINT-GERMAIN-EN-LAYE, *11 February 1667*

I have not neglected to report to the King about the willingness which you have encountered among the majority of officials in your court to pay the second third of the sum which they have committed to the East India trade. I must inform you that His Majesty showed considerable pleasure at the fruits of your labours, but at the same time he explained that he would distinguish clearly between those who were displaying their zeal for this cause by their strict punctuality, and those who had less scruples about avoiding their obligations; to which he added, and said that this was no idle threat, that he had resolved to exclude them from paying the *annuel*,[1] when it was the moment for them to do so, because they had failed to please him on an occasion such as this, which was so dear to his heart and of so great benefit to the state. . . .

(Clément, vol. II(ii), p. 439)

189. Pontac, first president of the *parlement* of Bordeaux, to Colbert

BORDEAUX, *24 October 1664*

When I learnt that the King had written to this city, to invite our citizens to enter the Indies company, I pointed out to the consuls to whom His Majesty's letter was addressed that they should use all their influence to exhort them to show their enthusiasm for this project. That did not produce the effect which was desirable if His Majesty were to be satisfied. Then, having learnt a few days ago from Monsieur Pellot, the intendant in this province, that the King was far from pleased with our citizens, and that His Majesty interpreted their refusal as a lack of affection for his service, I spoke two days ago to the magistrate of the Commercial Exchange, who is one of the most important residents of the city, and who knows well the strong and the weak, in order to persuade him to influence the merchants to join this association. At which he told me that he had begun this task, and that he would make yet further efforts with all possible speed, but he asked that I give him some time in which to influence their opinions and to make known to them the benefits they would derive from this enterprise. He added that, if His Majesty were to offer the right of citizenship to those who invested 4000 or 5000 *livres* in the company, he would discover a number of inhabitants who would accept these terms, for it did not seem likely that there were many who were rich enough to pay the 10,000 *livres* for the right of citizenship as was

[1] They were thus not permitted to pay the tax which guaranteed the hereditary nature of their offices—see p. 142, note 1.

stated in the orders and the agreement issued by His Majesty on this subject. I do not know whether you will find his proposition reasonable. . . .

(Depping, vol. III, pp. 358–9)

BORDEAUX, *10 November 1664*

. . . I have made known to the consuls and to some of the citizens what great energy they must expend in exhorting men to do their utmost for this cause, and that otherwise the King will examine the privileges of citizenship with such rigour that they will undoubtedly lose the most important part of them; that, if they were once lost, it would be difficult to re-establish them; and to convince them, I showed them what you had sent me on this subject. . . .

(Depping, vol. III, p. 360)

BORDEAUX, *28 November 1664*

. . . I have been told that the officers of the *cour des aides* have signed the roll in the name of their public prosecutor, which is a method of relieving themselves of the burden by circumventing the article which requires them to contribute at least 1000 *livres* each. Their conduct has served as an example for other courts who, I am informed, intend to imitate it, which is in my estimation completely contrary to His Majesty's intentions. I have a strong suspicion that some individuals among our citizens, who have insufficient resources to afford the whole sum of 1000 *livres* per person, have joined forces and invested the entire amount in the name of one of their number; but it seems to me to have much more serious consequences when a court like the *cour des aides* does the same thing. I thought it right to inform you, Monsieur, in order that you may decide on the most appropriate course of action. . . .

(Depping, vol. III, pp. 361–2)

BORDEAUX, *16 February 1665*

Those members of the *parlement* who have invested in the East India Company are very grateful to you for your kindness in telling the King of their zeal. . . . If all those who belong to the *parlement* have not signed, Monsieur, it is because there are some posts vacant, some officers who are out of the province, and some who are from families which do not have the resources. The others who could have signed are very few in number. I shall not, however, cease trying to persuade them to follow the example of their colleagues. . . .

(Depping, vol. III, pp. 363–4)

183

190. The archbishop of Lyon[1] to Colbert

LYON, *28 November 1664*

If I have sent you no report about what is happening here concerning the East India Company, it is not because I have been idle; but I have been waiting until enough people were enrolled for the sum involved to be considerable. I said to you, Monsieur, when I took leave of you, that I hoped it would be between 500,000 and 600,000 *livres*; we have done so well that I can tell you 1,000,000 is assured, on condition that there will be in this city one of the regional chambers of direction, as was promised by the company in Paris to Monsieur our mayor and without which few merchants would be prepared to invest in it. . . .

(Depping, vol. III, pp. 365–6)

191. Fortia, intendant at Riom, to Colbert

CLERMONT, *23 December 1664*

I have extracted from the courts of this province their undertaking to arrange the delivery of one third of the sums which they have invested in the East India Company. . . . The gentlemen of the *cour des aides* of Clermont-Ferrand have sent a reply that, before sending the third, they await your decision on a letter which Monsieur the first president has written to you. . . . They are the only court which still has not given up its share. . . .

(Depping, vol. III, pp. 370–2)

192. Anonymous letter to Colbert

IN AUVERGNE, *16 December 1664*

I do not fear, Monsieur, that I am troubling you with the complaints which have arisen in this province against the violence used by the intendant, because they are as just as they are reasonable . . ., and I am certain

---

[1] The archbishop was also lieutenant general in the Lyonnais, and was acting governor in place of his brother, the duc de Villeroy, whose important place on the new royal council (see p. 6) kept him at court. Both men were on friendly terms with Colbert, sharing his economic aims and priorities—see, for example, pp. 227–8.

that neither the King nor his council intended that in this province he should use all the force and threats which he has employed to gain contributions to the Indies trade, in which it is known that His Majesty wishes there to be complete freedom. Our intendant does not share this view, and therefore, not content with the sums which the courts have given of their own volition, after he had made considerable efforts to persuade them, he has returned to the attack, saying that he has received orders from you to constrain them to pay more. He has employed the same pretext to intimidate the towns...; he has summoned individuals to his house where they, going there in good faith, have been forced to sign a commitment to invest in this trade whatever sum he may wish. . . .

(Depping, vol. III, pp. 372–3)

193. Anonymous letter to Colbert

(*1664*)

You have formed this great society of the Indies, which is the finest, most glorious and most useful plan which has ever been devised in France. However, many grumble and seek to find fault with it; the officials, among others, complain that they are being forced to join; they are putting it about that it is a trap to impose the *taille* on the nobles and others who are exempt from it, and that everyone will be compelled to participate, the church, the nobles and the third estate; that the next step will be to tax them every year, making new demands on them, soon using the pretext that some loss has been sustained or that there is a new enterprise to further which appears useful on the surface; and that finally the King will seize everything when it is least expected, as he has done with other sums. . . .

These pronouncements have dashed everybody's enthusiasm; even those who were convinced that the undertaking was sound and wished to join it dare not show it publicly; the officials are regarding as enemies those men who have done no more than to speak of it in favourable terms, and, as you know, Monseigneur, the officials are held in fear and awe everywhere; they are the men with the greatest prestige, wealth and authority; they give an impetus to everything, and everything depends on them. . . .

(Depping, vol. III, p. 374)

194. Fermanel, wholesale merchant, to Colbert

ROUEN, *23 January 1665*

The sums which the merchants of this town have invested in the Eastern company are not as substantial as you had hoped for. I beg you to accept that there has been no failure to make them realise the benefits to all commerce which they might expect to result from a company of such magnitude, and one enjoying the King's wholehearted protection; but there is such widespread hardship among them because of the many losses they have suffered, that they would have the utmost difficulty in finding large sums to invest in a venture from which they can hope for profits only in three or four years time. . . . Today I am holding another meeting in the town hall, to inform them of your dissatisfaction on learning that some of them had stopped short of enrolling for the sum of 1000 *livres*, and to persuade them to increase their contributions. . . .

(Depping, vol. III, pp. 382–3)

D. Commercial expansion versus municipal privilege

If the merchants of Lyon demanded certain privileges in return for their investment in the colonial companies (*190*), they were at least cooperating with Colbert in one of his cherished schemes for economic expansion. Some privileged commercial centres took a less constructive course; they wished to preserve their rights and immunities without exhibiting any willingness to implement the commercial policies of the central government. Yet, of all the other great French ports—Bordeaux, Brest, Caen, Calais, Dieppe, La Rochelle, Le Havre, Nantes, Paris, Rouen, Saint-Malo—none could rival Marseille for its almost total devotion to its own interests at the expense of those of the state.[1] This was particularly serious because it was the only large seaport on the Mediterranean. Colbert had nothing to say in favour of the Marseillais who, throughout his ministry, seemed to want to prevent commercial expansion lest it undermine their monopoly of trade in the port (*195*). The consuls vigorously defended the privileges of the city (*196*), thus joining the merchants in openly flouting the principles on which the economic policies of Colbert were based (*197*).

195. Colbert to Rouillé, intendant at Aix

SAINT-GERMAIN-EN-LAYE, *13 January 1673*

. . . If the city of Marseille were as it should be, it would be in a fit state to attract almost all the trade with the Levant, and even to draw towards

[1] For further pettiness and chicanery by the ruling élite of Marseille, see pp. 80–1.

itself all merchandise from the Indies, as it formerly did. But as the behaviour of the merchants of this city is so corrupt that there is no police
force, and there is no honour among them, and as they are heavily burdened with the taxes resulting from a million instances of trickery on the
part of the city consuls, they will need an influence as powerful as yours if
they are to be put in a position where they can profit from their favourable situation. . . .

(Clément, vol. II(ii), p. 673)

PARIS, *8 September 1673*

I have received, by the latest post, the letter which you took the trouble
to write to me on 26 August. You should not be surprised that the Marseillais have spoken to you at such length about the Jews who have taken
up residence at Marseille; the reason is that merchants there do not
want commerce to expand, prefering simply that it should all be channelled through their own hands and be carried out according to their
methods. There is nothing more advantageous for the general state of
trade than to increase the number of men who practise it, which means
that what is of great benefit to the kingdom is not in the best interests of
certain individual citizens of Marseille. . . .

You must also make efforts to ferret out the evil ways used by the Marseillais merchants in their trading, which has given them throughout
Europe a reputation for bad faith that defies description. . . .

(Clément, vol. II(ii), pp. 679–80)

SAINT-GERMAIN-EN-LAYE, *28 December 1679*

I must admit that I was surprised to learn, in the memoir which was
enclosed with your letter of 16 December, about the number of ships
belonging to the merchants of Marseille in 1660 and 1670, and the number they have at present, as I find from the memoir that in 1670 they had
eighty-four, and in 1678 they had no more than fifty-six, which would be
indisputable evidence that declaring Marseille a free port[1] had not only
failed to bring them any advantage, but had even been harmful to their
trading; so that it would be better to revoke this declaration rather than
to preserve it.

But as you informed me that you had made use of officials from this
city in arranging the compilation of this memoir, I cannot but persuade

[1] Marseille had been declared a free port in 1669, in order to boost the Levant
trade.

187

myself that they have decided that it would be better for their city if there were to be revealed a great decline in their commerce rather than an increase. Therefore I am convinced that, when you have used other means to calculate the number of these ships, you will undoubtedly find that it is much larger, as it is impossible that the increased size of the city of Marseille, and the considerable volume of shipping which is continually to be seen in the harbour, are compatible with a reduction in trade and the diminution of her own ships.

(Clément, vol. II(ii), pp. 711–12)

196. Arnoul, intendant of the galleys, to Colbert

AIX-EN-PROVENCE, *15 January 1667*

... The citizens of Marseille ... must see the error of their ways, and must devote themselves to becoming efficient traders and reliable merchants if they can, without hunting so keenly for titles of chivalry and nobility which bring ruin upon them no sooner than they have amassed a little wealth. Because they are easy-going and idle, great talkers and spreaders of gossip, they like nothing better than to walk about on the quay with their swords at their side, wearing pistols and a dagger. . . . One thing which feeds their arrogance is the privilege of the citizens entailing that all other subjects of the King are treated in this city as if they were foreigners, namely that an outsider can acquire the rights of citizenship only by marrying a daughter of a Marseillais family. This has frightened the merchants away, or at least does not attract them to live here. . . .

(Depping, vol. I, pp. 778–9)

197. Colbert to Rouillé

SAINT-GERMAIN-EN-LAYE, *3 March 1679*

... I am quite prepared to state that the source of all the corruption which has occurred in the coinages of the kingdom has its origin in Marseille, because the merchants, not wishing to look for means of sending manufactured goods to the Levant, find it easier to send silver in the form of coin, thus buying their goods at far too great a price. As this trade devours large sums, it is certain that this is the place in the kingdom from which there flows into foreign countries a sizable part of the silver which has been collected through the labours of craftsmen and merchants in all the other provinces. . . .

(Clément, vol. II(ii), p. 695)

SAINT-GERMAIN-EN-LAYE, *20 April 1679*

In reply to your letter of 8 April, I must point out that, in everything which I have written to you about trade with the Levant and the shipping of silver which is being carried on, you will never find that I have suggested that this commerce with the Levant can be undertaken without sending any silver, because my feelings are never so extreme; it is simply that it is essential, by introducing various obstacles, to force the merchants to turn their attention towards those manufactures which could be shipped to the Levant, and to carry them in greater quantity, in order to reduce the trafficking in coinage and more especially to reduce the volume of trade carried by the English and the Dutch, who do send their manufactured goods there. . . .

To encourage them more strongly, it may well be necessary from time to time to visit some of the ships, and confiscate a portion of the coin which they are carrying, so that, fearing the consequences of these inspections, the merchants will feel obliged to carry more manufactured goods than they do at present. . . .

(Clément, vol. II(ii), pp. 697–8)

E. Trade and the international situation: Opposition to a 'national' economic policy; protection of shipping

The mild bullionism of Colbert offended the Marseillais merchants because it conflicted with their lazy and selfish approach to trading. In other areas too, such personal motives offer a partial explanation for the opposition to another of the economic policies dear to the minister—the waging of tariff wars, perhaps leading to naval and military encounters, against commercial rivals. Yet there were much deeper and more sincerely held objections behind the refusal to cooperate with this aggressive nationalist trading policy, stemming from the extreme provincialism and the varied nature of France. The best interests of the highly individual provinces and towns did not always coincide with the good of the state as devised by Colbert. Indeed royal policies not infrequently threatened to bring ruin to some areas at the same time as they offered prosperity to others. Therefore certain cities failed to obey the embargo on trade with the Dutch (*198*), and whole provinces asked to be exempted from the restrictive regulations promulgated by both sides in the conflict (*199*). Some regions of France were in fact more intimately linked with the economic activities of other countries than with those of their fellow Frenchmen, especially the provinces which were outside the customs union of the *cinq grosses fermes*.[1] Thus Brittany, whose trading fortunes depended on international commerce, was severely hit by the tariffs which separated her from her Hollander partners, and which therefore became a principal cause of the 1675 revolt in that province.[2] Colbert was himself aware that some tariff legislation could not be universally applied, though his concern seems to have been more with the feelings of friendly foreign powers than with the problems of the distant areas of France (*200*). Also many Huguenots appear to have preferred to trade with their coreligionaries overseas than with their Catholic fellow-countrymen (*201*).

Another bitter controversy centred on the provision of military escorts for merchant ships, both against the enemy and against pirates. Most merchants feared these hazards, but were reluctant to pay a sizable share of the costs involved in providing protection (*202–3*), while others did not want to arrive at a foreign port with a convoy of rival merchants. Nor did the escort vessels always behave in a manner which would mitigate these objections (*204*). Yet, despite these problems, the crown was at least determined that it alone, and not private speculators, should be responsible for the safety of shipping (*205*). A different kind of security would have been afforded by the insurance companies which were beginning to establish themselves, but these enterprises were mostly short-lived because they were run by greedy men who overreached themselves during the disruptive years of the Dutch War (*206*). In the face of these many obstacles created by the short-sightedness and selfishness of those involved in the various processes of trading and credit, the honourable merchant had a hard task in front of him, and Colbert was keen to extend his personal protection to those who suffered by reason of their honesty, giving them his support through temporary periods of unforeseen hardship and indebtedness.

Despite all the attempts of the central government to impose a national economic policy and to prevent unpatriotic contact with the enemy, trade continued with other countries and even with those against whom France had declared war. The tariff of 1664 recognised the existing division of the kingdom into the *cinq grosses fermes* and the provinces outside that union. The 1667 tariff went further, assuming an unreal degree of national unity, and its provisions provoked hostility outside and inside the realm. The Dutch War, that costly exercise in international bravado which was to reverse so many of Colbert's constructive reform plans, forced him to abandon this aggressive stance and to return to the more moderate rules of 1664.[3]

[1] The area of Northern France within which internal customs dues had been abolished—see pp. 200–1 and 204–5.

[2] See p. 238.

[3] The international and colonial effects of this policy are not relevant here, in an examination of the interrelationship of government and French society. These wider implications may be found most conveniently in C. W. Cole, *Colbert and a century of French mercantilism*, 2 vol., New York, 1939 (reprinted 1964), vol. I, pp. 422–50. Colbert always hoped that he might be able to reintroduce the 1667 tariff—see p. 89, above.

198. Colbert to the mayor and consuls of Nantes

PARIS, *14 April 1671*

I have already written to make it known to you that, as the King had been told that the Dutch were carrying raw sugar, which had come from the isles, from Nantes to their own country, in order to refine it and then to transport it into our kingdom and other foreign lands, it was important for you to take rapid and appropriate steps to prevent the continuation of this abuse, which is contrary to the King's intention that all the sugar coming from the French isles in the Americas should be refined in France. However, as you have not at the present shown the least concern about devising a means of satisfying this particular wish of His Majesty, I must inform you that, from today onward, he has instructed me to issue no more letters of authorisation to merchants of your town for trading with the said isles, until they have proposed the necessary means of remedying this abuse.

(Depping, vol. III, pp. 549–50)

199. The duc d'Aumont, governor of the Boulonnais, to Colbert

BOULOGNE, *27 October 1673*

I have not been able to disregard the insistent prayers of the merchants and seamen in this province that I should write to those who are in command at Oostende and Nieuwpoort, saying that, if they wished to leave the fishing-boats free to fish, without harassing them, we would act in the same way towards them in this country. Will you have the goodness to let me know, were the enemy to accept this suggestion, which I do not doubt, whether His Majesty will agree to it. It is of the ultimate importance for the peoples of these coasts that their fishing shall not be disturbed. I am sending you, Monsieur, a copy of a treaty which my father prepared, with the King's permission, in conjunction with the Archduke on this subject. I believe that there would be no difficulty in renewing it in due course, if you judged it to be wise. . . .

(Hamy, p. 104)

200. Colbert to Colbert de Terron, intendant of the navy at Rochefort

SAINT-GERMAIN-EN-LAYE, *30 August 1669*

Yesterday evening I received your letter of 21 August. I know only too well the importance of the discrepancy between the duty which is levied on sugar throughout the *cinq grosses fermes* and that on the river of Bordeaux, and therefore you may be assured that I shall lose no opportunity to make them equal. But care must be taken lest foreigners become obliged to find ways of doing without our wines.

You know that Cromwell has not drawn upon them for between eighteen months and two years, and we are at present negotiating a treaty with England, in which we shall perhaps suggest a partial reduction in the duties which have been imposed during the last few years. . . .

(Clément, vol. II(ii), p. 486)

201. The lieutenant general at Caen to Colbert

CAEN, *11 February 1665*

. . . The majority of the merchants in this town subscribe to the so-called reformed religion; as they have easier access to, and more familiarity with, England and Holland, because of the conformity of their religion, they carry all the trade in cloth and other merchandise which comes from those lands. . . .

(Depping, vol. III, p. 700)

202. Colbert to d'Aguesseau, intendant at Bordeaux

SAINT-GERMAIN-EN-LAYE, *19 February 1672*

As the King ought to declare war on the Dutch in a short time, it is highly important that you quickly arrange a meeting of some of the principal merchants of Bordeaux and that, after you have made known to them His Majesty's intentions in this matter, you should examine with them the precautions which should be taken to safeguard their trade. . . .

There are three courses which might be adopted: the first is to allow freedom of trade, which will be very hazardous and will lead to innumerable losses; or it can be prohibited entirely, which is the expedient agreed on by the Dutch; the third course is to forbid and prevent by every means the departure of ships without an escort, and to set down fixed times for them to leave our coasts in company with these armed vessels.

It is essential that you examine promptly, with the said merchants of

Bordeaux, which of the three methods is the best and that you then advise His Majesty accordingly.

(Clément, vol. II(ii), pp. 646–7)

VERSAILLES, *25 March 1672*

In reply to the letter which you took the trouble to write to me on 12 March, and since the merchants of Bordeaux consider that the course of action most beneficial for commerce, after the declaration of war, will be to make use of escort vessels . . ., it is necessary for you, if you please, to keep in close touch with Monsieur de Terron,[1] in order that you may together adjust the sailings of vessels from Poitou to those from Guyenne. . . .

(Clément, vol. II(ii), pp. 652–3)

203. Colbert to the bishop of Saint-Malo

VERSAILLES, *16 March 1672*

I have reported to the King about the representations you have made to the merchants of Saint-Malo in order to predispose them to provide two vessels with arms which will be used for the maintenance of commerce in the kingdom, and about the offer they made to you of giving 45,000 or 50,000 *livres* towards this expense. On which His Majesty instructs me to tell you of his high hopes that, through your diligence and zeal for his service and for the general good of the province, you will make them understand how important it is, in such an urgent matter, for them to make an effort to contribute towards the cost of these armaments a sum which is proportionate to the value of their trade; and he has no doubt that you will persuade them to raise their offer to 90,000 or 100,000 *livres*. . . .

(Depping, vol. III, p. 599)

VERSAILLES, *9 April 1672*

. . . I did not doubt that, as it involved dealing with the most ignorant merchants and citizens, men who are not accustomed to carry out the promises which they give, our success would be no greater than it has in fact been; but, as His Majesty has ordered the issuing of instructions for closing the ports of Brittany, and at the same time has authorised a de-

[1] Colbert de Terron was intendant of the navy in the Atlantic.

cree confiscating the taxes paid to the municipality, which I am sending by this post to the *sénéchal* of Saint-Malo so that he may publish it, perhaps this news will make them wiser in future, and they will be more ready to show to His Majesty some signs of their obedience. . . .

(Depping, vol. III, pp. 599–600)

VERSAILLES, *29 April 1672*

You will already have seen, by the decree which has been sent granting to the citizens of Saint-Malo the re-establishment of their municipal taxes, and by the orders which have been issued giving them leave for their vessels to depart for the fishing grounds of the New World, that His Majesty has approved the submission they have made to his wishes, by giving 30,000 *livres* to be used for arming the squadron which is designed to guard these said vessels. . . .[1]

(Depping, vol. III, p. 600)

204. Colbert to Colbert de Terron

16 August 1669

. . . The Western company has sent a complaint to the King which is of the utmost importance. They say that those of His Majesty's warships which have been to the French isles in the Americas have carried large cargoes of merchandise, and that, before leaving for home, they load up with sugar, tobacco and other goods as freight. . . . As there is nothing more contrary to the King's interests than to permit these vessels of war to carry commercial goods, you must employ any means, no matter how severe, to prevent it . . .; if they are allowed to take such liberties, the company and the commerce of French shipping will be ruined. . . . To remedy this, His Majesty has thought it appropriate to issue the enclosed ordinance and letter, in order to make his intentions known to you. . . .

(Clément, vol. II(ii), pp. 482–3)

205. Colbert to Chamillart, intendant at Caen

VERSAILLES, *10 November 1673*

In reply to your letter of 2 November, I would indeed have departed from

---

[1] This was not an extra sum, as Cole suggests (in *Colbert and a century of French mercantilism*, New York, 1939, Vol. I, p. 387), but part of the original offer. The letter of 9 April had been sent because they had gone back on their first proposal.

my duty had I led you to believe that the King was pleased to learn that the merchants had levied a tax of 24,000 *livres*, to be given to Messieurs de Beaumont and de Breteuil as payment for the protection which they have received from them while their ships are fishing; I can assure you that His Majesty shows so little inclination for individuals who establish themselves as protectors of his subjects that he has instructed me to send orders to four of his warships, which have been stationed in the Channel expressly for the protection of fishing, to destroy the vessels of the said Messieurs de Beaumont and de Breteuil unless they withdraw promptly. At the same time, His Majesty is ordering his council to issue a decree with all speed, forbidding merchant proprietors of fishing vessels to pay anything to the said Beaumont and others. . . .

(Clément, vol. II(ii), pp. 683–4)

206. Colbert to Sève, intendant at Bordeaux

SAINT-GERMAIN-EN-LAYE, *3 March 1673*

In reply to your letter of 24 February about a proposition which had been made to you concerning the chamber of insurance, the same has happened at Bordeaux as happened in Paris and anywhere else one might mention, namely that the merchants who wished to become involved in insurance, enticed by the profits which they have made during the first three or four years, have rashly insured everything during the last year and, as they have lost a great deal, have almost all withdrawn their investments. Thus you should not be astonished that the company in Bordeaux has also perished; perhaps it will be quietly re-established, and those who become associated with it in future may well show a little more circumspection. . . .[1]

(Clément, vol. II(ii), p. 675)

F. The Commercial Ordinance

The evolution of Colbert's economic policy was similar to that of his financial and judicial plans. During the 1660s the royal agents in the provinces were gathering endless detailed information on which the central government would ultimately be able to base its long-term economic strategy; meanwhile pressing matters were dealt with on a piecemeal, day-to-day basis. The vital needs of the

[1] Although stringent rules for insurance were laid down in the Marine Ordinance of 1681, it was not until 1686 that another viable company began operations.

royal treasury demanded some immediate expansion of the economy, but the minister preferred in these early years to concentrate on the less controversial field of colonial trade than to challenge the forces of privilege by attacking local barriers and restraints on commerce within the kingdom.

In March 1673, the fruits of a decade of research into the economic life of France were published in a single document, the Commercial Ordinance, which was intended to regulate commercial activity with other states and within the realm itself (*207*). Unfortunately for Colbert, this ordinance, like its judicial counterparts,[1] was destined to become little more than a monument commemorating his utopian vision, because the realities of French social life prevented its effective implementation. Had it been promulgated in the years before the Dutch War, when the crown was in a stronger financial position, it might have made some impact on the conservative way of life in the provinces. As it was, this expensive and unnecessary war ensured that the ordinance marked the end, not the beginning, of Colbert's hopes for the total overhaul of the economy.

The Commercial Ordinance struck at the centres of corruption and inefficiency which were hampering the search for prosperity, stating at length some of the crucial reforms which he had outlined in his analysis of the problems confronting him in 1664.[2] Savary shared the strong conviction of the minister that such innovations were essential (*208*).

207. The Commercial Ordinance

VERSAILLES, *March 1673*

As commerce is the source of the nation's wealth and of the riches of individuals, we have for many years made every effort to cause it to flourish in our kingdom. This it was which led us firstly to create among our subjects a number of companies, through whose agency they are at present able to obtain from the furthest lands those goods which formerly could be acquired only through the intervention of other nations. This it was which then made us pledge ourselves to promote the construction and arming of a large number of vessels for the advancement of navigation, and to employ our armed strength on sea and land in the maintenance of security. As these enterprises have been crowned by all the success for which we had hoped, we have felt obliged to make provision for their continued existence by a series of regulations which are capable of ensuring that the merchants will prefer honesty to fraud, and of anticipating those obstacles which deflect them from their tasks, through lengthy lawsuits

[1] See pp. 135–8.
[2] See pp. 173–6.

whose costs consume the greater part of the ready cash which they have acquired.

For these reasons etc., it is our pleasure to issue and to order that which follows.

Section I—Of apprentices, and of wholesale and retail merchants
3. No one shall be admitted as a merchant unless he has reached the age of twenty, and unless he produces the letters and certificates of his apprenticeship, and of the work he has undertaken since. . . .
4. The candidate for the mastership shall be questioned on single and double entry book-keeping, on letters and bills of exchange, on the rules of arithmetic, on weights and measures, and on the valuing and the quality of merchandise, in so far as these are relevant to the kind of trade in which he intends to participate.

(Section II is concerned with brokers and bankers' agents.)

Section III—Of the accounts and registers of wholesale and retail merchants and of bankers
1. All merchants, whether wholesale or retail, shall keep a register containing a record of all their trafficking, their bills of exchange, their debts owed and owing, and the funds spent on running their business.
2. All brokers and bankers' agents shall keep a daily record, in which shall be listed all the parties to each transaction arranged by them and which can be referred to in case of a dispute.
3. The books of the merchants, both wholesale and retail, shall be signed on the first and last leaves, by one of the commercial judges in those towns where there is a commercial court, and in the others by the mayor or by one of the consuls, without any charge or duty. . . .
4. The records of brokers and bankers' agents shall be signed and each page initialled by one of the commercial judges. . . .

(IV is on the subject of associations formed by merchants; V–X are on bills of exchange and their usage, and on the means of obtaining restitution from defaulting parties.)

Section XI—On insolvency and bankruptcy
10. We declare to be fraudulent bankrupts those who have misrepresented their wealth, have invented creditors or have exaggerated the sums owed to true creditors.
11. Wholesale and retail merchants and bankers who, at the time of

their bankruptcy, cannot produce their registers and records, duly signed and initialled in accordance with our instructions above, shall be considered as fraudulent bankrupts.

12. Fraudulent bankruptcy shall be brought to court with all speed and shall be punished by death.[1]

13. Those who have aided and abetted a fraudulent bankrupt . . . shall be condemned to pay a fine of 1500 *livres* and double the amount of the wealth they have concealed or of the imaginary debts they have demanded on behalf of creditors.

Section XII—On the jurisdiction of the commercial courts[2]

1. We declare that the edicts of November 1563, establishing a commercial court in our great city of Paris, and all other edicts and declarations concerning commercial jurisdiction, registered in our courts of *parlement*, shall be applicable to all the courts for commerce.

2. These judges shall take cognisance of all bills of exchange drawn up between merchants. . . .

4. The judges shall deal with disputes about sales involving merchants and craftsmen, where the goods were to be resold or used by them in their profession. . . .

5. They shall also concern themselves with the wages, fees and expenses of the agents and servants of merchants, but only when concerned with trade.

6. The judges shall not deal with disputes about foodstuffs, or about the improvement and furnishing of buildings, even between merchants, unless such things are concerned with the profession of one of the two parties.

7. The judges shall hear disputes about insurance, loans to ship-owners, promissory notes, bonds and contracts concerning seaborne trade and the cargoes of ships.

9. They shall equally be required to carry out our orders, when they affect matters within their competence. . . .

---

[1] The severity of punishments for fraudulent bankrupts and their accomplices, more rigorous than any other in the ordinance, underline the fact that this was a widely prevalent and extremely disruptive practice in the field of commerce. See p. 200.

[2] A number of towns had these special courts, which were designed to give speedier justice to busy merchants than they would obtain in the ordinary courts. Rules for procedure within them were systematised in the Civil Ordinance of 1667, section XVI (see p. 137), and this present ordinance now delineated their jurisdiction more clearly.

15. We declare null and void all warrants, writs, summonses and judgements, given by our judges and by lords in the seigneurial courts, which contradict those already issued and delivered by our commercial judges. . . .

(Isambert, vol. XIX, pp. 92–107)

208. Jacques Savary: *The Compleat Merchant*

Chapter Three: That the ignorance, imprudence and ambition of merchants are common causes of failure and bankruptcy
The regulations of the month of March 1673 have firmly established the rules for trading . . .; yet I submit that this will not be sufficient to prevent the bankruptcies which occur as a result neither of malice nor of deliberate planning, but are caused by the ignorance, imprudence and ambition of merchants rather than by their dishonesty. There are some particular things which a man must know before he enters into commerce. . . .

Firstly their ignorance arises because they lacked instruction during their own early days, not having been apprenticed to skilled merchants who possessed all the qualities needed for success in trade.

Secondly, they have not worked for long enough under other merchants, in order that they might acquire the relevant experience to act wisely.

Thirdly, when they present themselves for reception as a master into the gild of merchants which they wish to join, the president and guardians do not question them at all about the principal points or trading, about the quality of the goods they handle, their lengths and widths, the substances of which they consist; on the methods of book-keeping, both double and single entry; on letters and bills of exchange; so that they are often accepted as masters when they have just finished their apprenticeship, and are ignorant and incapable of trading. . . .

Their imprudence also causes them hardship, because they burden themselves with excess goods, beyond their resources. . . .

Their ambition, and their intention of making a quick fortune, also cause bankruptcy, because this greed leads them to lend excessively to all comers, and particularly to the nobility, who pay only when they choose, and to young men under 25 who, on reaching their majority, can easily shed these promises and obligations which they have taken on. Such loans consume all their capital. . . .

I have further noticed that the troubles which befall the majority of merchants result from their heavy expenditure, whether it be on rent for houses or on wages and food for their agents and domestic servants; or their needless outlay on excessive dress, on banquets and gambling, and all too often on the pleasures of women, which wastes their time as well, and time is a precious commodity for a merchant; or because of the large sums stolen from them by their agents and servants. . . .

Success and wealth usually crown the efforts of merchants if they have a thorough knowledge of the methods of trading in which they are engaged, drawn from the wide experience they have acquired through long service under other merchants before setting up their own business. . . .

Chapter Sixty-four: Of bankruptcies . . .: fraudulent bankruptcies, and how those responsible should be punished

. . . With regard to merchants who arrange fraudulent bankruptcies, through a premeditated plan to rob and unjustly carry off the wealth of their creditors, they merit the wholehearted dislike of all their creditors and of the public, also deserving an exemplary punishment because a fraudulent bankrupt is more wicked and contemptible than a highwayman; for the reason that men who travel through the countryside and are always in danger of being robbed therefore carry arms with which to defend themselves, making rigorous efforts to prevent anyone from taking away their property; but it is not the same with a merchant, because the public are not suspicious of him . . ., presuming that he will make good use of the resources they have entrusted to him . . .; thus merchants who declare themselves fraudulently bankrupt have planned to misappropriate the wealth of the public, and ought to be more vigorously pursued than the highwayman. . . .

There is nothing so pernicious, nor so dangerous to the state and the public, as the fraudulent bankrupt. . . .

G. The quest for uniformity and unity: Weights and measures; internal tolls and customs dues; the financing and improvement of road and river routes

The expansion of French trade into colonial markets, the increase in her merchant and naval fleets, the opportunities for prosperity and the sudden reverse in fortunes caused by wars—all these aspects of Colbert's external economic policy affected life only in the great seaports and their immediate hinterlands.[1] The rest of France was almost oblivious of these grandiose enterprises. The quarrel

[1] C. W. Cole, *Colbert and a century of French mercantilism*, New York, 1939, vol. I, ch. VII, offers an admirable summary of all spheres of Colbert's economic policies, their development and consequences.

between the central government and the non-maritime provinces turned on the innumerable local privileges which were jealously guarded by local hierarchies but which hampered the flow of commerce throughout the kingdom. If Colbert had deliberately begun his reform of trading practice in the less controversial field of overseas expansion, a confrontation with restrictive forces within the kingdom could not long be postponed.

There were three main projects at the heart of the plan to revive internal commerce, apart from the relevant regulations contained in the Commercial Ordinance. They were the unification of weights and measures, the simplification and reduction of local tolls and customs dues, and the building or rebuilding of roads, bridges and canals. Weights and measures varied from province to province, even from town to town, as Savary makes clear (*209*). The royal officials themselves were not above using lighter weights in assessing duties on goods, and it was always difficult to prove which was the standard measure, and which the variant. Colbert wished to institute a uniform system partly for the sake of efficiency, but also because the existing irregularities offended against the search for simplicity and order which characterised all his work. There is little evidence that he actually succeeded in changing French practice, and Savary thus became a useful manual for a merchant who needed to master these complexities.

France was divided into two areas as far as customs dues were concerned—the customs union of the *cinq grosses fermes* and the so-called 'foreign' provinces. The former included almost the whole of Northern France, save Brittany, Artois and French Flanders, and within the union internal dues had been abolished. Nevertheless heavy duties were payable on goods passing between the *cinq grosses fermes* and the rest of France, as can be seen from the tariff of 1664 which replaced them by a single levy (*210*). This tariff at least accepted the existence of the customs union as an undeniable fact, whereas the 1667 tariff failed largely because it tried to treat the whole of France as if it were a single unit for excise purposes.[1] It is not surprising that the 1664 edict had to be restored in 1678, because the barrier between the *cinq grosses fermes* and the foreign provinces was as strong as ever. Many of the tolls outside the customs union were, of course, legally established and therefore difficult to suppress. Not only did most of them remain, but Colbert even had to consider financing major road and bridge works by instituting new tolls on completed projects. This was frequently because in the *pays d'élections* the royal officials lacked the power, in the *pays d'états* the provincial Estates lacked the inclination, to finance and direct schemes of this size, and it was therefore necessary to entrust the whole matter to a single individual or to a small business group. They would undertake the task in return for a share of the profits, paid by means of some levy on future users of the finished route. When the finance was to come from state resources, the king was willing to provide treasury help only in *pays d'élections*, never in the *pays d'états* (*211*), believing that those more independent and obstructive provinces should be prepared to vote funds in proportion to the advantages they would receive (*218*). Difficult in peacetime, it was almost impossible to avoid recourse to private wealth for the financing of public works in

[1] See p. 190, including note 3.

war. Even in the *pays d'élections*, the crown would contribute only towards projects of importance, the burden of the rest falling on the localities (*213*), and Colbert often gave priority to trading arteries rather than routes to speed administrative communication with the capital (*214*). Once again the minister was compelled to compromise with his principles, because here were two conflicting policies—the improvement of highways and waterways, and the abolition of internal tolls and barriers. The latter was often sacrificed to the former. For the intendant all these plans meant extra work, and provide further instances of the way in which certain intendants exceeded their authority (*215*).

Thus, with the impossibility of making substantial grants from state funds, the central government had usually to turn towards private citizens of an enterprising nature. Some labour could admittedly be provided, albeit unwillingly, through the old custom of conscription, but the main burden of paying regular wages to workers and of supplying materials fell on the entrepreneur himself. Such men frequently accumulated immense debts (*216*), and it was therefore these worthy individuals whom the provincial Estates penalised when they refused to grant additional revenues. Colbert cherished the schemes so greatly that he was even prepared to offer some limited financial incentives from his hard pressed treasury in war-time to guarantee their completion (*217–8*). The Estates had the ultimate escape route of failing to provide the sums which had been agreed, but, as the costs of projects rose and the periods of construction were extended again and again, they eventually began to take a stern line about further expenditure and became totally uncooperative (*219*). The canal of Languedoc (*216–9*), which was built to join the Atlantic to the Mediterranean, was only the most notable among a number of plans for building canals, rendering rivers navigable and expanding or repairing the road network. All encountered the obstacle of inadequate finance, denied them by local bodies whom the central government was powerless to override. If the Estates raised difficulties about voting the required amounts, the town consuls might simply redirect money which had been specifically designated for such purposes (*220*).[1] Thus internal communications remained slow and inadequate, hampered further by the bands of robbers, footpads and vagabonds who prevented many valuable cargoes, including revenues on the way to the royal treasury, from reaching their destination.

Having failed to create a single customs unit in the kingdom, Colbert at least tried to unify the administration of the internal taxes on commerce, but after years of effort he reluctantly agreed that variations in provincial practice made this impossible (*221*). Sometimes the reform of commercial dues was demanded by a particular province, but this was prompted by the need to simplify a profusion of separate levies, not by a wish to break down provincial frontiers in favour of a larger national economic unit. Too many local vested interests were involved for that to be a popular course.

The central government did attempt to regulate other fields of commercial

---

[1] See pp. 71 and 73–6 for examples of these malpractices.

practice—for example it tried to limit interest rates to 5%; but an ineffective or unreliable bureaucracy and the heavy demands on the royal finances prevented the implementation of these edicts. Impressive on paper, the achievement of Colbert in the daily practice of commerce was far from spectacular.

209. Jacques Savary: *The Compleat Merchant*

Chapter Nine: Rules for converting foreign measures into those of France
It is self-evident that to succeed in trade, in the buying and selling of goods, it is necessary for apprentices to master not only all the diverse units of measurement used inside and outside the realm, but also how to convert them, one into another; that is why I am giving the rules for doing so here, in order that they may practice them during their apprenticeship. . . .

Chapter Eleven: Concerning the differences in weights in the cities of France and foreign countries, compared with those of Paris, and the rules for their conversion

At Lyon
The lb. weight at Lyon equals 14 oz; 100 lbs. equal 86 Paris lbs. and 100 Paris lbs. equal 116 Lyon lbs. . . .

At Avignon, Toulouse and Montpellier
The lb. equals 13 oz.
100 lbs. in these cities equal 83 lbs. in Paris.
100 lbs. in Paris equal $120\frac{1}{2}$ lbs. there. . . .

At Marseille
The lb. is 13 oz. or thereabouts.
100 lbs. at Marseille equal 81 lbs. in Paris.
100 lbs. in Paris equal $123\frac{1}{2}$ lbs. at Marseille. . . .

At London
The lb. equals in Paris $14\frac{5}{8}$ oz.
The Paris lb. equals in London 1 lb. $1\frac{3}{8}$ oz. . . .

At Antwerp
The lb. equals in Paris $14\frac{1}{8}$ oz.
The Paris lb. equals at Antwerp 1 lb. $2\frac{1}{8}$ oz. . . .

210. Edict reducing entry and exit duties on foodstuffs and merchandise. . . .

(1664)

. . . As we clearly saw that the tax-relief which we accorded to our subjects was able to reduce their misery and to make it easier for them to survive, but was not able to attract prosperity to them in order that they might taste its sweetness, and that only commerce could produce such great benefit, we have worked from the beginning to create favourable circumstances for its re-establishment. . . .

And as the soundest and most certain way of reviving trade is the reduction and regulation of all duties levied on goods entering and leaving the kingdom, we ordered our well loved and trusty subject Monsieur Colbert, counsellor in our royal council and intendant of our finances, having responsibility for taxes and commerce, to prepare a comprehensive report on the origins and present state of all these said duties. . . .

As a result of this report, we saw clearly that it was absolutely essential, if trade were to be re-established within the kingdom and outside it, which was the aim that we had set ourselves, to reduce these dues to one single levy on goods entering and another on goods leaving, and also to diminish them considerably. . . .

Therefore we have ordered:

That the duties of the *rêve* and *domaine forain*, those of *haut-passage* created by the edicts and declarations issued about their collection in the years 1369, 1376, 1378, 1382, 1488, 1540, 1549 and 1581 for the *traite domaniale* of Ingrandes, the new tax of Anjou created in 1599, the *trépas* of the Loire, the 15 *sous* on a cask of wine of the *sénéchaussée* of Saumur, and for the revaluation of the said dues as decreed by the declaration of August 1632, the increase ordered in the exit duties on certain kinds of merchandise and foodstuffs in the provinces of Normandy, Poitou and Anjou by three declarations of September 1638, and the 5 *sous*, 12 and 6 *deniers* in the *livre* added to these levies by the edicts and declarations of the years 1643, 1645, 1654, 1657 and 1658..., shall be and shall remain converted in the provinces of Normandy, Picardy, Champagne, Burgundy, Berry, Bourbonnais, Poitou and Anjou, the duchies of Beaumont, Thouars and the castellany of Champtocceaux, into one single exit duty which shall be paid at the first and nearest office for merchandise and foodstuffs in accordance with the tariffs which we have had drawn up in our council of commerce, as attached under the counter-seal of this edict, and which are to begin on 1 October next.[1]

Then, with regard to entry dues . . ., they too shall be similarly converted into one single entry duty. . . .

(Clément, vol. II(ii), pp. 787–93)

211. Colbert to Souzy, intendant at Lille

SCEAUX, *27 August 1670*

. . . There is nothing more universally accepted in this kingdom than that public works are carried out at the King's expense throughout those provinces where His Majesty has a right to impose whatever levy seems fitting to him; but with regard to those provinces which have Estates, public works are at their expense, and the King never interferes save to see that they are well and thoroughly carried out. . . .[2]

(Clément, vol. IV, p. 451)

212. Colbert to Morant, intendant at Aix

VERSAILLES, *17 June 1682*

Monsieur de Vendôme has presented a petition here addressed to the King, of which I am sending you a copy. As it is a question of the public benefit to be derived from the erection of a bridge between Beaucaire and Tarascon, His Majesty wishes you to examine with great care whether this bridge would be of considerable use to the two provinces of Languedoc and Provence. In that event, His Majesty would think it more appropriate that these two provinces should construct it, for the reciprocal advantage of their commercial life, rather than his granting a licence to build it to an individual who would then levy a toll upon it. . . .

(Clément, vol. IV, p. 539)

[1] All the levies referred to in this paragraph were export duties, and the array of import duties was similarly long. The edict was effective in suppressing many of them, but some were still being collected illegally even after the all-embracing single tax was in operation. The various taxes are fully discussed in C. W. Cole, *Colbert and a century of French mercantilism*, New York, 1939, vol. I, pp. 420–2.

[2] Some *pays d'états*, notably Languedoc, carried out these obligations with a considerable sense of responsibility.

213. Colbert to Le Blanc, intendant at Rouen

SAINT-GERMAIN-EN-LAYE, *28 February 1679*

With reference to the memoir you have sent me about works to be carried out during the present year in the generality of Rouen, the King has instructed me to tell you that he intends to bear the burden only of those which are of some consequence, such as bridges over rivers, major paved roads and others of this kind; when it comes to smaller projects, like improving, levelling or laying cobbles along a roadway which is in bad repair and is only about fifty or sixty yards long, or some similar scheme where the cost will not exceed 1000 or 1200 *livres*, His Majesty wishes you to ensure that it is done by the community concerned. . . .[1]

(Clément, vol. IV, pp. 478–9)

214. Colbert to Machault, intendant at Soissons

SAINT-GERMAIN-EN-LAYE, *23 February 1681*

With reference to the works to be undertaken during the present year within your generality, you should notice that the road to Paris is used only by the coaches and carriages which usually take this route, because, with regard to wine, grain and other foodstuffs and merchandise coming to Paris, they are all transported by water. Thus the road to Paris is not at all needed for the supply of food or for the maintenance of commerce, nor therefore for the benefit of the people. But as the road taken by the wagons carrying wine from Champagne and the Soissonais to Flanders is more useful, because it is by means of such wines that money is attracted to these provinces, it seems to me that works on this route should be preferred to the task of easing travellers on their way to Paris. . . .

(Clément, vol. IV, pp. 518–19)

215. Colbert to d'Ormesson, intendant at Lyon

VERSAILLES, *15 April 1683*

In reply to your letters of 5 and 8 April, I must inform you that you ought

[1] For the financing of local routes within the municipalities themselves, see p. 81.

closely to examine the edicts by virtue of which you are authorised to enquire into tolls; and, unless I am sadly misled, you will find that the edicts regulate the tolls and the tariffs on which they are to be based, and state that these tariffs must be posted clearly and in a public place. It is particularly the execution of these edicts which you are to watch over. But with regard to disputes which can arise between the toll-collector and the merchant or boatman who is to pay the dues, I am not persuaded that you will find the responsibility to be yours; because it is surely a general principle of the King's direction of affairs that merchants and carriers should not be required to come and plead before you over a dispute of so little consequence; and you will find that there is a great deal of difference between an investigation into whether a toll should be levied or not, or on what basis it should be levied, and the hearing of minute details which cause conflicts between toll-collectors and boatmen.

I must further tell you that there is nothing more contrary to the spirit of the King's orders than that you should establish formal sittings, with an office for a clerk of the court and a jurisdiction involving the appearance before you of advocates and prosecutors, because it is certainly not the King's intention to multiply the tribunals of justice in the provinces.

The reason which you give, that the justices of the lords who have the right to the toll would be judging cases involving their own interests, spoils the argument by proving too much, because this same reason would militate against all the justices of lords who have the right to administer higher justice, and that was why judges of appeal were established. . . .

(Clément, vol. VII, p. 298)

216. Riquet to Colbert

1 March 1669

The loan of 200,000 *livres* to pay for those lands acquired for the building of the canal was discussed and decided at the meeting of the Estates of this province the day before yesterday. . . .

The loan of the sum of 500,000 *livres*, which is to be handed over to me for the completion of the canal, was also debated and resolved at the same meeting. . . .

I must admit, Monseigneur, that the exorbitant expenses which I have incurred in the course of my work, and which I still pay out daily in the intention of finishing my project during next year, have left me in a state of financial hardship which you could scarcely conceive; but I see myself escaping from this misery through the 500,000 *livres* I have mentioned, and I have no doubt that I shall acquit myself of my said enterprise within the time I promised you, that is to say next year. . . .

(Depping, vol. IV, pp. 27–8)

217. Colbert to Bazin de Bezons, intendant at Toulouse

PARIS, *30 November 1672*

I am enclosing the decree of the royal council concerning the affairs of Monsieur Riquet, in which you will see that the King wishes the province to borrow 1,600,000 *livres* to reimburse him for what is owed to him. To that end, His Majesty has agreed that the Estates may keep 100,000 *livres* from the ordinary taxes of the province which are paid to the receiver general. . . .

His Majesty desires that Monsieur le duc de Verneuil,[1] you and the other commissioners presiding at the Estates, should use every means you think necessary to effect the said loan of 1,600,000 *livres*. For which purpose, he does not doubt that Monsieur le cardinal de Bonzi[2] will occupy himself, using all the authority which his position gives him, in persuading the Estates to grant him satisfaction, the more so as this is the only way of furthering work on the port of Cette and on the canal connecting the two seas, of whose benefits the entire province is aware.

His Majesty instructs me to tell you that he permits you to distribute up to 20,000 *livres* among the deputies of the third estate in order to ease the discussion and ensure that the decision is made with one voice, if that is possible. But he wishes you to carry out this distribution in conjunction with Monsieur le cardinal de Bonzi, and moreover to do so only in cases where you judge it to be absolutely essential, because His Majesty does not want the deputies to become accustomed again to receiving favours for doing what he desires. . . .

You will also find enclosed five or six letters of credence which you can use with reference to the bishops and nobles as you deem it appropriate. . . .

(Clément, vol. IV, pp. 81–2)

[1] Governor of Languedoc.
[2] Archbishop of Narbonne and president of the Estates of Languedoc.

218. The cardinal de Bonzi to Colbert

MONTPELLIER, *17 December 1672*

. . . We assembled again last Thursday; I found the mood of the deputies to be much calmer, and I had spoken to each of them individually . . .; we all agreed that the assembly could not refuse this loan; that the assurances given us by His Majesty in the decree of the council about the payment of interest were not only sufficient and completely infallible, but that there was no reason to want or seek any further surety. . . .

(Depping, vol. I, pp. 289–93)

219. Colbert to d'Aguesseau, intendant at Toulouse

3 February 1679

I have learned from your letter of what took place over the implementation of the proposal I made to you that the province of Languedoc be required to assist Monsieur Riquet in his financial difficulties by arranging a loan to him of 300,000 *livres*, and that Monsieur le cardinal de Bonzi and you have found the deputies of the Estates utterly opposed to this loan. In which I cannot see that they have any good reason, since they would have been reassured by your efforts and your diligence that the sum would have been properly used in a project which is of great consequence for the general well-being of the province, and by the certainty of repayment according to the privilege granted to the province and confirmed by the King. . . .

(Depping, vol. IV, pp. 63–4)

220. Comenge, lieutenant general of the admiralty at the Narbonne depot, to Colbert

NARBONNE, *12 May 1664*

It will be very easy for me to carry out the task which you have done me the honour of setting me, by informing you of the quality of commercial life in the area of my jurisdiction, which is in a state of utter ruin and decay . . .; ships cannot reach here because of the appalling condition of the canal, which is almost completely silted up, and so little attempt at restoration has been made that in each of the last three years less than 200 *livres* has been spent, although the King has always allowed the consuls of this town to levy a *robinage*,[1] which is usually farmed out at more than 4000 *livres* per year, and is designed to finance repairs to the said canal and its entrance channels; it was ordered by a decree of the council of 2 May 1642 that the dues collected by the *robinage* tax could not be diverted to other purposes no matter what the cause, and that the leases authorising the farming of the tax were to be drawn up in the presence of the officers of the admiralty, with the consuls in attendance, and that the said officers were to compile an annual report on the condition of the said canal in order to allocate to the lowest bidder the job of carrying out repairs; none of which is done because the eighty members of the town council are able to dispose of these funds according to their pleasure, have always opposed my taking cognisance of the matter, and have lodged an appeal with the royal council against the said edict; and as this appeal is being financed from municipal funds and they do not care greatly care whether it cost 10,000 or 12,000 *livres*, I have not sufficient power to contest their case . . .; I humbly ask you to give me your protection in order that the canal and channels may be restored, which is the unique means of reviving the original lustre of the commercial life of this town. . . .

(Depping, vol. III, pp. 345–6)

221. Ordinance concerning the customs dues in the province of Normandy

FONTAINEBLEAU, *June 1680*

. . . After having regulated the levying and collection of the taxes associated with our general farm of the customs within the jurisdiction of our *cour des aides* of Paris, by our ordinance of this present month of June, it remains for us to do the same in the area controlled by our *cour des aides* of Normandy; and, although it would have given us great satisfaction if we had been able to equate the two and create a single body of laws to apply throughout the jurisdictions of both our courts, nevertheless the different customs which obtain in our province of Normandy have obliged us to issue a separate regulation, in doing which we have had as our ultimate

---

[1] *Robinage* was a duty on goods travelling on canals between inland ports and the sea.

210

aim the welfare of our peoples that we seek to increase on every occasion. . . .

(Isambert, vol. XIX, p. 251)

H. The investigation of industrial production and the general regulation of industry

In industry and agriculture, as in commerce, Colbert showed little interest at the local level of the market town and its surrounding countryside, concentrating his attention on those aspects which affected the economic status of France in the world of international trade and warfare. His priorities were therefore to make the kingdom self-sufficient, to increase the stock of precious metals in the treasury, and to maintain effective armed forces for the protection of the realm in the wars which, though undesirable, were ultimately inevitable. In agriculture he accordingly emphasised the production of timber for shipbuilding, horses for the cavalry, and enough animals of other kinds to prevent the need for importing them from other countries. Fisheries were encouraged because they were schools for future naval and mercantile sailors. In the manufacturing industries he wished to establish in France those manufactures whose products had at the moment to be imported from other nations, luxury goods in particular, and he wanted to develop the export of high quality French produce which would be paid for by overseas buyers in the gold and silver he so keenly sought.

During the early years of his ministry, Colbert busied himself in gathering detailed information about industry, in order to formulate general regulations which would unify the varying practices of the different provinces into a single code, applicable throughout the whole country. The information was collected partly by the intendants, who were instructed to seek answers to specific questions, and in certain provinces by the governors, who produced rather wider surveys of industrial life, not prompted by a list of demands from Paris and therefore sometimes revealing extensive gaps in the knowledge of provincial resources as already possessed by the central government (*222*). The crown thus seldom learned anything totally new from the intendant, because that official confined himself to the brief prepared by the royal minister. The governor, in contrast, sent details of anything which he thought that the ministers would find interesting.

The first fruits of these enquiries were contained in the general regulations of 1669 (*223*), including many from the years before 1661 which were now revised and arranged systematically. This was in no sense a final statement, and investigations continued, novel situations arose and modifications were made. The execution of the 1669 rules was under the overall supervision of a new official, the inspector general of manufactures (*224*), although he had to work through the existing bureaucracy and above all through the proud and privilege-conscious gilds in the towns. In 1672 Colbert did send out a special team of officials, to examine how well the new regulations were working, and ten years later he was still discussing whether some permanent inspectorate was required. If so, it

211

would have to be financed out of a local levy on industrial production, and it should not be staffed by men resident in the province, who would have all the drawbacks of *sub-délégués*.[1] In laying down these instructions for manufactures, Colbert had to choose between two conflicting policies. His general principles of royal administration prompted him to reduce the independence of the gilds, but his insistence on high standards of quality led him unavoidably to the conclusion that he must cooperate with these privileged bodies, because they alone had the necessary staff to ensure that the rules were obeyed. For once, therefore, he supported a local privileged élite group, and saw with some satisfaction that his new code was being enforced. Yet the gilds, eager to safeguard the prosperity of their members, were not keen that their craft should be expanded. They preferred to exclude newcomers and thus ensure that the master-craftsmen were never short of work. This did not accord with the plans of Colbert, but he was compelled to choose between quality and quantity, ultimately selecting the former.

The minister was determined to systematise the size of manufactured goods, as well as their quality (*225*), in order that they should be respected abroad (*226*) as well as at home, and should compete with foreign products (*227*). Yet, although the royal and gild officials might discover infringements of these rules, the offenders often escaped punishment because the task of arresting them and bringing them to justice was entrusted to the municipal authorities whose devotion to duty was not widely celebrated.[2] Unfortunately there was no alternative group of judicial officers to carry out this aspect of the industrial legislation. Most town councils contained no manufacturers (*228*), and the consuls were simply unwilling to take on this additional burden (*229*); when they did attempt to shoulder the responsibility, their lack of knowledge and their inefficiency caused them to reveal a striking ineptitude, as a large number of documents testify. Some municipalities were administered by men with a keener eye for the profits of commerce, who issued regulations which were beyond their competence and incurred royal displeasure as a result (*230*). The worst instances of the exploitation of manufacturers come from the few towns where the consuls were drawn from the merchant class alone, showing that each group in the various stages of the commercial process preferred to undermine the position of others rather than to cooperate in promoting expansion and prosperity (*231*).

222. The duc de Chaulnes, governor of Brittany, to Colbert

SAINT-MALO, *4 September 1672*

. . . It would require a whole volume to give you an account of the affairs of Nantes, Monsieur, which I found in complete chaos. . . .

[1] See pp. 23–4 and 26–7.
[2] See pp. 68–76.

The merchants...told me that..., at the same time as I was pressing them to expand their trading, they had been deprived of their sole means of continuing to do so, by not being allowed to enjoy the reduction in duty on goods passing along the Loire. . . . I explained to them that their exclusion from this concession had not been caused by any change of royal policy, but simply because it was thought that the refined sugar which they carried had come from foreign colonies, and had not been refined at Nantes where there were not known to be any refineries. But, having chosen to investigate this matter, I have the honour to inform you that there are in fact two refineries at Nantes, of which one has been established a long time ago and is in regular production, while the other would be in the same state were it not for the suspension of the royal concession. I have watched the first one at work, and have moreover seen the men who were building two more and which were nearly complete until work was interrupted for the same reason; therefore, as soon as free passage is restored, we shall shortly have four. . . .

(Depping, vol. III, pp. 608–11)

223. Instruction . . . about the implementation of the general regulations for manufactures, registered at the *parlement* of Paris, His Majesty being present, 13 August 1669[1]

4. The royal inspector shall discover whether there is a craft gild in towns where industries are established, and whether the master craftsmen have inscribed their names on the register kept by the town clerk, on that of the civil court and on the roll of the gild . . . . And until this has been done they shall be forbidden to practise their craft, so that no one whose name is not on these registers . . . can work as if he were a master, by which means a community and corporation will be formed whose members will be skilled and whose doors will be closed to the untrained.
8. To keep every community of industrial workers in good order, it is essential that a register be kept, and initialled by a consul . . ., in which

[1] This document is concerned with the carrying out of the general regulations, and is not the list of regulations themselves. They may be found translated in full in C. W. Cole, *Colbert and a century of French mercantilism*, New York, 1939, vol. II, pp. 383–93. The first thirty-three clauses deal with the specific requirements for the size, strength and quality of cloth, the remaining twenty-six with the membership of gilds ?nd the inspection of products.

shall be recorded firstly the general regulations for manufactures, and the instructions and statutes concerning that particular place; and after that the list of names and surnames of every master of the craft, the indentures of apprentices, those meetings and discussions of the consuls in charge of manufacturing which are concerned with the gilds, and in fact everything which relates to them. . . .

9. A gild chamber shall be created in the town hall or, if there is none, in the most convenient place for transacting the business of the community and for the inspecting and marking, by the consuls in charge, of the merchandise which shall be brought there on certain days at appointed hours by the craftsmen and workers. . . . And as the merchants have a specialised knowledge of the good quality and faults of merchandise, and as it is in their interest that goods should be perfect, it is equally necessary that the said consuls shall have one of the most worthy merchants elected to aid them in their inspection and marking, who shall attend twice weekly for a three-month term of office, after which another shall be elected. . . .

10. The inspector must check that the general regulations have been distributed by the consuls to every craftsman and to the merchants; and where this has not been done, he must require the consuls to have them printed and sent at once to every master whose name is on the register, each of whom shall then record his acceptance of the regulations in the same register. . . . The cost of printing and distribution shall be charged to the gild.

15. The consuls shall make a tour at the first opportunity of every craftman's workshop, to ensure that their goods have been brought into conformity with the regulations on size. . . .

16. They must also make a general tour each month of the homes of the domestic workers. . . .

59. The inspector shall compile a report on the state of towns where trade and manufacturing are established, describing their nature and quality, seeing how the goods are made, noting their good and bad points, applying himself to ways of perfecting them by taking samples, and recording the measurements and the price of each item, the quantity produced each year and how many craftsmen of each kind there are in every town.

63. . . . If the mayor and consuls . . . do not conform to our orders about the correct implementation of these regulations, the inspector shall complain to Monsieur the intendant. . . .

(Clément, vol. II(ii), pp. 832–41)

224. Instructions from Colbert to Bellinzani, inspector-general of manufactures

PARIS, *8 October 1670*

He must begin his tour of inspection of all our manufactures by visiting Meaux and La Ferté-sous-Jouarre. In the town of Meaux some factories making moquette have been established, by a man from Tournai named Leclerc, and he must examine the agreement which authorised this manufacture in order to see whether it is being observed.

He must compile a summary of all aspects of this industry; must verify the number of looms working within it, and discover everything which could be done to expand and secure this manufacture so that we shall have no need for recourse to other countries for supplies of this fabric.

The said Leclerc is a timid man and it will be necessary to stimulate him, even by seeing whether one cannot give him some assistance in developing his factories. It should also be noted that one cannot rely on his honesty. . . .

He must then visit the velvet factories at La Ferté. . . .

He should ascertain secretly if Protestants and Catholics are admitted into these factories without discrimination. . . .

(Depping, vol. III, pp. 851–2)

225. Colbert to Voysin de La Noiraye, intendant at Tours

SAINT-GERMAIN-EN-LAYE, *22 August 1670*

I have received your letter of 16 August, telling me all that you have done both to compel the manufacturers to make their coarse woollen cloth in larger pieces, and to suppress the pulleys which they have used to stretch and broaden it.

I beg you to continue to watch closely that all rules and regulations are obeyed promptly. You can assuredly be no more usefully employed than in completely stamping out these pulleys and machines, whose sole function is to give the cloth a false appearance and therefore to cheat those who purchase it.

(Clément, vol. II(ii), p. 543)

226. Colbert to Le Blanc, intendant at Rouen

FONTAINEBLEAU, *21 October 1682*

. . . From reports which have reached me about the East India trade, I have learned of loud complaints that the linens of Rouen are of inferior size and quality to the standards prescribed, a development which will be greatly prejudicial to the province of Normandy; and I beg you to make detailed inquiries of the principal merchants as to what should be done . . . to restore the reputation which these linens formerly enjoyed in the Indies. But, in listening to the views of these merchants, I must remind you that their opinions never tend towards the general good, but only towards the furtherance of their own petty interests and trafficking, so that, while you may derive illumination from them, you should avoid following the courses they suggest on this point.

(Clément, vol. II(ii), p. 740)

227. Colbert to Bellinzani

PARIS, *6 November 1670*

. . . I am sending this letter to you at Abbeville. Do not fail, when you are there, to examine every means of perfecting the manufacture of cloth which is established in the town, and of making it as fine and beautiful as the light, variegated cloths of England and Holland. And as you will be able to see that there is a great difference between that produced in France and its English counterpart, we must use every available method to make ours equal in quality to those of that kingdom. . . .

(Clément, vol. II(ii), p. 576)

228. Colbert to Voysin de La Noiraye, intendant at Tours

SAINT-GERMAIN-EN-LAYE, *15 January 1670*

The merchant craftsmen in silk of the town of Tours have petitioned the King to exempt them from the jurisdiction which has been given to the mayor and consuls of the said town over the execution of the rules and regulations for manufactures, and to return this responsibility to the lieutenant general, claiming that the twenty-four consuls who compose the town council . . . have no knowledge of this industry, and that the craftsmen in silk have always been excluded from the ranks of the consuls. Although these reasons seemed to His Majesty to have great force, yet it is of the utmost importance not to attack the existing arrangements, both to avoid situations in which other towns in the realm would find excuses for similar alterations and to prevent the failure to obey the rules which would be fostered by the hope of obtaining concessions of this sort; therefore His Majesty has not acceded to the request of the silk workers. He has instructed me to tell you that he intends you to consider the remedies which could be applied to these complaints . . ., the best of which, it seems to me, is to reduce the number of consuls from twenty-four to twelve, suppressing the rest when the present holders die; of the remaining twelve, always to elect two cloth merchants and also two craftsmen in silk, and when six of them are appointed as judges of manufactured goods, to include at least one cloth merchant and one silk worker. I await your reply to this suggestion.

(Clément, vol. II(ii), pp. 511–2)

229. Colbert to Barillon, intendant at Amiens

12 September 1670

I am perpetually receiving complaints against the mayor and consuls of Amiens over their failure to enforce the rules and regulations for manufactures, and about the frauds and abuses committed in that town. I beg you to apply yourself with the greatest determination to rectify this situation and to ensure that they enforce the said regulations with severity; if they prove recalcitrant, it may be necessary to make an example of one of their number by suspending him and removing him from the magistrature.

(Depping, vol. III, pp. 839–40)

230. Colbert to Bouchu, intendant in Burgundy

SCEAUX, *24 September 1682*

A complaint has been made to the council about a regulation made by the mayor and consuls of Beaune concerning the sale of their wines, and I am sending you the decree of the council on this matter. It is the intention of the King that you have it registered at the office of the town clerk at

Beaune, and that you keep careful watch to see that it is punctually executed, as His Majesty does not intend to allow the said mayor and consuls to take charge of pricing their wines.

(Depping, vol. I, pp. 879–80)

231. Note sent to Colbert about the Amiens cloth trade

The cloth industry in the town of Amiens is one of the largest manufactures in the country. It consists of 600 masters, who employ a great number of workers and who, by using thread which is spun in the province, give a livelihood to 100,000 people.

This industry does not just sell its products in the towns and cities of the kingdom, but has them transported to Spain, Italy and other far distant places, even China.

The merchants on whom this considerable trade chiefly depends number no more than eight or ten, all related by blood or marriage, and always consuls in the town.

Their collusion enables them to buy their merchandise at whatever price they choose, as they send only one of their number to the auctions, which is a practice that no one could condone.

By this method a piece of cloth, which in the days before this monopoly the manufacturers could sell for between 60 and 65 *livres*, will now sell for no more than 45 or 50 *livres*, and in addition they are compelled to receive half the sum in silk which the merchants have brought, and which they have to buy at a third more than would be an acceptable price elsewhere.

. . . All the trade thus rests in the hands of seven or eight families who, during the last fifteen or twenty years, have acquired immense fortunes, and who have grown fat at the expense of the poor artisans from whom they have taken away the right of attending the fairs and of exercising the freedom in trade which is enjoyed by all the other subjects of the King.

In order to end this corruption which is so all-pervasive, so public and so harmful to commerce, it is requested that:

1. the manufacturers be free to attend the fairs, which the merchants have denied to them on their own authority alone, there being no laws, edicts or ordinances which exclude any of the King's subjects from attending fairs. . . .

2. that three fairs annually be instituted in the said town, in order to

end this corruption by giving the manufacturers the opportunity to sell their wares. . . .

(Depping, vol. III, pp. 615–6)

I. New inventions and foreign craftsmen; state aid for industry: Privileges, monopolies, tax concessions and incentives

The preoccupation of Colbert with the creation of a more favourable trade balance, reducing the import of manufactured goods from abroad and increasing the export of French industrial products, did not find favour with the gildsmen who were helping to enforce the new codes of regulations. To achieve his aim, the minister wished to entice foreign craftsmen who would set up factories in France and to encourage the invention of novel manufacturing processes. Both these policies threatened the closed society of the gildsmen, introducing a competitive element into industrial production which might reduce their prosperity. The crown thus had to protect inventors and immigrant craftsmen by grants of privilege and financial support, while the gilds put every possible obstacle in their path to success. Any individual or group who evolved some new method of expanding output quickly applied to the King for aid in ensuring that the profits from the discovery were enjoyed, at least initially, by those responsible (*232*). Of the two main fields of industrial activity which most concerned the central government—military supplies and luxury goods—the former raised special problems, because the state was the only potential customer and did not always provide inventive manufacturers with adequate demand for their products (*233*).

Luxury goods aroused objections if their importation was financed by exporting precious metals to the countries in which they originated. The moral condemnation of such lavish expenditure, which earlier ministers had included in legislation against luxury, was no longer voiced, and Colbert was prepared to allow the wealthy to adorn themselves and their property in a sumptuous manner so long as the goods were made in France. The only trappings of ostentation which were frowned upon were those, like gold thread, which actually used precious metals in the manufacturing process. Only the greatest subjects might wear them, and then each case was authorised by special royal letters patent. Merchants complained about these prohibitions and smugglers circumvented them, the authorities considering that the pursuit of illegal importers caused too much bad feeling between crown and traders (*234*). The manufacture of elaborate lace, silks, glass, mirrors, tapestries and non-precious metalware in France was positively encouraged, the minister hoping that ultimately the kingdom might export them to commercial rivals. Industrial experiments were tried in new areas (*235*), although the crucial factor in their survival and success was often the arrival of an expert foreigner. These men had more knowledge, but also more initiative and interest in commercial matters than the native French, and royal agents travelled throughout Europe in order to lure them into the realm of Louis XIV, sometimes successfully (*236*), sometimes not. On the other hand, the emigration of French workers was not to be allowed (*237*), and those abroad were to be brought home where possible (*238*). Some of these visitors soon established flourishing industries (*239*), though their continued prosperity depended on the skill, and therefore the health, of a single craftsman (*240*).

The crown was always ready to grant privileged status to those who ran these new enterprises (*241*), but these concessions might outlive their usefulness and stifle further expansion (*242*). When the central government heard criticisms of existing monopolies, it was quick to reconsider them (*243*). Support for new industry came not only from the crown, but in the *pays d'états* it was voted by the provincial Estates (*244*), and it also came from a group of wealthy and enlightened aristocrats (*245–6*) who were usually provincial governors and friends of Colbert. Another incentive was the remission of taxes to towns (*247*) and industrialists (*248*) who cooperated in these ventures, while an ordinary man who had three children working in factories was exempted from the *taille*, although such concessions were quickly revoked when their recipients became complacent. Bad craftsmanship was to be proclaimed as loudly as good (*249*) in an attempt to frighten those responsible, and the laziness of working-men, a very frequent complaint, was to be met with stern measures (*250*). Yet in some towns, where all levels of the population were unwilling to cooperate, there was little the government could do but repeat its exhortations, Auxerre above all acquiring a reputation for obstruction which rivalled even the chicanery of Marseille (*251*).

232. Barentin, intendant at Poitiers, to Colbert

POITIERS, *8 May 1666*

. . . I am sending you a memoir about a machine which a group of individuals in this town have invented, and it is a completely accurate account because I have seen the results myself; it is my belief, Monsieur, that if it should please you to propose to the King that he should grant the privilege for which its makers are asking, His Majesty would have no difficulty in agreeing to do so, which would help them to develop it; and as this machine can be worked by cripples and even by the blind, it will be of the greatest usefulness. . . .

Plan for a machine to make ribbon, so that one man can do the work of at least ten
A group of men at Poitiers have invented a machine with which, using the labour of one man, they can control ten looms making braid and ribbon. These said inventors most humbly beg the King that it may please him to permit them to enjoy the benefit of their invention and the fruits of their labours by according them, for twenty years, the privilege

of establishing themselves and their partners and of setting their machines to work in any part of the kingdom where they deem it appropriate, and by granting them the right to sell or transfer their privilege to others and to dispose of their machines, while forbidding everyone else, no matter what their rank, from making use of their invention during the years of this privilege, on pain of confiscation and of a 5000 *livres* fine to be paid to them. After which time the inventors will present their machine to the public. . . .

(Depping, vol. III, pp. 784–5)

233. The archbishop of Lyon to Colbert

LYON, *2 February 1666*

The testing of the newly invented cannons took place in my presence and that of Monsieur Dallier[1] last Saturday. The large ones consistently breached a wall at 900 paces. . . . As for those which hold only two pounds of balls and are fired resting on a fork, we could find no drawbacks and thought them very useful. The bullet was seen by us to hit the mountainside, where it dislodged the surface although it had travelled more than 900 paces. . . .

(Depping, vol. III, p. 755)

LYON, *13 January 1668*

Monsieur Emery, to whom you granted the privilege of having the sole right to cast cannon of the newly invented type, has at present no work and, having broken away from Monsieur du Puys, was planning to go elsewhere, had I not persuaded him to stay until he had offered you his services. As he does not have the honour of being known to you, he has requested me to write you this letter; his is undoubtedly an inventive mind, which could be retained in France for a small consideration.

(Depping, vol. III, pp. 757–8)

234. Colbert to the archbishop of Lyon

PARIS, *26 December 1670*

. . . I have until now been at a loss to understand the requests which have

[1] Receiver general of the finances in the neighbouring province of Dauphiné.

been made by the manufacturers of Milanese gold thread. They complain about the prohibition on the wearing of gold and silver; I do not know on what they base this complaint, seeing that the wearing of gold and silver in public has been forbidden for more than twenty years. . . .

They protest further that these goods are imported into France. You know that the King has expressly forbidden this, and I am always instructing the customs officers to let none enter; if they ask for preventive measures to be taken, I can assure you that I will arrange them without making any further difficulty. It is true that they have asked me to authorise official inspections of the premises of merchants and that I have refused, but this kind of search greatly disturbs commercial life and makes the merchants despondent, so that it must be used only as a last resort. . . .

(Depping, vol. III, p. 865)

235. Colbert to Chamillart, intendant at Caen

SAINT-GERMAIN-EN-LAYE, *28 August 1670*

I have looked at the samples of silk which you have sent me, and although they are rather coarse I am nevertheless convinced that the introduction of silkworms into the election of Avranches can bring nothing but great benefit to the subjects of the King. But as success depends on the planting of mulberries and on knowing whether the climate is suitable for bringing these trees here in the near future, which can be learned only by experiment, it is desirable that you should induce the people to plant some of them. Meanwhile, if you send me further information, I will consider it; and moreover, if there are any practical ways in which I can play a part so that these foundations may be laid successfully, I will be very willing to participate.

(Clément, vol. IV, pp. 233–4)

236. Janot, commercial agent, to Colbert

MIDDELBURG, *30 October 1665*

Monsieur van Robais, who used to run a cloth factory in this town, has just loaded all the looms, presses and other machinery that he can transport on to a little ship which is sailing for Saint-Valéry-sur-Somme, intending to go from there to Abbeville where it appears that he will

222

prosper and will make others eager to do likewise. . . .

I have not neglected to obey the instructions you gave me. . . . I have written to a number of merchants and craftsmen in Holland, in order to persuade them to make a sizable fortune for themselves by coming to live among us; I am awaiting news of the results. . . .

You could also try to attract tapestry makers from Antwerp, Brussels and Oudenaarde. . . .

(Depping, vol. III, pp. 751–3)

237. The archbishop of Lyon to Colbert

LYON, *26 September 1672*

A short time ago I had the honour to inform you that, acting on advice I had received that a Swiss merchant was enticing workers in the silk industry to settle in Geneva, I had put him in the castle of Pierre-Scize; not having been sent any instructions from you on this matter, I have handed him over to the commercial judges to be tried. As you have shown me on other occasions how dear these things are to your heart, and as it is highly important to the King's service that the desertion of workers be prevented, I am sending you a copy of the sentence which I have caused to be pronounced.

(Depping, vol. III, p. 759)

238. Colbert to Colbert de Croissy, ambassador in London

26 September 1669

. . . As the King intends that none of his subjects shall live in a foreign country without his express permission, it is important that you should make known to all Frenchmen living in England that His Majesty insists on the strict observance of the decree which has been registered in the *parlement*, requiring them to return to this kingdom within the time prescribed. In the meanwhile I ask you to compile a list of the names and ranks of all those living in England, and then to send it to me. . . .

(Clément, vol. II(ii), pp. 492–3)

239. Floquebert, lieutenant general at Reims, to Colbert

REIMS, *1 July 1665*

... If I may give you a detailed report on the newly established lace-making industry in this town, as you have instructed me, Monsieur Pierre Chardon, a Frenchman who has lived for a long time in Venice where he was known as Cardoni, arrived here on 26 May with his wife, three sons and two daughters. ...

At the moment there are, working in his house, six Venetian women, a further twenty-two from Flanders and thirty girls from this town, not including servants and domestic staff. There is every indication that this number will continue to increase daily. A little while ago, there arrived seven girls who had been sent from Paris. ...

(Depping, vol. III, pp. 732–4)

240. Memoir sent to Colbert by Dunoyer, member of the gild of mirror manufacturers

30 November 1666

The possibility of producing mirrors in France which are as fine as those of Venice is no longer in doubt, so long as the Venetian workmen wish to work here. ...

Although the advantages have been pointed out to them, they do not wish to teach their skills to the French..., so that the financial state of this enterprise ... depends not only on the whims of these gentlemen, but also on the length of their lives and even on their health.

It is indeed true that no work has been done for ten days, because the craftsman responsible for putting the materials into the pot-furnace has an injured leg, and neither Monsieur Antoine not any of the others can replace him and moreover do not wish to attempt it, saying that it is the most difficult of tasks and that one must study it from the age of twelve.

This stoppage has not halted the payment of their salaries and the wages of the workmen and clerks, who number nearly two hundred, nor the fires in our two great furnaces, which consume five cartloads of wood daily, because if the fire were out for a day they would be reduced to dust. ...

(Depping, vol. III, p. 790)

241. Privilege granted to Monsieur Guichard for the manufacture of cottons at Saint-Quentin

VERSAILLES, *17 February 1671*

. . . Having invited Pierre Guichard, merchant of our town of Saint-Quentin, to establish there a factory making cotton and linen cloths, we have been informed most humbly by him that, as this industry had never before existed in the kingdom, he has been obliged to expend considerable sums in attracting workers from abroad, both to build and to work the looms for weaving them. . . .

We have therefore permitted and accorded, and do permit and accord him the right to organise the manufacture, in our said town of Saint-Quentin and within ten leagues of it, of all kinds of cottons and linen, and expressly forbid all other persons, of whatever rank or condition, to trouble or disturb him and to imitate or counterfeit these said cloths, both within the town and within ten leagues of it, for ten whole and consecutive years beginning on the first day of March next. . . . Nevertheless we wish that those who manufactured similar cloths, both in the town and in its surroundings, before the publication of these presents should continue to do so as before. . . .

And in order further to encourage the petitioner to devote his efforts to the said industry, we have exempted and do exempt the house in which he resides and that of one of his partners from all billeting of our troops and soldiers; and, to attract more workers into this industry, it is our wish and pleasure that the said foreign workers who are employed there and have worked for six whole and consecutive years at this manufacture . . . shall be considered as native and born Frenchmen . . . and pay no tax or duty . . . on the understanding that they will always remain in our kingdom. . . .

(Clément, vol. II(ii), pp. 850–1)

242. La Bourlie, lieutenant general at Sedan, to Colbert

SEDAN, *4 December 1664*

Since I received your letter, I have called together the consuls and syndics of this town, to hear from them about the state of the factories producing Dutch and Spanish cloth, both that of Monsieur Cadeau and those of other citizens who are in this trade, and I took them to visit

Cadeau and to carry out an inspection in accordance with your wish and your instructions. There we found seven looms working.... I then went back to see those in the town, and found seven citizens who had three looms each, and of as high a quality as the others; they told me that they had to pay 55 *écus* per loom each year to Monsieur Cadeau, as prescribed in his grant of privilege, and that they could barely maintain production because of the heavy burden of this levy; but that the privilege expired on St John's Day 1666, and that they preferred to suffer with that hope of an improvement in their minds, than to leave the town and go elsewhere. It is certainly true that the King can consider the industry of Sedan to be one of the finest in the kingdom; the consuls have brought twelve of the principal and most prosperous citizens to speak with me, all of whom are ready to set up looms as soon as they are free to do so, have sent their children to be trained in Holland to this end, and are beginning to trade in wool ready for the day when the privilege expires. . . . I have been asked by the consuls and the forces of law and order to inform you, on this occasion, of the considerable damage which has been done to the community here by the long duration of this privilege. . . .

(Depping, vol. III, pp. 696–7)

243. Colbert to Rouillé, intendant at Aix

FONTAINEBLEAU, *1 September 1679*

The King has learned that in 1603 Monsieur Rayer or his colleagues obtained the monopoly of fishing for tunnyfish in the Mediterranean, that he and his colleagues have enjoyed this privilege until his death, which occurred recently, and that this kind of fishing is worth 12,000 *livres* per year. His Majesty has instructed me to tell you that he wishes you to find out whether it would be better for the province if His Majesty were to grant this right to someone whom he is pleased to name, or to open this sort of fishing freely to all the province.

In doing so, you must consider only whether this fishing is of such a sort that is necessary to lay out a large sum in order either to establish or to maintain it, because in that case it would be better for the King to grant it to someone who was able to support the expense.

But if this fishing can easily be done by all the fishermen of the province, then in that case His Majesty will not renew the monopoly and will throw it open completely to the public, provided that it is certain that this will yield as many or more fish, so that the kingdom will always derive the same benefit.

(Clément, vol. II(ii), p. 705)

244. Colbert to Bellinzani

ATH, *30 June 1671*

The Estates of Burgundy have, during their last session, allocated a sum of between 60,000 and 80,000 *livres* for the creation of new industries. It is essential that these funds be used wisely for the greater profit and advantage of this province. . . .

(Clément, vol. II(ii), p. 623)

245. Colbert to the archbishop of Lyon

VERSAILLES, *22 July 1672*

I have received the letter which you have taken the trouble of writing to me on 11 July, in which you tell me that you have had a furnace constructed at Neuville[1] for Monsieur Desessarts, and that since Easter he has cast 150 cwt. of steel. As the only problem to date has been the manufacture of a sufficient quantity of this material, it seems that, as long as he succeeds in producing 2000 cwt. per year, which you believe is feasible, there is reason to hope that the manufacture will maintain itself.

(Clément, vol. II(ii), p. 660)

246. The archbishop of Lyon to Colbert

LYON, *25 June 1675*

In order to comply with the instructions which I had the honour of receiving from you when I was in Paris, I have had made from the silk of Neuville two pieces of black taffeta; they have been sent by courier to Monsieur de Moulceau, who will have the honour of presenting them to you. Monsieur Octavio May, who is the man responsible for the inven-

[1] Neuville was the family estate of the archbishop's family—the Villeroy—see p. 184, note 1.

tion which gives taffeta its gloss, has supervised their manufacture; the thread for one of them has been made from Italian silk, that for the other coming from the Valence area. The said Monsieur May claims that he can obtain silk from the latter region which will make much better thread than that of Bologna; if this plan succeeds, many merchants have resolved to build mills like those of Neuville. . . .

(Depping, vol. III, p. 369)

247. Voysin de La Noiraye, intendant at Tours, to Colbert

TOURS, *11 September 1668*

In allocating the taxes, I shall take care to make it known to those towns which have applied themselves to manufacturing that the reduction in the *taille* which His Majesty has granted them is explained solely by this fact, and shall announce the contrary to the mayor, consuls and citizens of Le Mans, namely that they have been drprived this year of the relief which they could have hoped for, because of the lack of interest they have shown to date in the company of cloth manufacturers[1]. . . .

(Depping, vol. III, p. 691)

248. Chamillart, intendant at Caen, to Colbert

29 November 1666

. . . I have reduced the burden of taxation on certain merchants who are involved in the manufacture of Spanish and English cloth, London serge and cottons, and have relieved them from billeting in the towns of Caen, Bayeux, Saint-Lô and Valognes, which means that everybody, in order to obtain similar favours, is embarking on these new ventures. . . .

(Depping, vol. III, p. 775–6)

249. Colbert to all mayors and consuls

PARIS, *17 February 1671*

The King has decided, in order to bring the manufactures of the realm

[1] Two years earlier this company had been formed by six merchants of Le Mans and it replaced the weavers' gild which was dissolved in 1667.

much more into line with the statutes and regulations which have been publicised everywhere, that it is important to instil fear in those who manufacture or handle defective materials. It is for this reason that the King has issued in his royal council of commerce the decrees which you will find enclosed, in which it is stated that, in front of those places where the inspection and marking of merchandise is carried out, there shall be placed an iron collar on a pole, from which shall hang goods which are not of the quality prescribed in the regulations together with the names of the merchant and the worker who are at fault[1]. . . .

(Clément, vol. II(ii), pp. 607–8)

250. Colbert to the bailiff[2] at Chevreuse

SAINT-GERMAIN-EN-LAYE, *21 September 1669*
I have been advised that the principal reason why the manufacture of ribbons at Chevreuse has been prevented from expanding and improving is the lack of effort on the part of the workers, and also their debauchery. This has forced me to write to you in order that you may issue a prohibition, forbidding all publicans and other persons in the town from giving either food or drink to any worker in the said industry during working days, save at dinner time for one hour only, on pain of a fine of 10 *livres*. . . .

(Clément, vol. II(ii), p. 490)

251. Colbert to the bishop of Auxerre

SCEAUX, *15 September 1673*
. . . With reference to the manufacture of cloth, I am convinced that it is very advantageous to the town of Auxerre and that the expenditure which is allocated to it out of the municipal taxes is most useful and necessary.

The mayor and consuls do not realise what they are doing when they make difficulties about giving the aid and all the protection which is essential for the maintenance and expansion of this manufacture. Towns where the magistrates are sensible, and know how important it is to

---

[1] For a third offence the culprit himself was to be confined in the iron collar.
[2] The position of the *bailli* is explained above—see p. 65, note 1.

attract money by every sort of method, nurture manufactures with amazing care. But, as the town of Auxerre wishes to return to the state of laziness and self-abasement in which it formerly languished, and as it does not choose to profit from the means which I have offered it in order to lift itself from this unhappy situation, the other matters which press upon me—together with the state of my health, which is not such that I can work as hard as I used to—compel me to abandon it to its evil ways. If you, through your authority, are able to prevent it, I am sure that you will be doing the town a great service; but I am giving up this continual struggle against the pettiness of Monsieur Billard and the other governors of the said town.

(Clément, vol. II(ii), p. 680)

J. The natural resources of France, agricultural and mineral

Although the French boasted that their country was nearly self-sufficient because of its abundant natural riches, their governments during the seventeenth century showed much more interest in expanding manufactures and trade than in exploiting the land and its produce. Colbert continually exhorted intendants to encourage the increase of livestock, but the only help given by the royal ministers was the negative support afforded by their edicts prohibiting the seizure of animals as payment of the *tailles*.[1] The sole exceptions to this policy of passive exhortation arose when agricultural products had a military application, as in the cases of horses for the cavalry (*252–4*) and timber needed in shipbuilding.[2] Beyond that, Colbert confined himself to some very limited financial incentives aimed at favouring French meat at the expense of that imported from elsewhere, for ultimate export to the colonies of the New World.

The central government welcomed the development of mining, and indeed all mineral resources were by long tradition considered to be the property of the crown. Here too the actual prospecting had to be done by private enterprise and therefore by monopoly (*255*), and foreigners were often needed to provide the necessary skills (*256*).

Colbert was fortunate in having to contend with no serious famine, once the effects of the bad harvests in 1660 and 1661 had passed. Then grain had to be moved from one province to another (*257*) giving local privileged bodies a chance to exploit the plight of others (*258*). In most years no drastic government action was required, and therefore no general regulations were evolved. After the plentiful crop of 1668, the export of corn was permitted when the state of the market allowed. France was a land of such extent and variety that, even when some provinces suffered an economic setback, others could be called upon to help.

---

[1] See pp. 97–9. Taxes might also be reduced if a harvest had been poor.
[2] The forests came under direct royal control and had their own laws.

252. Circular from Colbert to all intendants

5 June 1663

As the King has deemed the restoration of horse-breeding throughout the provinces of his realm to be most important for his service and beneficial for his subjects, both in order to have the number of horses necessary for equipping his cavalry in war-time and to avoid the necessity of transferring large sums each year into foreign lands to purchase them, he has resolved to devote to it a part of the energies which he directs towards the running of his state and to promote everything which helps it to flourish. To which end he has chosen Monsieur Garsault, one of the equerries of his Great Stables, to visit every province in the kingdom and discover the state of horse-breeding and the means of re-establishing it once again, at the same time encouraging the nobility to participate in it. . . .

(Depping, vol. III, p. 663)

253. Decree of the royal council re-establishing horse-breeding in the kingdom

PARIS, *17 October 1665*

As the King wishes that particular care be taken to re-establish horse-breeding in the kingdom. . ., His Majesty has sent inspectors to examine existing studs and to find suitable places for creating new ones and, having bought a number of stallions in Frisia, Holland, Denmark and Barbary for breeding, intends to distribute those which are suitable for carriage-horses along the sea coasts, from the Brittany border to the Garonne, where mares of appropriate size may be found; and the Barbary horses in the provinces of Poitou, Saintonge and Auvergne; but in order to encourage those individuals who are entrusted with one of these animals designed for breeding, it is reasonable to accord them certain privileges as a reward for the efforts they are making towards fulfilling His Majesty's plans for the good of his service and his people. His Majesty, in his council, has commissioned and commissions Monsieur Garsault, equerry of his Great Stables, to distribute the said stallions in the places he considers most appropriate within the aforementioned provinces, and put them in the care of individuals whom he selects. . . .

His Majesty permits these men to charge 100 *sous* for each mare served. . . .

(Isambert, vol. XVIII, pp. 63–4)

254. Colbert to Bazin de Bezons, intendant at Limoges

2 May 1680

The paucity of foals to be found at the fair of Châlus leads me to believe that the revival of horse-breeding in this province has not been as successful as the King desired. Always apply yourself to the task of creating as much enthusiasm for it as you can; and as it depends to some degree on the stallions, there is perhaps nothing more vital than to buy half-a-dozen of the finest foals each year and to have them fed until the age of six or seven, at some place in the generality, in order that they may be used at stud when they are old enough. . . .

(Clément, vol. IV, p. 273, note 1)

255. Concession for mining

SAINT-GERMAIN-EN-LAYE, *19 April 1682*

From Jean-Baptiste Colbert . . ., superintendent and general reformer of mines and mining, greeting:

With reference to the plea presented to His Majesty by Monsieur de Liscouët de Coëtmen, saying that there are lead and tin mines in the parish of Carnot, in the diocese of Cornouailles in Brittany, which he wishes to open up, excavate and deepen in order to smelt and purify these ores, on payment to His Majesty of 10% of his profits and other income from the mines, if it please His Majesty to accord to him and his family for —— years the privilege of doing so, and excluding all others from participating, but compensating the owners of the land; and to permit him to build forges, furnaces and other things which he may need . . .; His Majesty will grant permission for him to do so. . . .

(Clément, vol. IV, p. 603)

256. Penautier, treasurer of the Estates of Languedoc, to Colbert

September 1667

As a knowledge of lead and copper mining and of signs indicating rich deposits is totally lacking in France, it will undoubtedly be necessary, if the plan to develop them is to succeed, to obtain the services of an experienced man from either Sweden or Germany, who has in particular the quality, through long experiment and observation, of finding the places and the rocks which are likely to bear abundant veins of copper suitable for mining, and who will be able to deduce, from exterior and interior evidence, as soon as work has begun to open up a mine, whether by the position and the character of the seams it will be rich enough to merit the labour and expense of pursuing it deeper into the ground.

By this means we shall not fall into the error which occurs daily in Languedoc, namely that one devotes oneself to the vigorous pursuit of a vein which often peters out and ends in nothing, and neglects those which sometimes have later proved to be the best and richest.

To remedy this evil, Monseigneur Colbert is very humbly requested to bring someone from Sweden of this calibre. . . .

(Depping, vol. III, p. 803)

PÉZENAS, *5 April 1669*

. . . From all that the Swedes have done here, it is an established fact that they know more than other men and, whatever one may say, we are indebted to them for the knowledge they have given us of how to judge seams and how to follow them. . . .

(Depping, vol. III, p. 804–5)

257. Louis XIV to the maréchal de La Meilleraye, governor of Brittany

PARIS, *18 February 1662*

I have given orders for the purchasing in Brittany of 1000 tons of corn, which is to be brought here as soon as possible, just as I have had it sent from other countries and from those provinces of my kingdom where the harvest has been better, with the intention of alleviating the famine which has been so severe this year in some areas. And as this is something very close to my heart, I have chosen to write you this letter in my own hand, to make it known that I wish you to facilitate the purchase and transport of this same amount of corn by doing everything which your office gives you power to do . . ., seeing that this is a matter of bringing relief to my subjects. . . .

(Louis XIV, *Oeuvres*, vol. V, pp. 74–5)

258. Louis XIV to the marquis de Saint-Luc, commandant in Guyenne

PARIS, *5 March 1662*

Since writing the enclosed letter, I have heard that it has been decided at the *parlement* of Bordeaux to send me a remonstrance, suggesting that only 10,000 *setiers*[1] of corn should be allowed to leave my province of Guyenne, instead of the 40,000 *setiers* which I have ordered from there to help the provinces in this region where it has been a bad year; and, because I know better than anyone else the needs of my subjects, I add these lines to my earlier letter to confirm that I intend, notwithstanding these deliberations or anything else to the contrary, that the amount of corn which I ordered shall be provided, and brought here from Guyenne immediately, to be sent to these areas and distributed to the poor people; for I am absolutely certain that, if it seems at present that there is not enough of it in that same province, this is only because they wish to sell it to me at a higher price, and not because they fear a shortage. You will therefore inform the *parlement* and the consuls of Bordeaux, once and for all, that I expect to be obeyed without any further retort or delay. . . .

(Louis XIV, *Oeuvres*, vol. V, pp. 79–80)

K. Conclusion: A conflict of priorities—economic expansion and the need to increase indirect taxation

The enlargement of the French merchant fleet and the expansion of French manufactures were two constant themes in the economic policy of Colbert, and to further those ends he was prepared to make extensive fiscal and financial concessions. Yet, in the difficult years after the beginning of the Dutch War, the increasing needs of the royal treasury forced him to retrace his steps. It proved impossible to reduce both direct and indirect taxes, to abolish internal tolls, to

[1] A *setier* was equivalent to about eight pints.

liquidate the debts of the towns, to suppress surplus office-holders and to unseat the financiers and usurers. Given that taxation had to be increased, he preferred to raise indirect taxes because they fell on a wider proportion of the population,[1] but this imposed restraint on the industries whose products were now to be more heavily taxed and frequently provoked disturbances in areas subject to the new levies. Although in 1680 Colbert could designate the excessive *aides* as one of the principal causes of the present economic distress,[2] just as he had done in 1664,[3] in fact those taxes—principally on wine but also on certain foodstuffs—increased steadily throughout his ministry (*259*). The greatest improvements which could be made in indirect taxation were in reducing the corruption of officials, standardising the rates throughout the country and simplifying the multiplicity of separate levies into single larger ones.[4] Even these plans proved too ambitious, but any success they achieved resulted only in improved receipts for the royal treasury—never in a reduced burden for the taxpayer. The indirect taxes and their collectors were always more unpopular than the *tailles*, and, while Colbert claimed that he tried to avoid increases on necessities such as salt,[5] the commodities he did single out frequently seemed near necessities to the ordinary people. The duties on tobacco and on the everyday metalware used by the bulk of the population caused great ill-feeling; although neither was a totally novel levy, those proposed by Colbert were more stringent and burdensome than any devised by previous ministers. These two edicts, together with a third insisting that all legal acts be transferred to specially stamped paper, were principal reasons for the 1675 rebellions in Bordeaux and Brittany.[6] It was another indirect levy, this time on wine, which sparked off a revolt in south-west France during 1664 and 1665.[7]

Thus Colbert made some advance in expanding the economy of the kingdom, but the scope of his activities was essentially limited by vested interests and local privileges. Most of his policies—for colonial companies, the canal of Languedoc, development of industries, simplification of taxes, tolls and tariffs, and many more—had been evolved by his predecessors as royal ministers. Sometimes he achieved more than they had, often he was defeated by the same forces which had been too strong for them. Even his successes were frequently short-lived, falling prey to the economic pressures which attended the lengthy wars of Louis XIV's later reign. Despite his efforts, France still remained a poor participant in the European economic race, where the smaller kingdom of England and the much smaller Dutch Republic led the field. For the hundred years which separated the

---

[1] See p. 83.
[2] See p. 89.
[3] See p. 174.
[4] See pp. 109–11, 201–5 and 210–11.
[5] See p. 118 and 120.
[6] See pp. 237–8, 241, 247 and 252. The tobacco and stamped paper taxes were regarded as particularly harmful by Colbert in his 1680 survey—see p. 89; yet he had been optimistic about the yield of the latter on its creation in 1673.
[7] See pp. 260–4.

death of Colbert from the French Revolution, two paradoxes continued to puzzle royal ministers and reformist writers—firstly that, although certain elements in society were undeniably rich, the treasury remained poor; secondly that, while most of them believed France to be abundant in natural resources and potentially self-sufficient, the considerable reluctance to develop these God-given advantages meant that many Frenchmen lived in a state of hardship and misery.

259. Table showing the yield of the *aides*

Year	*Livres*
1661	8,140,000
1662	9,931,000
1663	12,200,000
1664	13,720,000
1666	14,673,000
1675	19,600,000
1682	22,000,000
1683	22,000,000

(Clamageran, vol. II, p. 639)

8 REVOLT

The reign of Louis XIV, like those of other *ancien régime* kings, was punctuated by a number of short-lived and localised rebellions. The history of these insurrections reveals, often in their most extreme form, many of those characteristics of French society and administration which have been described in preceding pages—the obstructive behaviour of provincial Estates, *parlements*, municipal authorities and royal officials; the conflict between centralised government and provincial institutions, between royal power and local privilege; the way in which certain social groups sank their sometimes considerable differences and united in resisting the greater threat to their position as posed by the forces of the crown; and the difficulty for the ministers of punishing more than just the exceptional giant among the extensive ranks of the corrupt and the rebellious. The documents in this last chapter are concerned with only three of these disturbances—the 'Révolte du papier timbré' of 1675 in Brittany, the 'Guerre du Lustucru' of 1662 in the small province around Boulogne, and the uprising caused by taxes on wine in Guyenne during 1664 and the subsequent years. Although most revolts would not have taken place if the poorer classes of town and countryside had not been enduring a spell of unusual economic hardship, the occasion was usually provided by the crown through its imposition of some novel or increased fiscal levy. The underlying economic crisis might have been brought about by harvest failure as in 1662, or by measures designed to finance expensive wars as in 1675, but the new taxes which actually signalled the start of the rising could well be offensive because they attacked provincial immunities rather than because they were crippling in themselves. The result was nevertheless to unite the two elements in society, the poor and the privileged, who rose in opposition to the royal power while they sought redress for their very different grievances. The revolts were usually localised because economic hardship might itself affect only a relatively small part of the kingdom at a particular moment, because different provinces cherished different privileges, and because the central government wisely imposed controversial levies only on certain areas at any one time, with the specific intention of preventing just such a widespread reaction.

A. The Breton revolt of 1675: Provincial unity in opposing the crown

Brittany, conscious of its comparatively recent union with the French crown, was perhaps the most separatist and independent province of the kingdom, guarding its many liberties from attack by the royal power. The complaints which caused it to rise in open disobedience against government authority during the summer of 1675 were many, with different social groups and parts of the province stressing some more than others. The rebels in Upper Brittany, the eastern half of the province, were all agreed in designating three new taxes as their principal reason for taking up arms—the stamped paper tax which was to give the revolt its name and the impositions on tobacco and pewter.[1] In addition the merchants were annoyed because the anti-Dutch tariff legislation which had preceded the outbreak of war between France and the Republic, and the eventual closing of the Breton ports, had deprived them of unrestricted contact with their regular trading partners—the Hollanders and the English.[2] Brittany was outside the customs union of the *cinq grosses fermes*, and therefore had grown used to trading with other countries because no customs dues were levied, rather than with the rest of France which involved the payment of entry and exit dues.[3] The new legislation meant that the province was now trapped between the still operative old internal customs barriers and the new national economic frontiers. Further hostility among the Bretons was aroused by the attempts of the central government to undermine the privileges of the provincial Estates and to reduce the extensive seigneurial jurisdictions which continued to exist side by side with the royal system of justice.[4] In Brittany these private judicial courts, a legacy of the feudal past, had survived in greater numbers than elsewhere in the kingdom, and Louis XIV was determined at least to stamp out usurped noble jurisdictions, even if it would be very difficult to suppress the legitimate ones. As was its usual practice, the central government launched an attack—within the restricted geographical areas it had selected—on a number of controversial aspects of provincial life and privilege at the same time, hoping to provoke sufficient opposition that it could then magnanimously withdraw some of the offensive edicts in return for a compromise agreement with the province to the effect that its inhabitants would accept the remainder. In this case, however, the local reaction was much more violent than the government would have wished.

Revolt was an infectious disease, and Brittany was not alone in openly rejecting royal demands in 1675. As in so many seventeenth-century French uprisings, the first blows were struck by vagabonds and the humblest townsmen, although the nobles of the sword and the robe were not slow to encourage them discreetly; the *bourgeois* were more keen to preserve order, but they would not actively support the government in implementing its controversial policies; the *parlement* of Brittany, which had a history of insolent opposition to royal orders, made no real attempt to calm the rebels *(260)*,[5] unlike its sister court at Bordeaux which did order the execution of some of the culprits; in addition there is evidence that royal agents and tax-farmers sometimes saw it as in their own best interests to foment further disorders *(261–2)*.

[1] See also the introductory remarks on pp. 234–5.
[2] See pp. 189–94.
[3] See pp. 200–2 and 204–5.
[4] These policies had already caused considerable bad feeling at the 1673 Estates—see p. 54.
[5] See pp. 138–40 and 147–8.

260. The duc de Chaulnes, governor of Brittany, to Colbert

PARIS, *19 April 1675*

I wrote to the principal towns of Brittany as soon as I learned of the first uprisings which had been caused by the news of the insurrection at Bordeaux, and I have received replies which are full of obedience. . . .

(Depping, vol. III, p. 254)

PARIS, *22 April 1675*

I am sending you the letters I have just received by an express courier, whom Monsieur de Coëtlogon sent from Rennes to Monsieur de Pomponne. They will show you that at Rennes last Friday there was an uprising by a rabble of vagabonds, most of whom were strangers; that the town did its duty and played no part, and that the few nobles who were there have made professions of their devotion to the service of the King, so that, by the same letters, you will see that all is calm. . . .

(Depping, vol. III, pp. 254–5)

RENNES, *12 June 1675*

I told you, Monsieur, in my last letter, of the agitation which began just when I was ready to send the three companies to rejoin the battalion of the Crown. . . .

This outburst stopped me from doing so, as I did not wish to give the order until calm had been restored; but as all the suburbs had taken up arms in the most insolent way, and they are much larger than the town and full of riff-raff, and as there were widespread rumours that troops were approaching from all sides, and because of the special fears of the women, complete confusion had resulted. A crowd appeared and shouted in the square outside the Town Hall, near my lodging, where I had stationed a group of the *bourgeois* guards. I went down there twice and saw only women and children aged between ten and twelve, a few much older men having disappeared by this time. In the meantime I had learned that, in the suburbs, they had placed their men in a tower that they were guarding and at one of the town gates. I ordered all the companies of *bourgeois* to arm themselves, who then drove them from their positions and restored calm to the populace. . . . The true source of this uprising is the *parlement*; angered by what has happened at Nantes and

Guingamp, the procurators and other judicial officials have spread a thousand slanders in this town against the authority of the King, and such attitudes cannot be allowed to grow within a corporation of men who are in a position of power; it is the judgments which were delivered in these two towns against those guilty of sedition, and without the right of appeal to the *parlement*, which have led the members of this court to profit by my absence at Nantes and devise the plots of which we are now seeing the effect.

(Depping, vol. III, 255–6)

RENNES, *15 June 1675*

. . . You will know from my letters that my first plan was for Monsieur Coëtlogon to raise in this town four companies of soldiers, and I even told you that, as the decision had been approved by the Town Hall, I had already appointed two captains and that they had enrolled the necessary men; but, when it was made known to them what their tasks would be, among which was the protection of the tax-collection offices, they handed back their pay and refused to serve any longer, as a result of which I decided to mount guards from the companies of the *bourgeois* militia until the arrival of the battalion of the crown. . . .

I am keeping the town, that is to say the honest *bourgeois*, in a state of loyalty and am deriving from them all the help for which one could hope from such men. 'Their obedience to my orders, the guards they have formed and the positions they have occupied create a desirable impression all the time, because they show the rabble that they are not of their party. . . .

(Lemoine, pp. 125–30)

RENNES, *30 June 1675*

I did not feel that I ought to enlarge any further in the enclosed letter on the conduct of the *parlement*; but I thought you should know privately and in greater detail of the delight it has shown in allowing me to unravel this tangle without itself taking part. It has even tried to clear its name with the people by taking no action against them, which is in fact to give tacit approval to their angry attacks on the edicts; and I can assure you that it has been only too ready to receive their petitions. With regard to Monsieur the first president, he is full of zeal and good intentions; but he shows a feebleness which one could scarcely imagine; he has often said that the *parlement* will do everything I wish, and will proclaim it publicly;

but when, in the course of specific discussions, I suggested to him that it should send out deputations to the rebels and hold meetings with them, as its sister court in Bordeaux had done, he avoided the issue by pointing out the differences between these two uprisings. However, I cannot keep from you the only proposition which has been made to me, five days ago, on behalf of the *parlement*; one member of that body told me that it was the feeling of the *parlementaires* that they should meet and, over a matter as grave and important as this, should send a deputation to the King, asking him to revoke the edicts; that a similar deputation from the town should join up with that of the *parlement*, and that by this means it would be probable that the people would lay down their arms. I replied that I did not believe that loyal servants of the King would be of this opinion. . . .

(Depping, vol. III, pp. 260–1)

261. Madame de Sévigné to Madame de Grignan

LES ROCHERS, *30 October 1675*
. . . Would you like to hear the latest news from Rennes?
. . . The day before yesterday a man named Violon, who had started off the battle and the pillaging at the stamped paper tax offices, was broken on the wheel; he was quartered after his death, and his four quarters were exposed at the four corners of the town. . . . As he was dying he said that it was the tax-farmers of the stamped paper tax who had given him twenty-five *écus* to start the uprising. . . .

(Sévigné, vol. I, pp. 894–5)

262. The duc de Chaulnes to Colbert

RENNES, *2 June 1675*
. . . The ill-founded complaints that I have received from tax officials about the losses they claim to have sustained have prompted me to warn you about them. . . .

Monsieur d'Argouges told me yesterday that not only had it been impossible to vindicate the false report of a tax official at Lamballe, who had fired two shots from a pistol in his room at eleven o'clock in the evening, in order to provoke some sedition, after which he overturned everything in his room as though it had been looted, but that the official had been forced to confess the mischief he had done. . . .

(Lemoine, pp. 114–16)

B. Lower Brittany: A spontaneous peasant revolt

Almost uniquely among the revolts which occurred during the personal rule of Louis XIV, the 1675 rebellion in the western half of Brittany was not caused by various elements in provincial society who had united against the crown, but was an uprising of the poor peasants whose targets were the provincial élites—nobles, clergy, officials, townsmen, anyone in fact who was not of their own class—as well as the royal taxes which were already in existence or were rumoured to be under consideration; nevertheless their savage methods and their failure to distinguish among guilty and innocent victims sometimes bore little relation to their specific grievances (*263–9*). Indeed these humble inhabitants of Lower Brittany, speaking their own language and scarcely conscious of any loyalty to the kingdom of which their province was technically a constituent, were whipped up by an unscrupulous leader, Le Balp, into an almost chiliastic fervour which was not typical of other French revolts at this time. It was this spirit which led some of them to produce their revolutionary manifesto, the *Code paysan* (*270*), which is equally remarkable, although its demands received scant attention from the authorities once the insurgents had been suppressed. It is true that rules of land tenure and traditions of seigneurial jurisdiction made the Breton peasant less secure than other French peasants, but that does not fully explain the passionate nature of their protest.

263. The marquis de Névet, commander of the troops in the diocese of Cornouailles, to the duc de Chaulnes

LÉZARGANT, *19 July 1675*

. . . There also came to see me this morning a common man on behalf of twelve parishes around Châteaulin to show me a remonstrance which they had drawn up, in order that I might present it to you. I found its demands to be quite justified. In it they beg for mercy from the King and make no conditions either about the edicts or about anything else, but simply ask for justice against wicked nobles, magistrates and extortionate tax-collectors. This man even promised me on his life that in a short time he could arrange for every parish in the diocese to subscribe to its provisions, if I would give him permission to publish it, which is what I have done. . . .

(Lemoine, pp. 189–90)

264. The duc de Chaulnes to Colbert

RENNES, *26 June 1675*

. . . Calm is but slowly returning to the diocese of Cornouailles, and the people going back to their homes, since the 8th of this month when they rose up in the same way as the men of this town. But they are nevertheless still in a perpetual state of great agitation and have even turned against their parish priests, whom they accuse of treason. Monsieur le marquis de La Roche, governor of Quimper, wrote to me that on the 23rd a number of parishes assembled together, although without sounding the alarm bell, and attacked the house of a nobleman who received wounds from a number of blows; then they ransacked a local office of the stamped paper tax which is the current target of their insurrection, and he assures me that these people are in such a state of misery that further manifestations of their rage and brutality are greatly to be feared. . . .

(Lemoine, pp. 149–50)

265. The case of Le Balp and the marquis de Montgaillard: Statement by the marquise de Montgaillard against Pongan and Beaumont (1677)[1]

. . . When the peasants of Lower Brittany began to rebel, there were no troops whatsoever in this province. It was that which prompted the rebels to pillage more than two hundred noble houses without meeting any trouble. They marched off under guard all those whom they did not kill, nobles, priests and others, compelling them to go with them to pillage some other place, and thus increased the ranks of their troops from day to day in order to give their cause a better name and make men believe that people of standing had joined them. They even gave posts to those who went with them, no matter who they were, as in the case of the son of a nobleman who served as a lieutenant to his father's miller for the fifteen days until he managed to escape.

They killed everyone who opposed their will, whether for refusing to go with them or for refusing to sign documents which were presented to them. Messieurs de Carcelaun and de Saint-Pierre were hacked to pieces along with many others; the marquis de La Coste, the King's lieutenant

---

[1] Although this case was heard in 1677, it refers here to the events of 1675.

in the province, was on the brink of death from the wounds he received.

The prospect of such perils forced the nobles to leave the country-side. . . .

(Lemoine, pp. 258–9)

266. Petition of Gilles Dupré, innkeeper of Maël-Pestivien (1675)

. . . On 18 July last he was surprised to find his house invaded by one Mengui, guardian of the peace, of the village of Kerlern, with Thomas, called Manchot, Charles Kervern and other accomplices, who were armed with muskets, pistols, picks, bill-hooks, iron-tipped forks and other offensive weapons, and showed themselves to be overcome with wine and in a state of great agitation; they, having entered the said building, beat and tormented the supplicant, his wife and his servants with gross insults and violence, smashed the furniture, furtively went off with anything movable and committed pillage and theft of an unprecedented kind, even driving nails into three casks of wine which he had there, drinking their fill and allowing the rest to flow freely . . ., saying that this was the hour of their absolute dominion, and sneering at the King our sovereign lord and at his edicts, as well as at his justice. . . .

(Lemoine, pp. 305–6)

267. The bishop of Saint-Malo to Colbert

RENNES, *30 June 1675*

. . . In Lower Brittany the peasants of a number of parishes in the neighbourhood of Quimper have risen against the nobility and against an imaginary salt-tax which certain malicious minds have led them to fear will be imposed on them. . . .

(Lemoine, pp. 170–1)

SAINT-JEAN-DES-PRÉS, *23 July 1675*

. . . The peasants from some of the parishes around Pontivy threatened to come, last Sunday and on Monday which was a feast-day, to burn and pillage the house of a farmer of our taxes called Lapierre and certain others, whom the rabble designated as extortioners, and they were as good as their word for in fact, in broad daylight on the Sunday, about a good two thousand of them appeared as an angry mob in the town of Pontivy and hurled themselves upon the house of the said Lapierre, broke down the door, looted all the furniture they could carry, took all the wine in the cellar, which comprised some four hundred and forty hogsheads, and rolled them into the street where they broke them open and drank the contents, save for a few which they rolled or carried outside the town in order to share out later among themselves; when they were well and truly drunk, they returned to the house, smashed the rest of the furniture and demolished part of the building; the poor *bourgeois*, whose town stood wide open to them, dared not oppose them nor resist their violence, and each of them piled up and locked away all that he could find in his house in the way of furniture and papers, fearing that these things would otherwise be looted, but these scoundrels were not content with that and threatened during the evening that they would return the following day to mete out the same treatment to a large number of other households, which they proudly set about doing yesterday morning.... But the *bourgeois* were a little less frightened than they had been on the preceding day, and a man named Lavoir, who was at the castle of Madame de Rohan, resolved, together with the seneschal of the town and a number of citizens, to leave the castle bearing what they had collected together in the way of shotguns and muskets and to fire upon this riff-raff, who for the most part had no firearms and were a much smaller number than on the preceding day; this plan was put into action so well that they killed fifteen or sixteen and wounded many more, with the result that the rest of the peasants took fright and retired to the countryside, still shouting that they would return in greater force the next day and visit them again, but as their anger normally overtakes them only on feast-days, when they become thoroughly drunk and then begin some disorder, there is every sign that they will not undertake any new enterprise at the earliest before Thursday and Friday, which are also feasts, and not during these two working days. . . .

(Lemoine, pp. 194–7)

268. The duc de Chaulnes to Colbert

PORT-LOUIS, *13 July 1675*
Since I learned that calm had almost returned to the diocese of Quimper,

I have heard that popular agitation has spread to the diocese of Léon where a mob of two or three thousand men have attacked the country-house belonging to Monsieur de Trévigny which in truth was built almost entirely by means of forced labour services. . . .

(Lemoine, p. 182)

269. Transaction between the religious of the abbey of Langonnet and the vassals of the abbey

14 July 1675

There have appeared before us—the undersigned notaries of the juris-diction of Langonnet—the Reverend Father Prior and the Religious of the abbey of Langonnet who declare that they will not claim the right to demand from their men and vassals of the parish of Tréaugan any tithe on buckwheat and promise to accept the annual rents of their said vassals in kind without the right to increase them, also promising to enclose the woods of Douvant, Couvau and Rosmartin and Costréaugan or, failing that, to permit the said vassals to pasture their animals there on payment to the said abbey of the fowls traditionally due for this concession. . . .

(Lemoine, pp. 182–3)

270. The Peasant Code[1]

Copy of the rules drawn up by the honourable inhabitants of the fourteen united parishes on the coast between Douarnenez and Concarneau, to be observed therein without exception until Michaelmas next under pen-alty of a broken skull.

1. That the said fourteen parishes, joined together in the cause of the liberty of the province, shall send six of the most worthy men in the parishes to the next Estates, to explain the reasons for their uprising, and that their expenses shall be paid by their communities, who shall provide each of them with a red cap and jacket, blue breeches, and a coat and other clothing appropriate to their position.

2. That the inhabitants of the fourteen united parishes shall lay down

[1] 2 July 1675. Printed in A. de La Borderie, *La révolte du papier timbré advenue en Bretagne en 1675: histoire et documents*. Saint-Brieuc, 1884.

their arms and shall stop all acts of authority until Michaelmas next, as a special favour to the nobles whom they shall call on to return to their country-houses as soon as possible; failing which they shall forfeit the said favour.

3. That it shall be forbidden to sound the alarm bell and to summon an assembly of armed men without the universal consent of the said union, and those who disobey shall be hanged from the belfries. . . .

4. That the right to demand a share of the harvest and to require labour services, as claimed by the said nobles, shall be abolished, as they are a violation of Armorican liberty.

5. That to establish more firmly the peace and goodwill between the nobles and the honourable inhabitants of the said parishes, they shall arrange marriages among themselves, on the understanding that, when the daughters of nobles choose their husbands from the common people, they shall ennoble them and their descendants, who shall share equally among themselves the wealth they inherit.

6. That it is forbidden, on pain of being hanged from a gibbet, to give shelter to the salt-tax collector and to his children, and to provide them with food or with any other goods; on the contrary, it is prescribed that they be tormented as if by a mad dog.

7. That there shall be levied, for no matter what tax, not more than 100 *sous* per hogshead of wine from outside, and 1 *écu* for that from vineyards within the province, provided that innkeepers and landlords shall sell the former at 5 *sous* and the latter at 3 *sous* per quart.

8. That money from the ancient hearth-tax shall be used to buy tobacco, which shall be distributed with the consecrated bread at parish masses, for the gratification of the parishioners.

9. That the rectors, vicars and priests shall be paid a fixed salary for their services to their parishioners, and shall not be able to claim the right to any kind of tithe, or to demand any additional payment for all their other religious duties.

10. That justice shall be administered by able men chosen from among our honourable citizens, who shall be paid a salary, as shall their clerks, so that they cannot claim any fee for sitting from the parties concerned, on pain of punishment;—and that stamped paper shall be held in execration by them and their successors, to which end all the acts and writs which have been written upon it shall be copied on to other paper and shall then be burned, so that even the memory of stamped paper shall be entirely blotted out.

11. That hunting shall be forbidden to everyone, whosoever he be,

from the first day of March until mid-September, and that dovecots shall be burned down and permission given to kill pigeons in the fields.[1]

12. That it shall be permissible to go to the mills when one chooses and that millers shall be compelled to give back flour of the same weight as the corn.

13. That the town of Quimper and others nearby shall be constrained by force of arms to approve and ratify these present regulations, on pain of being declared enemies of Armorican freedom and their citizens punished on the spot; it is forbidden to take any produce or merchandise there until they have satisfied these conditions, on pain of a broken skull.

14. That the present regulations shall be read and published with the announcements at high mass and in the square of every town and in every parish, and affixed to the crosses which shall be placed there.

(*Signed*) The Skull-breaker and the People

C. The suppression of the Breton revolt: Punishment and compromise

When the government had to suppress a revolt, it followed its customary course of pardoning the many and severely punishing the most culpable few. The policies of the centre and the provinces diverged so frequently, each side being able to provide reasonable evidence for its stance, that it would be unwise of the crown to impose excessive penalties on people who were only following the best interests of their region as they saw them. It was better simply to punish those whose methods were violent by any standards, and seek a compromise with the rest. The desire of the ministers was to reimpose peace as quickly as possible, because there were insufficient troops to sustain lengthy local wars, and the problems of military indiscipline and inadequate pay for the soldiery soon undermined the maintenance of order and calm. Moreover, foreign enemies keenly followed, and even encouraged, these troubles which diverted the attention of the government from its international involvements.

The demands of the farming year of necessity interrupted the activities of the rebels and the sheer appearance of troops frightened some of them into submission (*271*). The crown, through the governor of Brittany, was careful to take account of the separatist feelings of the province as a means of reducing tension (*272–4*) and to avoid inflicting suffering on those areas which had remained loyal (*275–6*). When the fire of the rebel cause had been quenched, the governor struck hard, aiming his blows at the privileges which the people so proudly cherished rather than at a mass of individuals (*277–8*), although the Breton *parlement* undoubtedly deserved its fate. The province was quick to show its docile acceptance of the royal will, which was prepared to be magnanimous in return (*279–80*), and this spirit of cooperation lasted for a few years. Yet, despite the generous inten-

[1] The noble right to keep pigeons was particularly burdensome to the peasant, who was not allowed to kill the birds as they raided his precious crops.

tions of the governor, the reality of a military presence in Brittany had been as destructive and oppressive as ever (*281*).

271. Madame de Sévigné to Madame de Grignan

PARIS, *24 July 1675*
. . . I am waiting . . . for a spell of peace in Brittany before I set off there. . . . We have no wish to go and throw ourselves into the fury which is turning our province upside down. It increases daily. . . . It is thought that the harvest will disperse these mobs of rebels; because in the end they will have to gather in their corn. There are six or seven thousand of them, of whom the most skilful do not understand a word of French. Monsieur de Boucherat was recounting to me the other day how a priest had received a clock in the presence of his parishioners which had been sent to him 'from France' (for that is what they said). . . .

(Sévigné, vol. I, pp. 767–71)

LA SILLERAYE, *24 September 1675*
. . . Some forty or fifty of our poor Lower Bretons had gathered together as a mob in the fields, and, as soon as they saw the soldiers, they threw themselves down on their knees and cried 'mea culpa': they are the only words of French they know; just like our Frenchmen who say that in Germany not a word of Latin is said at the mass except 'Kyrie eleison'. Nevertheless they will not fail to hang these poor Bretons: they ask only for wine and tobacco and they are put to death. . . .

(Sévigné, vol. I, pp. 859–60)

272. The bishop of Saint-Malo to Colbert

SAINT-JEAN-DES-PRÉS, *23 July 1675*
. . . As for me, Monsieur, eight or ten days ago I took it into my head to send to Monsieur le duc de Chaulnes at Fort-Louis one of the missionaries from my seminary who is a Lower Breton by birth, speaks the language of that area fluently, and has a very gentle and winning manner in dealing with people, in order that he, on the pretext of visiting his parents all the way over at Saint-Paul-de-Léon, would travel through the whole

of Lower Brittany and could talk to the peasants in their own Breton tongue as if he were one of them, thus replacing their parish priests in whom they no longer have any confidence; he was to try and persuade the rebellious parishes to submit and come to seek Monsieur le duc de Chaulnes through their representatives, imploring him to intercede on their behalf in begging the King's mercy and in obtaining his pardon; this plan succeeded so well that Monsieur le duc de Chaulnes has sent me his warmest thanks and told me that by this means many parishes have already shown themselves repentant and have sent deputies to him with this aim in view; however, the troubles which broke out yesterday and the day before at Pontivy[1] will no doubt cause us to lose all this ground which we have made, and will set such an evil example throughout the whole of Lower Brittany that I begin to despair of our ever succeeding in the future in calming spirits as primitive as these by gentle methods. . . .

(Lemoine, pp. 199–200)

273. Decree of the duc de Chaulnes

RENNES, *12 June 1675*

As we have been informed that many parishes near Châteaulin took up arms only on hearing the ringing of the alarm bell, which we have ordered to be sounded when enemy vessels appear off the coast, and as we consider that they had no evil intentions, we now order them to lay down their arms until such time as the service of the King obliges them to take them up once more, and we assure them that they will not be pursued by the law; in addition we declare to be disturbers of the peace of the community all those who have sown the rumour that the King wished to impose the salt tax or a levy on corn, for nothing is more contrary to his intentions which are to maintain this province in all its privileges.

(Lemoine, p. 125)

274. The duc de Chaulnes to Colbert

RENNES, *15 June 1675*

. . . On the 10th I sent the three companies of troops to rejoin the battalion, and they passed through one of the suburbs without any trouble, although disorder broke out again that evening once the effects of wine

[1] See pp. 244–5.

had made themselves felt; no longer able to use the presence of troops within the town as a pretext, they spread a thousand rumours that others were coming in much larger numbers than these three companies. As this emotion was caused only by the fear of soldiers, I believed that it would soon subside. The rebels wished to take advantage of it and try to obtain from the *parlement* the revocation of the edicts, and spread the rumour that they would go next morning to demand that the town crier be sent out to publish abroad the revocation. . . . But they did not dare to come; the whole morning of that day, which was the 12th, was on the contrary very peaceful, but when I received news that the peasants of Lower Brittany were causing a commotion because of the rumour which had been spread that His Majesty wished to impose a tax on corn and salt, I resorted to the certain remedy of summoning the Estates, and this announcement has produced the best possible effect; men laid down their arms in the suburbs, and there just remained a few riff-raff on guard at one of the gates leading to them.[1] One can safely say that all was peaceful on the following day and yesterday, which was the procession of the Holy Sacrament. . . .

(Lemoine, pp. 125–9)

275. The duc de Chaulnes to Louvois[2]

PORT-LOUIS, *3 August 1675*

I have learned on the return of Monsieur de Beaumont of the decision taken by His Majesty to send a considerable body of troops into this province and, as I hear from Monsieur de Jonville that no order has been made for paying them while they are stationed in the towns, I believe that you will not take it amiss, Monsieur, if I take the liberty to point out to you the consequences of treating those towns which have remained loyal in the same way as those areas of the countryside which have risen up, thereby failing to distinguish between those who have followed the path of duty and those who have departed from it. The towns alone have stemmed the tide of sedition and, if they were to be punished by having to pay for the cost of troops, it is to be feared that on a similar occasion the

[1] The summoning of the Estates had a calming effect only on the people of Upper Brittany of course. The revolt in Lower Brittany continued throughout July, as documents above have shown. But for towns like Rennes, the revolt was over.

[2] The marquis de Louvois, as the minister responsible for war, dealt with the military aspects of the involvement in Brittany.

memory of their punishment would lead them to take extreme action which would be prejudicial to the interests of the King, especially so because I have kept them in a mood of obedience through the hope of the favours they would receive if they did not follow the example of Rennes and Nantes. . . .[1]

(Lemoine, p. 211)

276. Louvois to the duc de Chaulnes

VERSAILLES, *12 August 1675*

The letter which you have done me the honour of writing to me on 3 August has been given to me. As the troops going to Brittany have orders to carry out any instructions you may give them, it is for you to send them to whatever places you think will be most useful for the service of the King; and with regard to their maintenance and supplies, it is His Majesty's intention that while they are marching through the province they shall live off the people; but those whom you station in loyal towns shall be given full pay by the crown which the commissioner Monsieur de Jonville shall hand over to them punctually. And as His Majesty is confident that you will send them in against the rebellious areas, His Majesty intends that while they are there they shall live at the expense of the countryside, and that when they are encamped Monsieur de La Rapée, who is marching with them, will arrange for the provision of their bread ration, animals and forage for their subsistence, which shall be taken from those parts which revolted.

(Lemoine, pp. 214–15)

277. The Amsterdam Gazette

29 October 1675

Paris, 22 October. Letters from Rennes in Brittany announce that Monsieur le duc de Chaulnes has arrived there with 3000 men of the King's troops, with orders to transport the *parlement* from that town to the town of Vannes, in case the people should be unwilling to pay the sums

[1] The loyal towns referred to here are of course those of Lower Brittany, where the revolt was mainly the work of peasants and the towns were a target. In Upper Brittany, towns like Rennes and Nantes led the revolt, even if their wealthier *bourgeois* showed less enthusiasm for it.

required of them to be given as compensation to those men who have an interest in the tax-farms.

31 October 1675
Paris, 25 October. The troops who have been sent into Rennes are living there in whatever manner they please; they are on guard night and day, and the townsmen have never been in such a state of dismay. The *parlement* has been transferred from there to Vannes, the presidial court to Lamballe, and the Jesuit college has been closed down. . . . The majority of the peasants in the surrounding countryside have run away and are seeking shelter, some this way, some that, with the result that the nobles now find themselves without tenants in their farms.

278. Madame de Sévigné to Madame de Grignan

LES ROCHERS, *20 October 1675*
. . . Monsieur de Chaulnes is at Rennes with four thousand men; he has transferred the *parlement* to Vannes; that is a most grievous blow. The downfall of Rennes will bring with it that of the whole province. . . . I am far from being afraid of these troops; but I share the sadness and the sorrow of all the province. People do not believe that the Estates will meet; and if they do, it will be to buy off once more the edicts which we bought off two years ago for 2,500,000 *livres*[1] and which have now been imposed on us again, to which will perhaps be added a price for the return of the *parlement* to Rennes. . . .

(Sévigné, vol. I, pp. 884–5)

LES ROCHERS, *27 October 1675*
. . . There are five thousand troops at Rennes, of whom more than half will pass the winter there. . . . Twenty-five or thirty men have been selected at random and are going to be hanged. The *parlement* has been taken away; that is the final blow, for without that Rennes does not even bear comparison with a town like Vitré. . . .

(Sévigné, vol. I, pp. 891–2)

[1] For Madame de Sévigné's verdict on this earlier dispute over the edicts, See p. 59. (Pp. 53–9 are all concerned with the Breton Estates of 1673.)

279. The French Gazette

16 November 1675

Dinan, Brittany, 11 November. The duc de Chaulnes, governor of this province, declared open our Estates on the 8th of the month. The following day was occupied with the traditional formalities, in the reading and the verification of the powers of the commissioners. Yesterday Messieurs de Boucherat and de Harlay Bonneuil, the first and second commissioners (the second acting as spokesman and making known the wishes of His Majesty in a most eloquent speech), announced the request for a free gift of 3,000,000 *livres*. The assembly not only agreed to it at that very moment, on a single resolution and a unanimous vote,[1] but, to underline the sorrow felt by the province for the past rebellions, it directed that a deputation consisting of the bishop of Saint-Malo, president of the clergy, the duc de Rohan, president of the nobility, and the seneschal of Nantes, in the name of the Third Estate, should go to His Majesty and expressly beseech him to overlook and to forgive in the future the bad impression of the whole province which the crimes of a few rebels have created.

280. The Amsterdam Gazette

5 December 1675

Paris, 29 November. The deputation from Brittany has obtained from the King a general pardon for all the disorders in that province, and they have set off on their return to Rennes; Monsieur de Pommereuil will take the amnesty there which the King is sending to the Bretons who, as a sign of their gratitude, have given His Majesty a free gift of 3,000,000 *livres*; he will present the amnesty to the Estates of their province.

281. The duc de Chaulnes to Louvois

REDON, *9 February 1676*

I cannot put into words, Monsieur, the havoc wreaked by the troops on

---

[1] This was a satisfactory outcome for the crown, because the enforcement of the edict on metalware and the pursuit of seigneurial jurisdictions were regarded by some royal supporters, including the duc de Chaulnes, as very costly considering the small potential financial yield—cf. pp. 58–9.

the march; the battalion of the Queen, leaving Rennes in order to go to Saint-Brieuc, has pillaged every house within four leagues of its path, and, as the troops displeasure at not having been allowed to do as they wished may lead them to take some kind of revenge, I hope you will approve when I ask you to send a circular letter to each colonel and captain, ordering them to see that their cavalry confine themselves to their duties. . . . Otherwise this province will be treated as if it were enemy territory. . . .

(Lemoine, pp. 230–1)

D. The 'Guerre de Lustucru' of 1662: A 'classic' provincial revolt

Whereas the peasants of Lower Brittany had introduced some unusual elements into the 1675 rebellion, the 1662 disturbances around the Channel port of Boulogne corresponded to a type of revolutionary movement which was reproduced in many parts of France during the seventeenth century. Although there was genuine hardship in that year, after the bad harvests of 1660 and 1661, the actual cause of the troubles was the imposition by the crown of a new tax whose sole purpose was to break the exemption from the *tailles* which the province claimed as a historical right. The tax was not in itself crippling; the dispute was simply a trial of strength between royal and local power, as Louis XIV openly states in his *Memoirs*.[1] The innovation was presented as if it were a generous concession (*282*), but the men of the Boulonnais were not to be fooled, the privileged orders making no attempt to restrain the wave of popular discontent, and a minority of nobles even falling victim to it. In general, however, the unity of social groups against the crown seems to have predominated, and such disputes between classes were untypical.

The suppression of the revolt was equally predictable. Much of it collapsed at the sight of the royal troops; a few men were savagely and rapidly executed and a number of others designated for the galleys; the leader was to be punished spectacularly, as a warning to others; and the rest of the province was to be humbled by an attack on its privileges and its pride, rather than by more conventional judicial penalties (*283*). Eventually only a proportion of those destined for the galleys were finally required to go (*284*), and of those some were unlikely physically to reach the ports where the fleet was based (*285*).

282. Register of the Council of State

Fontainebleau, 19 May 1661

As the King has been informed that the Boulonnais has suffered heavy damage because of the continual passage of troops, both cavalry and in-

[1] See pp. 8–9.

fantry, during the recent wars, and as moreover in those years a number of levies were imposed on that same province for the purpose of provisioning, financing winter quarters, making payments to enemies and other such expenses, and as His Majesty wishes that his subjects living in that province should enjoy the fruits of the peace which he has just procured for the whole of Europe, and to this end will reduce all taxation to very modest sums which are easily raised, His Majesty in council has ordered and orders that through Monsieur d'Ormesson, *maître des requêtes* at the court and intendant in the generality of Picardy, he will impose a levy of 30,000 *livres* annually on all his taxable subjects in the province of the Boulonnais, beginning in this present year. . . .

(Hamy, pp. 254–5)

283. Machault, special royal commissioner in the Boulonnais, to Colbert

MONTREUIL, *15 July 1662*

. . . The Boulonnais was formerly a county belonging to the family of La Tour du Bouillon. In 1551 . . . its peoples ceded it to King Francis I . . . on the condition that the privileges which they had enjoyed, while under the tutelage of the counts of Boulogne, be preserved. . . .

Since 1551 the kings have, from time to time, issued new letters of confirmation of these privileges, in order that they might be thus fully enjoyed, until 1658 when vital needs of state obliged His Majesty to seek some assistance from all his peoples, and he imposed a levy of 81,700 *livres* on the province for the maintenance of his troops. . . .

The decree ordering the tax was carried out. The people paid it, and the nobles were exempted on their noble property, the tax-farmers on the profits of their farms, so that all this levy fell on the ordinary people.

As the tax could rightfully last only as long as there was a war, the King immediately after peace was signed reduced it to 30,000 *livres*. And it is currently this tax, which the people believe to have been nullified by the declaration of peace, which has provoked this revolt. The people have risen up; the flame has spread from village to village; numerous vagabonds and layabouts have joined with them; their ranks have swelled; the nobles, who feared that they would not long maintain their exemption and especially so in peacetime when their services were no longer necessary, have not shown anger at this insurrection, preferring that the rebels might succeed and therefore deliver them from the cause of their fear. Thus, Monsieur, has this evil grown. . . .

I forgot to tell you that this province does pay an *aides* tax. . . .

As for the salt tax, they have never contributed to it, and thirty years ago there was a man named Carry who, having proposed on his own authority to Boulogne that an attempt should be made to establish it, was hacked to pieces by the populace. And since that time the word 'Carry' is so seditious a term throughout the province that the moment it is hurled against someone, he is immediately exposed to the fury of a people who know no mercy. . . .

(Hamy, pp. 287–90)

MONTREUIL, *10 July 1662*
. . . In the meanwhile, Monsieur, I have spent today gathering information and evidence from the large number of witnesses of the revolt who are here.

They include officials, gentlemen and others, some of whom can give eye-witness reports. There are also many men of noble birth, who have come here because they share our aims, for they have been pillaged and maltreated by the peasantry for refusing to support them. . . .

(Hamy, p. 280)

IN CAMP AT HUCQUELIERS, *11 July 1662*
The plan of which I have already told you, for subjugating the rebels of this province, has had the utmost success. From the moment that all the troops assembled within sight of their positions and made ready to attack them, at this village in which they had barricaded themselves, they took refuge in the castle and then, after some exchanges of musket-shots, surrendered unconditionally and laid down their arms.

Nearly five hundred of them thus fell into my hands, and I have put them under guard prior to taking them to Montreuil tomorrow. You can see from this great number that the King's plans for restoring his galley fleet will be assured of success.

We have taken the rebel leader, a man named Clivet, and one or two of his company. I can think of no torture too severe for such exploits. Meanwhile, Monsieur, the whole province will almost certainly remain completely calm. I am making every effort to press ahead with criminal proceedings so that order may be restored and the law be effectively enforced from the first possible moment.

Monsieur le duc d'Elbeuf under the articles of war has ordered the immediate hanging of three of them. This kind of sentence is customary on

257

such occasions. When I shall have concluded the cases against these rebels and have had them punished, there will be nothing left to do in the King's interest than to ensure that the allocations by Monsieur de Saint-Pouanges[1] of the tax of 30,000 *livres* for 1661 are observed and honoured. I even believe it will be possible to make them pay a further tax for this year as well. . . .

(Hamy, pp. 281–2)

MONTREUIL, *27 July 1662*

I am sending you a copy of the judgment which I delivered this morning. You will doubtless find it appropriate enough for frightening the whole province, and the examples which have been made will serve to restore everything to the state in which it should be.

I have designated for its execution those places where the revolt was most openly professed. . . .

Judgment

. . . We order that the house in which Clivet was living shall be demolished from top to bottom and razed to the foundations, and in its place a pyramid shall be built, and a similar one in both Samer and Marquise, to which shall be affixed a copper frame, holding a summary of this judgment and of the events which gave rise to it;

And moreover that the bells of the said Samer and Marquise, because they served as a means of sounding the alarm, calling together rebels and making them charge the King's troops, shall be taken down for one year. . . .

We have forbidden and forbid, also for one year, all fairs and markets in these said towns, and prohibit all subjects of the King from selling, buying, taking, bringing away, or trading in any merchandise and other produce there during that said time, unless they are necessary for the subsistence and life of the people. . . .

We expressly prohibit and forbid all inhabitants of the province of the Boulonnais, of no matter what rank and condition, to take up arms, and to assemble or gather together for any kind of pretext, and to utter the word 'Carry' and others tending to provoke sedition, on pain of death. . . .

(Hamy, pp. 298–9)

---

[1] Saint-Pouanges was intendant at Amiens, and was the second cousin of Colbert.

Monsieur, I am sending you a copy of the judgment I delivered this morning against Clivet. . . .

Judgment

. . . We have declared and do declare the said Bernard Postel, lord of Clivet, duly guilty in fact and in law of the crimes of sedition, rebellion, disobedience of the King's orders, of armed riot and unlawful assembly, and moreover of having been the leader and commander of the said seditious and rebels, of having pillaged, burned down and raided many houses in the said province of the Boulonnais and further of the assassination committed by him of Monsieur Belleville, in reparation for which we have declared and do declare that all his heirs have forfeited their position and are deprived of the title and quality of a noble, and at the same time we have condemned and do condemn him to make honourable amends, wearing a shirt, with his head and feet naked, a noose around his neck, and with placards in front of and behind him bearing the words 'Chief of the rebels', accompanied by the executioner of the high court, in front of the cathedral of Our Lady of Boulogne, and there on his knees, holding in his hand a burning torch weighing two pounds, to ask pardon from God, from the King and from the law for his said crimes, which being done he shall be conducted to the main square of the old town of Boulogne where the executioner shall cut off his arms, legs and thighs while he is alive on a scaffold which shall be erected for this purpose, and he shall then be laid and exhibited on a wheel, his face turned heavenward, to live for as long as God shall please. . . .

(Hamy, pp. 318–20)

284. The French Gazette

July 1662

Monsieur de Machault has been sent a decree of the council, announcing that proceedings will be instituted against 1200 of the most culpable; that those who are aged twenty and under, or seventy and over, together with the crippled and the sick, shall be set at liberty; and that from the rest, 400 of the fittest shall be selected to serve for ever in the galleys.

285. Poulletier to Colbert

MONTREUIL, *31 July 1662*

Monseigneur, when I arrived in the town of Montreuil in order to take the condemned prisoners to the galleys, Monseigneur d'Elbeuf told me that there were 400 of them and that they should leave at the first possible moment, which is what I am hoping for; but they are in a very poor state, for all are completely naked and most are ill, some dying every day. However I think that when they are in the fresh air their health will improve. . . .

(Hamy, p. 300)

E. The 1664 revolt in Guyenne: Local protection of the rebel leaders

This insurrection began as an attack on a wine tax, and demonstrates the inability of the central government to catch the chief culprits. This was partly because the forces of law and order were inadequate, but also because the local topography and men of influence in the area both conspired to hide the fugitives. At least the crown resorted to the one method which concealed its inefficiency and proclaimed its determination to bring the criminals to justice—the hanging of their effigies in public. Thus honour was partially satisfied (*286*).

286. Pellot, intendant at Bordeaux, to Colbert

BORDEAUX, *26 May 1664*

. . . A mob composed of men from Hagetmeau[1] and the surrounding area have driven out by armed force the guards and collectors of the Bordeaux wine tax,[2] who had been installed there for some time past. At first there was some resistance on the part of the said guards and collectors during two attacks which were made on different occasions, and in which men of both sides were killed and wounded; but as they feared that they could no longer hold out, and that they would be burned inside the house which they were defending, the insurgents having attempted to do this by every sort of means, if with little success as yet, the said guards and collectors withdrew during the time when the rebels would seem to have

[1] Or Hagetmau.
[2] This tax, the *convoi*, was a uniquely Bordelais levy on wines, and not one of the regular *aides*.

dispersed, though with the intention nevertheless of returning to the attack on another night. As these inhabitants of Hagetmeau have been pardoned for other revolts which they have instigated on this same matter, out of consideration for Monsieur le maréchal de Grammont who is their lord, and as they had promised to accept these tax offices and obey their instructions, all of which seems to have had a contrary effect and to have made them more impudent and tiresome, I believe that it would be wrong to overlook this new sedition, which has gone too far to avoid the punishment which it merits. Thus it is important that His Majesty should send orders as soon as possible to the two companies of dragoons who are in this province, that they come to this place and remain here until the trials of the culprits are completed and the punishments carried out. . . .

(Depping, vol. III, pp. 68–9)

MONT-DE-MARSAN, *6 August 1664*

. . . This insurrection at Hagetmeau has certainly been very considerable and quite relentless. Not content with driving out by force the guards of the wine tax, as you already know, the rebels have not dispersed since that time and have committed numerous violent acts and murders, including the killing in Hagetmeau of a father, mother and son on the grounds that these people of the town were sympathetic towards the said guards. When Monsieur Debrussy, the director of the wine tax, came to the said Hagetmeau on my instructions to re-establish the said guards there, to try to arrest the rebels and to inform them of the cases against them, in order that I could then try them, the rebels were found to have erected barricades and they fired on him and on the guards and dragoons who accompanied him. . . . They continued to attack in large numbers on subsequent nights. . . . It is claimed that there are some nobles in this conspiracy and that men have been provided by thirty or forty neighbouring parishes. . . . Complaints have been made that the troops have pillaged the town of Hagetmeau and burned houses, and that looting also took place in the houses of nobles and in nearby villages; but as in Hagetmeau they had to be broken into, because the inhabitants had deserted them, it was very difficult to stop soldiers from making themselves comfortable with whatever they might find in empty houses, and it was necessary for them to help themselves to the provisions which were there in order to live. As for the burnt houses, there was indeed one which overlooked the barricades and which, if the rebels could have seized it, as they were continually trying to do, would have made it impossible for the troops to have remained here; therefore the officers, for reasons of security, were obliged to have it burnt, and because of the wind the fire spread to three or four other houses of no importance. As for the neighbouring villages and the houses of nobles, they caused no trouble there, although they did go there to take prisoners; but this was carried out in an orderly manner, and they found almost all these villages barricaded and deserted, which is a sign of their complicity and rebelliousness. . . .

(Depping, vol. III, pp. 69–70)

MONT-DE-MARSAN, *20 August 1664*

We have dispensed some fine justice here to the rebels, and with all possible publicity. Two have been hanged, two condemned to the galleys. The principal authors of the insurrection have been condemned to be broken on the wheel in effigy, the nobles who are their accomplices to have their heads cut off, and the others accused to various penalties, while all the condemned, together with the communities who supported their causes, are to pay damages and compensation to the tax-farmer and to those who have suffered. . . .

(Depping, vol. III, p. 71)

AGEN, *3 October 1664*

. . . There are still some remnants of disorder in the Hagetmeau district. The man named Audijos, whom I sentenced in his absence to be broken on the wheel, roams the countryside with fifteen or twenty insurgents. By day he visits isolated houses and even villages, where he pillages and commits a great deal of violence, by night he withdraws and sleeps in the woods. In the parish of Costure, he has murdered the priest for publishing a decree forbidding anyone to give shelter to him as leader and to the others who have been condemned by my judgment. Three or four days ago, he laid an ambush for the guards of the wine tax, killing two on the spot and wounding others. Everything possible has been done to catch him but so far without success, because this area is very difficult and wooded, and horsemen cannot easily travel from one side to the other as it is crossed by big and sturdy hedges of thick wood, and it has many deeply rutted tracks whose high banks offer the rebels the means of firing downwards from behind the hedges, after which they retire into the woods where they cannot be pursued. . . .

(Depping, vol. III, pp. 72–3)

AGEN, *19 December 1664*

Attacks on the guards of the wine tax have in no way abated around Hagetmeau. . . .

The two companies of dragoons who are on the spot are making no great impression on this problem, either because they have been weakened by the drafting of some of their number who are collecting the *taille* in the elections of the generality of Bordeaux, or, which seems more probable to me, because the officers do not set about their task with any vigour; it being certain that on many occasions they have been warned that Audijos and the rebels were near their quarters, and yet they did not go out to attack them, even though they had orders to do so. . . .

(Depping, vol. III, p. 79)

SAINT-SEVER, *3 May 1665*

. . . Having received advice that Audijos was at Montaner in Béarn, I sent dragoons there bearing orders from me and a *pareatis*[1] from the *parlement* of Pau authorising his arrest; but as soon as they were seen in the area, the alarm bells sounded from every side. The people flocked together so that Audijos, who had heard the warning, had time to save himself. . . .

(Depping, vol. III, p. 84)

SAINT-SEVER, *9 May 1665*

. . . I did also write to you that I had heard that Audijos had been received by the consuls of Taisc in Béarn only a few days ago, and that I would enlighten you in greater detail about this information. I have since learnt for certain that Audijos was not there, but instead that it was two of his principal accomplices who have assisted him in all his evil doings; that they were friends of the consuls, and that they were allowed to leave without being arrested after being permitted to camp for the night near the town. . . .

(Depping, vol. III, pp. 87–8)

---

[1] Letters of *pareatis* authorised the execution of a legal judgment outside the area of jurisdiction of the court responsible for the decision.

SAINT-SEVER, *20 November 1665*

I am sending you, Monsieur, the draft I have prepared of a pardon in favour of the people of Chalosse and the surrounding area. I have given a summary of the facts, omitting many details. I have excepted only Audijos and the chief and most dangerous rebels, three or four from the Chalosse district, and five or six from Bayonne whose names have been given me by the best intentioned citizens. . . .

(Depping, vol. III, pp. 114–5)

AGEN, *9 August 1666.*

. . . Since last December, when the said Audijos returned from Spain, he has been living in Couture, his birth-place. . . . When he has need of men, his accomplices Plantier and Baillet gather together for him some thirty or forty men, from six or seven neighbouring parishes. . . . Since his return to the Chalosse area he has not once attacked the officers of the wine tax, but has devoted himself to killing and pillaging those in the area whom he believes have given evidence against him. . . . It is thought that Audijos and Plantier are still in hiding somewhere in that area. . . .

(Depping, vol. III, pp. 121–2)

EPILOGUE

In 1682, a year before the death of Colbert, the court of Louis XIV took up permanent residence in the elaborately and extravagantly enlarged *château* of Versailles. Yet that sumptuous setting, which dazzled the outside world, masked the declining power of the central government which surrounded the king. In 1661 the monarch and his new councils had hoped to change French society and to reform the administration, but, as the costs of war had slowly emasculated the independent strength of the royal treasury, the ministers had been forced to rely on the traditional and separatist institutions and officials forming the bureaucratic hierarchy of France. This meant that conservative provincialism prevailed, and plans for creating a unified and centralised state had to be abandoned. Moreover these attempts at reform had provoked an increasing unity among different privileged groups in the localities, as they sought to resist the innovations of the central government whose 'national priorities they did not share. Behind the courteous exchanges which passed between Paris and the provincial capitals, there was a growing mood of hostility.

The disastrous cost of the Dutch war could have been mitigated by peaceful policies in the 1680s, but the king preferred to take a more aggressive and expensive course. Listening to the bellicose war minister Louvois, who was dominant in the royal favour during the last years of Colbert, and to the fervent religious orthodoxy of his mistress and his confessor, he embarked on the persecution of Protestants and was soon caught up in the first of the two lengthy wars which lasted for most of the remaining years of his reign. Coupled with a series of bad harvests, the kingdom was reduced to great misery. Louis XIV had once marvelled that his realm appeared so prosperous and his treasury was so poor. Now the only signs of wealth were to be seen among the financiers who profited from the distress of both government and subjects, and among the nobles who continued to spend lavishly on gaming, luxury and changing fashions. The government had little time for the destitute, save for its attempts to prevent vital taxpayers from perishing, and it was therefore to the nobility and the privileged that the peasant turned for protection against the seemingly unreasonable demands of the crown.

Although some nobles spent money on a scale which exceeded their means, those with real wealth still steadfastly refused to invest it in what they regarded as the socially inappropriate enterprises of commerce and industry. The kingdom thus lagged ever further behind in the European race for prosperity. Even for those who had begun life in the world of business, the goal was still the purchase of office and ultimately ascent into the *noblesse de robe*.

Thus the plans of Colbert remained largely unfulfilled. At court the royal ministers were overburdened with work, as were the intendants in the *généralités*. Therefore decision-making was slow, and more had to be done by the traditional bureaucracy of venal office-holders in the provinces. It was now impossible for the crown to reduce the number of officials, to escape from the clutches of financiers, to implement its impressive edicts on fiscal and judicial reforms. The attempt to impose new indirect taxes resulted in a sequence of Pyrrhic victories for the central government, because the cost of overcoming opposition almost outweighed the yield of the taxes and did irreparable harm to the prestige of the royal administration. The subtle undermining of privilege was beyond the power of the crown as long as its armies were busy and its treasury empty. When revenues for later years began to be anticipated and spent in advance, the problem worsened. At the death of Louis XIV in 1715, the internal situation in France offered little evidence of the strong government and glorious spectacle by which Europe characterised the reign of that great monarch, whom many nations hated but all respected and feared.

266

INDEX

267

Index

Financiers, 83, 92–4, 97, 265

Governors, 5–6, 8; as effective administrators, 27–31; encouragement of economic development, 28, 30, 176, 184, 191, 208, 211–13, 221–3, 227, 233–4; quelling of revolt, 28, 239–43, 245–6, 248–55, 257–8; as defenders of weak subjects, 102

Industry, present state of, 173–4, 176, 211–13, 215; plans for reform of, 18–19, 129–30, 169, 174, 176, 211–18, 234–6; regulations for, and infringements, 175, 211–14, 219–20, 228; gilds, 211–14, 219; royal inspectors, 211–15; the maintenance and increase of quality, 211–16, 220, 228–9; good and bad monopolies, 218–21, 224–7, 230, 232; native manufacture of foreign goods and encouragement of foreign craftsmen, 9, 169, 211, 215–16, 219–28, 230, 233; military industries, 169, 211, 219–21, 230–2; other encouragement of manufactures, 169, 211, 230, 232–3; new inventions, 220–1; incentives, 220, 228; harmful effect of tolls and dues, 213, 217–19; harmful effect of municipal administrators, 212–14, 216–19, 220, 228–30; laziness of workers, 220, 229

Intendants, social origins of, x; reasons for wanting to be, 16; general powers, limits on powers and rules for conduct of, 16–17, 23–6, 31, 97; relations with other officials, 23–5, 93, 95–7; general instructions for investigations, and reports, 17–21, 102–3; observation of other royal officials, 16–17, 23–4, 95–7, 99, 102, 104–6, 108–10, 113–14, 140–1; reporting corruption of officials, 23–4, 65, 67, 80–1, 97, 102–3, 112, 146; as supervisors of tax collection, 18–20, 83, 86, 95, 97–118, 228; role in commercial administration, 184, 186–9, 192–5, 205–6, 209; role in industrial administration, 215–19, 220–2, 226–8, 231–2; as judges, 112, 261–2; investigation of and reports on specific topics, 17, 119–20, 124–5, 205–6, 260–4; secret enquiries, 18, 125; role in administration of the *pays d'états* and municipalities, 17, 20, 22–3, 26–7, 36, 48–50, 61–2, 65, 67–76, 79–81, 186–9, 209, 217–18; discussion between central government and intendants, 157–9, 178–9; as sounders of local opinion, 192–3; as agents for royal propaganda, 121–2, 127; delegation of their powers, 23, 26–7, 212; briefness of reports, xvi; abuse of powers and inadequate reporting, 21–5, 95–6, 101, 180, 184–5, 187–8, 206–7; overwork of, 61, 83, 112, 266; ignorance of neighbouring areas, 118

Law courts and officials, *see also* Office-holding; reform of the courts, 4–5, 129–54; reform of the law, 129, 131–8, 157; reform of punishment, 152–5; galleys preferred to imprisonment, 152, 154–5; use of torture, 138; extraordinary royal tribunals, 92–4, 156, 158–61; conflicting jurisdictions and consequent appeal cases, 2, 20, 25, 84, 92–3, 95–6, 118, 123, 130, 134, 147, 169; commercial courts, 196–9, 237; courts' defence of their powers, 124–5; delays in justice and attempts to eradicate them, x, 14–15, 130, 135–7, 139, 145–56, 169; collusion with criminals, 129, 149–50; interference of judges in administration, 112; role in revolt,

268